ALAN SHEARER

PORTRAIT OF A LEGEND

EUAN REEDIE

C000020842

JOHN BLAKE

Published by John Blake Publishing Ltd,
3 Bramber Court, 2 Bramber Road,
London W14 9PB, England

www.blake.co.uk

First published in paperback in 2007

ISBN: 978-1-84454-390-8

British Library Cataloguing-in-Publication Data:

A catalogue record for this book is available from the British Library.

Design by www.envydesign.co.uk

Printed in the UK by CPI Bookmarque, Croydon, CR0 4TD

1 3 5 7 9 10 8 6 4 2

Papers used by John Blake Publishing are natural, recyclable products made from wood
grown in sustainable forests. The manufacturing processes conform to the environmental
regulations of the country of origin.

Every attempt has been made to contact the relevant copyright-holders, but some were
unobtainable. We would be grateful if the appropriate people could contact us.

CONTENTS

CHAPTER ONE

A Bittersweet Finale

Two key questions dominated the closing stages of Alan Shearer's career. First, would he beat Jackie Milburn's Newcastle goalscoring record? Second, could he finally win some silverware with his boyhood heroes? The first question was answered emphatically in February 2006, but the response to the second one, in the context of Newcastle's recent history and abject form at the beginning of the year, looked likely to be a resounding 'No'.

At least Shearer was exempt from the vitriol cascading down from the St James' Park stands towards the under-performing men in black and white. The Newcastle supporters were desperate for him to bow out with a long-awaited record and trophy to his name. Instead, the disenchanted Newcastle hordes were, perhaps a little unfairly, pointing the finger of blame at one man, and one man alone, for their wretched fortunes: manager Graeme Souness. The year before, Souness, who had astutely aligned himself with Shearer and played a key role in the Newcastle kingpin's decision to postpone his retirement, had seemed poised to win over those who had opposed his appointment. But now, almost 12 months on, the Newcastle legions were rapidly losing patience with the Scot and his apparent inability to mastermind a reversal in fortunes for a side in inexorable decline.

'Souness out' refrains were regularly roared out by the disgruntled Magpies' masses as Newcastle toiled in January: scraping a 2–2 draw at Middlesbrough; labouring to a 1–0 win over Mansfield Town in the FA Cup thanks to Shearer's goal which equalled Jackie Milburn's record; enduring an insipid defeat away to Fulham; and succumbing to Blackburn at home.

A lengthening injury list added to the Scot's mounting woes, with the likes of Michael Owen, Scott Parker, Belozoglu Emre, Stephen Carr and Shola Ameobi all sidelined, prompting Souness to consider the prospect of the insurmountable loss of his talisman: 'God forbid if anything was to happen to Alan Shearer,' said Souness. 'If it did we'd be in terrible trouble. I don't think anybody needs me to tell them how disastrous that would be.'

Thankfully, Shearer was spared further injury heartache in January, but his beleaguered manager's suffering endured and elicited little sympathy from Newcastle chairman Freddy Shepherd, who contradicted the Scot by saying, 'Sometimes people can look at the negatives too much. Yes, we have injuries but people shouldn't forget that we still have a lot of quality players and experienced internationals available.'

Even Shearer told the BBC that his side's extensive injury list should be not be used as an excuse for Newcastle's ineptitude. Souness's critics pointed out that the former Liverpool legend had been allowed to spend £50 million on transfers during 2005. It was universally acknowledged that some of his signings had failed to make the impact at St James' Park their hefty transfer fees merited.

The anti-Souness lobby was shunting the Scot out of his job. 'You're going to be sacked in the morning,' gloated the Blackburn fans after their team pilfered a victory at the end of January thanks to a disputed 75th-minute goal from Morten Gamst Pedersen. Their claim seemed to have some validity when Shepherd summoned Souness to St James' Park to discuss his future following this sorry loss, although both were said to be reluctant to effect a parting of the ways for different reasons. Souness was a fiercely proud man who had always insisted he would never resign, while Shepherd was keen to avoid paying the Scot the £3 million in compensation he would be owed if he chose to dispense with his services.

A 2–0 win at Cheltenham Town in the FA Cup fourth round at the end of January provided a lifeline for Souness and gave Shearer the chance to renew acquaintances with his first professional club, Southampton, with whom Newcastle were paired in the fifth round. Souness was cheered by the return to fitness of Scott Parker, Belozoglu Emre and Shola Ameobi, who all played part of the game against Cheltenham. Was salvation just around the corner? Sadly not, as his fate was sealed with a 3–0 thumping at Manchester City, leaving Newcastle perilously close to the relegation zone in 15th place. Freddy Shepherd had seen enough and handed Souness his P45, prompting Shearer to say, 'I can only have sympathy for Graeme. He worked his socks off trying to get things right here. But he was hampered by a horrendous injury situation that no team could have coped with.'

Cue yet more frenzied calls for Shearer to be installed as Newcastle manager. The likes of Sam Allardyce, Sven-Goran Eriksson, Martin O'Neill and Steve Bruce also emerged as favoured candidates with the bookmakers. However, Shearer was insistent that he did not want to be considered for the post, commenting, 'I would like to go into it one day but now certainly isn't the right time. I think the Newcastle job is a great one for someone though. Whoever gets it right here will find themselves put up on a pedestal by a huge football club with a great following. It's a tough job but a great one.'

ALAN SHEARER

Thankfully for Newcastle supporters, he compromised enough to become assistant to the club's academy supremo, Glenn Roeder, who was installed as caretaker manager until the end of the season. It had all the potential to be a managerial dream team that could haul struggling Newcastle out of the mire and into the upper reaches of the Premiership where European qualification beckoned. It was also, according to Roeder, another step towards Shearer eventually taking charge of the club he cherished.

He said, 'Alan Shearer sees himself as a future manager and so do I. But timing is everything in life and I agree with him that it is not right for him at the moment. I can see Alan being just like Stuart Pearce, who learned from the brief managerial experience he had at Nottingham Forest, went away, studied the game, got every qualification you can have. And what a difference it has made to him at Manchester City. That's why these qualifications are important.'

Yet there were suggestions raised in some quarters that Shearer could potentially undermine any future manager given what some people perceived to be his excessive influence on affairs at St James' Park. Just ask Ruud Gullit and Bobby Robson. However, a bullish Shearer insisted, 'I'm only going to be a player for another three months, so that won't be a problem for whoever comes – not that I see it as a problem anyway. Everyone is entitled to an opinion, but I was bought to score goals and, thankfully, I've done that. Other people can say what they want. My role is to try my best on the football pitch, and that's what I've always done.'

His brilliant best on the football pitch was in evidence once again when he memorably surpassed Jackie Milburn's Newcastle goalscoring record in his side's 2–0 victory over Portsmouth at St James' Park. Newcastle, too, as is often the case for a team after a change in manager, looked a completely different outfit from the dispirited and disjointed bunch that had blundered during the final throes of the

4

A BITTERSWEET FINALE

Graeme Souness era and, in their next game, overcame Aston Villa 2–1 away. In the next three games, which Shearer missed due to a calf injury, Newcastle conceded no goals at home as they beat Southampton 1–0 in the FA Cup fifth round, drew 0–0 with Charlton and disposed of Everton 2–0. The Roeder revolution was in full swing and Newcastle's flourishing fortunes continued when Shearer returned, and scored, in a 3–1 home win over Bolton in the Premiership. Shearer was at his belligerent best, contesting every decision of referee Alan Wiley he deemed to be incorrect, and receiving a yellow card for his troubles.

A visit to Old Trafford to meet Manchester United has never been a happy hunting ground for Shearer and this was again the case in March when Sir Alex Ferguson's men cruised to a comfortable 2–0 victory over Newcastle. Shearer suffered the traditional taunting from the United supporters, who could not resist venting their spleen about the striker's rebuff of their club one last time. Newcastle and Shearer could also not compete with a rampant Liverpool, who romped to a 3–1 victory at St James' Park.

Meanwhile, as only months remained until the planned end of Shearer's career, Glenn Roeder mused on how to fill the gaping void Alan's departure would leave. Widespread rumours had surfaced in the press that Manchester United's Ruud van Nistelrooy had been earmarked as a possible replacement for the retiring hero, leading Roeder to admit, 'That's the type of quality we are looking at. When you are trying to replace a record goalscorer, it's impossible as far as I'm aware to find someone in the mould that Alan is as a player and as a person.'

By now, Newcastle seemed to have assured Premiership safety and could now turn their attentions exclusively to the FA Cup, which represented Shearer's last chance of silverware. However, when Newcastle were drawn away to Chelsea, who were stampeding towards a second successive league championship, Shearer must have groaned inwardly. He could barely disguise his dissatisfaction with the tie Newcastle had been handed in public, either.

He remarked, 'You've just got to work hard and then we'll see what happens at Stamford Bridge. There's no point pulling the wool over anyone's eyes. We've got a very, very tough tie, but who knows. There haven't been too many shocks in this season's FA Cup and if we won it would be regarded as a shock.'

Glenn Roeder went even further by suggesting that, if Shearer was provided with the chance to play in the FA Cup final, it would rank alongside what has entered folklore as 'The Matthews Final', when Stanley Matthews inspired Blackpool to a thrilling 4–3 win over Bolton Wanderers in 1953.

Ominously for Shearer, however, Newcastle's last four league visits to Stamford Bridge had resulted in defeats of 3–0, 5–0, 4–0 and 3–0 and his club had not won at Stamford Bridge since 1986, during caretaker-manager Glenn Roeder's playing days.

This unhappy trend continued as Shearer was a fading force well shackled by John Terry, who scored the only goal of an unmemorable match. Rather than bow out with a match-winning goal, Shearer marked his final FA Cup appearance with anger, vehemently protesting against Robbie Elliott's sending off following a second booking administered for a debatable foul on Shaun Wright-Phillips in the final minute. Shearer was duly cautioned for dissent to seal his misery.

He later raged, 'It was a blatant dive. There was absolutely no contact and I thought that at the time. I have seen it again on a replay and it was definitely the case.'

Typically modest, Shearer also wanted to deflect attention away from himself, adding, 'It doesn't matter that this was my last FA Cup tie. This is about Newcastle United and it always has been. It's not nice when you get knocked out of this great competition, but there's only one team who can win it and it's not going to be Newcastle.'

A BITTERSWEET FINALE

'For such a great player as Alan to have won the Premiership [with Blackburn] and nothing else is a shame,' John Terry said, 'because he has probably been the best player in the Premiership over the years and is an absolute legend.'

Surely a finale more befitting of Shearer's Boys' Own tale could have been scripted? But as the *Daily Telegraph*'s Tim Rich pointed out, 'What separates sport from all other forms of mass entertainment is its indifference to happy endings. Had this been cinema, an art form Alan Shearer has graced, you could have guessed the finish from the opening credits. The FA Cup would have been lifted at Wembley – no stadium overruns in Boys' Own Land – and the last scenes would have been shot by the brown metal garage doors in Gosforth where Shearer first learned how to hit a target.'

Shearer later attempted to play down the disappointing dearth of club silverware to his name having finished up on the losing side in two FA Cup finals. He said, 'I have lived my boyhood dream. I have played in front of the most loyal fans in the world, captained my country, played for the club I supported as a boy and broken the goalscoring record of an absolute Tyneside legend [Jackie Milburn].'

Hear, hear. That Shearer did not fill his mantelpiece with trophies and awards should not diminish his considerable achievements as a footballer and icon to millions.

As Tim Rich stressed, 'When Richard Burton walked into the Miners' Arms in Pontrhydyfen to ask, "Are you all right for cash?" they did not love him less because Burton had never held an Oscar. Shearer is certainly all right for cash and many things beside.'

So, would Shearer's final weeks and months as a Newcastle player now unfold in unspectacular fashion, devoid of incident or interest? There was still the hitherto undreamed, albeit diminishing, prospect of Europe to play for, although a 3–1 defeat at Charlton at the end of March seemed to extinguish that flickering hope.

ALAN SHEARER

And, as the realisation dawned on other Premiership managers and players that Shearer was only games away from retirement, plaudits and praise for him were bound to proliferate.

Tottenham manager Martin Jol offered the following compliment to Shearer before his side met Newcastle at St James' Park in April: 'I think he is one of the few people who are living legends. Ian Rush is another, but normally you are not a legend until you die. Alan Shearer already is one.'

Jol even went as far as to suggest, somewhat optimistically, that Shearer was performing well enough to play for England again in that summer's World Cup. He added, 'I think if you told people tomorrow that he would like to play for England again, you would consider it seriously. As a number nine, I don't feel there are many better players. I wouldn't say he should still be playing for England because he has made his decision. But what I am suggesting is that if he said that maybe he wanted to have another go you would accept that he is capable, and he's not the youngest any more.'

Perhaps Jol talked Shearer up too much, as the much-praised striker lived up to the hype and hyperbole by despatching a penalty in Newcastle's 3–1 humbling of Spurs. A 2–1 victory in his final match against Middlesbrough helped to partly assuage his FA Cup misery, while he converted another penalty and calmly slotted in a second – his 13th goal in a turbulent season for Newcastle – in his side's exhilarating 3–1 vanquishing of Wigan at St James' Park.

He might have failed to deliver club honours in his farewell season, but Shearer believed winning a place in the UEFA Cup was becoming an ever-more realistic proposition.

He said, 'Europe would be great and it is certainly realistic now. We are level with Wigan and Bolton on points so there's an outside chance we could get there after a long hard season. It would be a great way for me to sign off.'

A BITTERSWEET FINALE

However, as it transpired, Shearer concluded his career in bittersweet fashion with a goalscoring flourish and memorable 4–1 victory over old rivals Sunderland at the Stadium of Light, before leaving the field as a hobbling, disconsolate figure who had succumbed to injury yet again.

First, the positives, as what turned out to be Shearer's final league appearance for his club saw them secure their biggest win in a Tyne-Tees derby for 50 years – a Jackie Milburn-inspired Newcastle side routed Sunderland 6–2 at St James' Park in 1956. There was also perfect symmetry in the fact that Milburn, too, was in his final season for Newcastle. Shearer, who admitted his side has been 'absolutely rubbish in the first-half' as they trailed 1–0 to a Justin Hoyte goal, was part of an extraordinary Newcastle fight-back in the second 45 minutes as four goals were rattled in as Sunderland disintegrated.

Michael Chopra equalised, before Shearer smashed in his 206th and final Newcastle goal from the penalty spot. He then left the pitch to a chorus of derision from the Sunderland fans as a knee injury – sustained from a heavy challenge from Julio Arca – caused him to limp off after 71 minutes. Newcastle added a further two goals from Charles N'Zogbia and Albert Luque to further humiliate their North East rivals, but this crushing victory was overshadowed by the terminal implications of Shearer's ailment.

The news that Newcastle fans and Shearer had dreaded was released days later: the unfortunate striker had torn his left medial ligament to confirm his premature retirement from the game. Unlike years gone by, there would be no chance of a comeback against all the odds, which had left medics stunned and amazed. This was it. This was the end and how excruciating it was for every Newcastle fan.

This depressing sense of finality was enough to make grown men weep, although former Newcastle centre-forward Malcolm Macdonald was cheerier than most and punctured the prevailing mood of despair on Tyneside with the following upbeat assessment of Shearer's league match.

He told the *Evening Chronicle*, 'I don't feel sorry for Alan. I feel elated. Can you think of a better way of leaving the stage? He skippers Newcastle to a 4–1 victory over Sunderland on their own patch having laid his penalty bogey against the Wearsiders by scoring the goal that nosed his team in front for the first time. And Shearer left having smashed into a tackle with three red-and-white shirts converging on him. That is what United's skipper is all about. It was Roy of the Rovers stuff.'

He might have gone, but he was certainly not forgotten, as his ubiquitous presence at St James' Park bore testimony in Newcastle's next home match against West Brom.

Paul Gilder, of the *Journal*, described the scene: 'Be it the 25-metre version which hung from the Gallowgate End, or the six-foot alternative leaning on the wall of the home dugout, there was no escaping the domineering image of Alan Shearer at St James' Park on Saturday. On a day when one of the finest players to have worn a black-and-white shirt announced his career was over, it was fitting Shearer should find himself the centre of attention, with recollections of his past glories overshadowing the achievements of those he will leave behind this summer.

'Neither Glenn Roeder, the coach who has rescued Newcastle's season, nor Shola Ameobi, the striker who assumed Shearer's mantle in a manner which met with approval from the club's record goalscorer, could outshine a man who, at 35, is a living legend. Neither would have wanted to.'

A swashbuckling 3–0 victory for the Magpies was made all the more special by the cacophonous cheers that greeted Shearer's appearance in the dugout. Glenn Roeder was understandably extremely moved by this poignant outpouring of emotion from the Geordie faithful.

A BITTERSWEET FINALE

He reflected later, 'I turned around and said to him, "Alan, that makes the hairs stand up on the back of my neck so Christ knows what it does to you." That is why he has lived the dream and, in Alan's eyes, that must be better than winning trophies. To have the love of your own people must be a wonderful thing.'

If passion was at fever pitch for this match, it soared to stratospheric levels when Shearer took his last strides on the St James' Park pitch for his testimonial against Celtic on Thursday, 11 May. The encounter between an Alan Shearer XI, featuring Newcastle players present and past – including Rob Lee and Les Ferdinand – and the Scottish champions was invested with additional poignancy given that all the proceeds would be given to charity.

Shearer said, 'It's been an honour and a privilege to have served this club. I hope that by pledging some money to charity and other worthy causes that people less fortunate than myself will also benefit in some way from my football career... Now I will have my final opportunity to say farewell to the fans who have supported me so well throughout my career.'

Shearer also announced that he would be leaving a legacy to football by setting up a two-year scholarship for one outstanding 16-year-old per year, in conjunction with Newcastle's academy.

Thankfully, after all the intense frustration and disappointment about the unceremonious end to Shearer's distinguished career, an occasion bearing all the hallmarks of a hero's send-off was staged at St James' Park when the testimonial match took place. The night included pomp, pageantry, pyrotechnics and one peerless footballer, engulfed by tears and cheers from a 52,000 crowd. A deafening roar greeted the arrival of Shearer, while placards bearing his name and a giant Number 9 provided an eye-catching and intensely emotional sight. The Celtic supporters, renowned for their vociferous vocal backing, also played a significant part in proceedings, twirling their scarves above their heads at one point during the game, which prompted the Newcastle fans to follow suit in a stunning show of unity and football fervour.

The game itself wasn't bad, either, as the Shearer XI edged out Celtic 3–2 with guess-who scoring the winning goal? In a perfectly stage-managed finale, with the scores level at 2–2 with only minutes remaining, the Newcastle XI were awarded a highly dubious penalty after Les Ferdinand tumbled in the box. Up stepped Alan Shearer, who had replaced Michael Chopra in the dying minutes, to strike home the winning goal in time-honoured fashion. Referee Mark Clattenburg, who adhered to the 'Shearer must score' script and ignored the rules for once, seemed to suggest to Celtic goalkeeper David Marshall which way he should dive to allow Shearer to finish in style. Shearer did the rest, with what was the last kick of the game. Then the Geordie hero treated his devotees to one final glimpse of his trademark goal celebration, wheeling away with his right arm held aloft in front of the Gallowgate End.

After lapping up the cheers and unbridled acclaim of the St James' Park masses in a lap of honour with his children, a clearly emotional Shearer, his voice trembling, mused, 'Where else in the world would you get that? I had more than one tear in my eye to be honest, but I defy anyone not to have a tear in their eye with an atmosphere like that.

'Newcastle will always be my club, it always has been. I would just say – look at every kid in every playground in the North East and the joy they get when they score a goal. I'm exactly the same. This [St James' Park] has been my playground for the last 10 years.'

So what were his highlights during 10 highly memorable years playing for the club he supported since childhood?

'I have to say my first game here against Wimbledon was special because I achieved something that I always wanted to do, which was play here, score a goal here and wear the number-nine shirt,' added Shearer. 'But I think the thing that will stick with me forever will be the reception after I got the record goal, the 201st against Portsmouth. The feeling when I score a goal is fantastic, but that day, they lifted the roof off for me. There was a spell about 10 minutes after I'd scored when they were still going crazy. When people talk about the hairs on the back of your neck standing up, that was definitely the case for me that day.'

Shearer continued, 'The Portsmouth one, the semi-finals at Old Trafford – I'm not so sure that stand has rocked like it did in those games,' he said when asked which matches came to mind most readily. The Inter Milan game away was great because of the 14,000 or 15,000 Newcastle fans behind that goal.

'There have also been disappointments as well – the two finals that we played in. It was just our luck that we were playing teams that one was going for the double, one was going for the treble. But I think the biggest disappointment for me was the Sporting Lisbon game last year, when we had done so well to get our noses in front and get a good lead. That week, really, was a bad one. We went on to the FA Cup semi-final after that with players suspended and players injured, and that was a disappointing week.

'But you have to have the bad times as well as the good times. That's what's been good about the 10 years – it hasn't all been plain sailing, we have had to work hard to get where we are, to get what you want.'

And that was that, or so Shearer thought.

But Newcastle being Newcastle, a city which loves to worship a legend like no other, the Geordies could not resist paying homage to their favourite son once again the day after the testimonial match.

In an event entitled 'Black and White Day', organised by the *Evening Chronicle* and the Newcastle-Gateshead initiative, schools, offices, shops and the general public were encouraged to don black and white colours and arrange special events in tribute to Shearer.

Among those taking part, according to the *Evening Chronicle*, was Harewood Court residential home in Cramlington, which held a Zimmer-frame football match.

ALAN SHEARER

Meanwhile, Newcastle Civic Centre had a black and white flag draped over its central tower, while, as the newspaper reported, 'City Sightseeing buses in Newcastle were also offering free tours for customers sporting black and white colours. Schools across Tyneside encouraged their children to leave their uniform in the wardrobe and come to class in black and white shirts.

'Kelly Scott, a teacher at Moorside First School in Newbiggin-by-the-Sea, Northumberland, said, "Shearer is a legend and we just had to get involved. All the children are Toon fans and they loved the chance to wear black and white."'

Farewell, Alan Shearer, and thanks for the memories.

CHAPTER TWO

Football Crazy

1970 was undoubtedly one of the 'thirty years of hurt' for embattled English football fans that were alluded to by comedians David Baddiel and Frank Skinner in their unforgettable Euro '96 anthem, 'Football's Coming Home'.

Four years after becoming world champions on home soil, England wilted in the searing Mexican heat, succumbing to an agonising 3–2 extra-time defeat against old foes West Germany in the 1970 World Cup Quarter Final. This crushing loss signalled the end of a golden era for English football, as legends such as Bobby Charlton called time on their illustrious careers. However, only a matter of months later, someone whose name would, in years to come, be included alongside Charlton in best-ever England XIs, came into the world.

Alan Shearer was born on 13 August 1970, the son of working-class parents, Alan a sheet-metal worker for American Air Filters and Anne, a local council worker. He and his big sister Karen spent their early years in Park Avenue, Gosforth, a council estate on the outskirts of

Newcastle, and enjoyed a respectable, working-class upbringing, despite the poverty of the area. Alan said in *The Times* in 1998: 'I was fortunate. We weren't by any means a well-off family, but we never went short. The house we lived in is still there now with the cobbles outside. I'm very proud of that. It wasn't a great area, but we were very fortunate to have a roof over our heads and I still realise that now. There are many people in the world that are not as fortunate as we have been, but having said that, my dad worked his socks off – six days a week – to get what he wanted and to bring us up. And my mam.'

'For he's football crazy, he's football mad.
The football it has taken away the little bit o' sense he had.
And it would take a dozen servants to wash his clothes and scrub
Since Paul became a member of that terrible football club.'

You would be forgiven for thinking that the chorus of this 1960s football song by Robin Hall and Jimmy McGregor was penned with Shearer in mind. His formative years were dominated by the game.

A pair of brown double doors leading to a block of student flats and a small patch of grassland represented, for Shearer and his soccer-mad chums, any one of a number of legendary football theatres, such as St James' Park or Wembley.

Hour upon hour, day after day, the young Shearer relentlessly kicked a ball about with childhood abandon, imagining he was a Newcastle legend like Malcolm Macdonald or Wyn Davies. Little did he know that his fairytale would one day come true and that it would feature goals galore, multi-million-pound transfers and that he would achieve legendary status with both his hometown club and his country.

There was never any doubt that football would become his drug, his passion, as his father Alan indoctrinated him with his love of the beautiful game as soon as he could walk. Shearer recalls that his father used to take him into the backyard for a kickaround. Encouraging an embryonic football passion was the first phase of Mr Shearer's masterplan. Now it was time to imbue his impressionable son with an appreciation of his second great obsession – Newcastle United.

He was determined to ensure that Shearer would be steeped in his favourite club and, at the age of three, presented the wide-eyed toddler with a Newcastle United strip and a pair of boots. There could be no turning back – it was the beginning of an inextricable union that was bound to last a lifetime. On alternate Saturdays, he and his father would make the pilgrimage of thousands in Newcastle to worship at the Tyneside temple of football – St James' Park.

The Toon Army loves its footballing gods and, in the early 1980s, Kevin Keegan was the player who was their deity and the object of their veneration. The man nicknamed 'Mighty Mouse' had already become a legend with Liverpool in the 1970s, with his incredible work-rate and his effervescent forward play earning him immense admiration from fans and players alike. His subsequent spells at Hamburg in Germany and Southampton had been less auspicious, but the next chapter in his career, between 1982 and 1984 at Newcastle, would capture the hearts and minds of a passionate public, including a young Alan Shearer.

Forming a swashbuckling attacking Tyne triumvirate with Peter Beardsley and Chris Waddle, Keegan helped orchestrate a Geordie revival, which culminated in Newcastle achieving promotion to the old First Division in 1984.

When Keegan made his Newcastle debut against QPR in 1982, the clamour to catch a glimpse of him was extraordinary. Shearer recalls that he was among some 10,000 devotees queuing up hours before kick-off before cramming into the Gallowgate End, which was throbbing with expectancy and excitement. 'When Keegan ran out with the rest of the team, the whole place just exploded,' he reminisces in his autobiography. 'I couldn't take my eyes off him. His runs, his work-rate, his ability on the ball and his refusal to give up anything as a lost cause: it was hypnotic stuff and I just couldn't get enough of the Keegan magic.'

Imagine the joy of the captivated Shearer when his new hero scored the only goal of the game with in front of the Gallowgate End and its adoring legions. If the enthralled youngster had had any doubts about football being his future vocation, they were well and truly eradicated by this moment of magnificence. He would now live, sleep and literally dream football and Kevin Keegan, ensuring he watched his idol at every home match.

Even better, at the age of thirteen, he got up close and personal to the Tyne titan after winning a local newspaper competition to spend a day training with Keegan and his Newcastle team-mates at their training ground. Although his mother's response to the question, 'Explain in no more than twenty words why you want to spend a day with Kevin Keegan' was fairly banal, it worked and he spent a day agog while Keegan and co put on a master class. 'He was extremely friendly and approachable – just what everyone in the North–East had come to expect from him,' says Shearer in his autobiography. 'I have to admit I was a bit tongue-tied when I met him, but to have my picture taken with him was just about the biggest thing that had happened to me in my thirteen years so far.' Embarrassingly for the young fan, he was wearing a Liverpool tracksuit, as his second favourite team at the time was the Merseyside outfit.

It was against the Anfield Road side that mulleted Magpie Keegan made a characteristically showman-like farewell in his last game for Newcastle. Shearer was one of the ball boys for the game and, with a mixture of sadness and awe, he watched as Keegan was whisked back into the heavens by a helicopter.

As he left, he tossed his No. 7 jersey into the sky never to be seen again – or so Shearer and the crestfallen crowd thought at the time. He could never have envisaged being reunited with Keegan some twelve years later, four years after King Kevin had begun his reign as Newcastle manager. Inspired by the Messianic impact of Keegan, Shearer dedicated himself to following in his illustrious footsteps by playing football at every opportunity.

At his first school, Grange First, he cultivated his skills in six-a-side competitions. As enthusiastic young footballers are wont to do, blissfully unaware of tactics in gloriously anarchic, harum-scarum fashion, he charged after the ball at every opportunity.

In an interview with BBC Radio Newcastle, Shearer articulated his adolescent ardour for football: 'I was one of those greedy little scruffy kids at school that thought I could play anywhere. I took the free-kicks, I took the throw-ins, I took the corner kicks and wanted to take everything. It was the buzz of scoring goals that got me into that position if you like.

'I think you are actually born with a talent to be in the right place at the right time and sniff out where that ball is going to land in the box. Is it going to land at your feet and are you going to put it into the net? I actually think it is difficult to teach someone that. You can coach them to be a better finisher. But I'm not too sure you can coach them to be in the right place at the right time.'

Although he had not yet established himself as a striker, Shearer was nevertheless beginning to emerge as central a figure for his school sides as he would later become for both his club and his country.

He became captain and midfield lynchpin of his next school, Gosforth Central, for whom he made an indelible impression – an inveterate and much-loved match-winner.

Proof of his incalculable worth to his school side was uncovered in 2000 by *The Times*' Oliver Holt. He wrote: 'Earlier this week, an event organised by England's sponsors, Nationwide, in Newcastle gave an unexpected insight into the determination that has driven the centre-forward since he was eleven. Some children from his old school, Gosforth Central, had come to meet him on the banks of the Tyne and one had dug up some school match reports written by a teacher. Every one had 'M.O.M. – Alan Shearer' written at the bottom.

Invariably, the games seemed to be played in driving rain and high winds on sodden, muddy pitches. Shearer excelled in all of them. At the bottom of a report of a 3–2 victory over their fiercest opponents, Chapel House, which brought Gosforth Central their first trophy, the teacher had written: 'Man of the Match – I suppose with the three goals and the endless encouragement, it has to be ... Alan Shearer.'

In one game, the precocious Shearer scored a colossal thirteen goals. Little wonder, then, that his sports teacher, Jimmy Nelson, tried to cancel the games if Shearer ever fell sick.

While he was excelling on the football pitch, he was completely apathetic to academia and often hid his more-often-than-not pitiful school reports from his mother. 'I wasn't interested in doing any of my lessons,' confessed Shearer in his book *Going for Goal* as reported in the *Daily Mirror*. 'I couldn't wait for break or lunchtime so that I could get the football out. When my teachers explained that there was very little chance of making it as a footballer, I ignored them. There was nothing else on my mind. Once, when we had to complete a careers form, I wrote, for a bit of fun, that I wanted to be a dustman. My dad gave me a clout for that and made me put down "joiner" instead. But both he and I knew my heart was set on playing football and nothing else.'

Shearer's performance in the classroom may have been lamentable – although he did leave school with an English CSE oral qualification – but his displays on the pitch were habitually noteworthy.

He continued to be an exemplary leader to his team-mates when he moved on to Gosforth High School, captaining their football teams from Under-14 to Under-16 level. Jimmy Nelson, the master in charge of Shearer during this period, recalled in the *Independent* in 1997: 'We share our site with Grange First School and I first became aware of Alan when he was a nine-year-old there. They used to play six-a-side in the playground, using skittles for goals, and our caretaker, Norman Teasdale, ran the team. I can remember him saying to me: "We've got this player coming across to your school and he's going to be a star." I never thought one day that Alan would be worth £15 million, but I always thought he had a good chance of being a footballer. He was a very aggressive young player. He played in midfield for my team so we could make the most of him. He used to get hold of the ball and make those surging runs he does now. I can remember one match, we were playing into a gale-force wind and he ran the full length of the pitch to score.'

Nelson added that the school was proud to use Shearer as a role model for its children. He said: 'We take great pleasure in the way he conducts himself. We had a spot of bother with bullying last year and when we held an assembly about it the theme was: "What would Alan Shearer do in the same position?" It's great to have a role model like Alan.'

Meanwhile, Shearer's progression in the football world continued to gather momentum as he began playing for a bastion of soccer excellence in the North-East, Wallsend Boys Club, originally built and funded by Swan Hunter shipyard workers for youngsters in the area in 1903.

Based in Wallsend, on the outskirts of Newcastle, the Tyneside football factory has over the years nurtured a rich vein of Geordie talent – including Peter Beardsley, Steve Bruce and Michael Carrick – to become arguably Britain's most famous soccer academy. Its pre-eminence in the North-East owes much to the fact that only boys living within a five-mile radius can join the club.

Shearer was one such lucky lad and, under the tutelage of Wallsend coach Les Howey, was switched from midfield to striker, where his voracious appetite for goals could reap the richest of dividends.

It was during one game, in which Wallsend were coasting to victory 13–0, that his lack of success in front of goal prompted his father to offer him a financial incentive. 'We were winning 13–0 and I had squandered several chances, as well as hitting the bar a few times,' said Shearer in his book *Going for Goal*, as featured in the *Daily Mirror*. 'My dad was goading me from the sidelines. He used to call me Smoky because of my love for smoky bacon crisps. He yelled: "Bet you a pound you can't score, Smoky." That was a challenge I couldn't ignore. In the next five minutes I had three touches and scored a hat-trick.'

Such scintillating scoring became commonplace for the young Shearer, and it led to him becoming fêted, and also good-naturedly ridiculed, by his team-mates, one of whom, Steve Bailey, explained to the *Daily Mirror* in 1996: 'We called him 'Chink' because when he smiled his eyes screwed right up, almost disappearing. And 'Helmet Head' came about because he had a funny hairstyle. His fringe stuck flat against his forehead – he looked like he was wearing a Roman helmet.'

Yet Wallsend officials were not as impressed with Shearer's displays and admit to this day being slightly surprised at his remarkable rise to prominence. His chairman at the time, Sid Sharp, told the *People* in 1994: 'Alan has surprised me a bit with the progress he's made. He wasn't anywhere near as good as [Peter] Beardsley when they were youngsters. Alan used to get knocked off the ball at times, but he's become so much stronger now. Full-time training has made a big difference.'

Another Wallsend official, Peter Kirkley, also did not anticipate the glittering career that lay ahead of Shearer. He disclosed to the Newcastle *Evening Chronicle* in 1995 that Shearer had only arrived at Wallsend because his father had alerted a scout, Brian Clark, to his son's abilities. Kirkley said: 'When he [Shearer] played for us at Wallsend Boys Club, no one could have imagined that such a glittering career stretched before him. Except him probably: he had a great belief that he'd be a player. His self-belief was his major asset: that and his determination. He had a huge burden on his shoulders, because he was always paired with players almost a year older than himself. His birthday is in August and the cut-off point was September. However, he loved that, he'd rather test himself against older players.'

He added: 'Alan was a striker who was always scoring. He wasn't the tallest or biggest. I've always smiled at his nickname 'Big Al', but when he had the ball you could turn away, you knew it was a goal. Shearer's secret has always been that he plays to his strengths, not his weaknesses. He has great assets and he plays within them. Others make the mistake of trying to do what they cannot.'

Between the ages of ten and fifteen, Shearer spearheaded Wallsend's attack with Jason Richardson, a speedy attacker who consistently overshadowed his forward partner.

Richardson eventually became a YTS trainee at Newcastle when Shearer went south to Southampton, but was finally axed after failing to make the grade at St James' Park.

In 1998, The Newcastle *Evening Chronicle* interviewed Richardson, who admitted Shearer's superior work ethic was fundamental to his success. He said: 'Alan used to go running after we had training sessions to keep fit and be better. I was young and a bit daft – I didn't think it was bad just turning up 15 minutes late for training.'

Like many Wallsend old boys, Shearer has never forgotten how his time at Darsley Park aided his rise through the footballing ranks. He has repeatedly sought to ensure Wallsend profit from his fame and fortune.

In October 2003, for example, he donated the Newcastle shirt he had worn when he scored his 250th league goal against Southampton to the famed football academy on Tyneside. The prized possession raised £5,000 at an auction for his former club, outstripping the £4,500 that the Brazil shirt worn by Pelé had once raised. Shearer remarked of his gesture: 'I was only too happy to help the club because without such places the Premier League would not exist.'

In March 2005, meanwhile, he teamed up with Tyneside laminating firm, UNIKA, to present Wallsend with its first-ever minibus. Then, in October 2003, he and a galaxy of top stars who had been reared at Wallsend attended a dinner to mark the retirement of long-serving member, David Beardall.

Shearer enthused in the *Evening Chronicle*: 'Professional football desperately needs the likes of Wallsend Boys Club, despite all the money being flashed around, and mustn't forget it. It may be awash with millions and it may have gone berserk again through Roman Abramovich at Chelsea, but top football owes a debt to these grassroots clubs.

'Their [Wallsend's] record is unbelievable. We have the best right here on the banks of the Tyne. When you consider the players they have developed and how much they have been sold for ... millions upon millions of pounds. They have an incredible system.'

It was during his time at Wallsend that Shearer's potential was spotted by one of the host of talent scouts that prowl the touchlines of youth games, scouring the field for a jewel among a sea of mediocrity.

Legendary North-East scout Jack Hixon's eagle eyes caught sight of the youngster playing for Newcastle City Schoolboys Under-13 team at Benfield Park, a discovery that would change his and Shearer's life forever. Not only would Hixon introduce Shearer to the professional game, but the pair would develop a lifelong friendship which would see them stay in daily contact by telephone.

Hixon recalled in the *Independent* in 1997 that Shearer's sheer will to win and application had made a significant impression on him: 'The thing that impressed me right from the start was the competitive element in Alan's play, his combative spirit. He wasn't a particularly big lad, but he had a lot of strength. He stimulated my interest by his sheer drive and aggressive running. He wanted to get forward and make ground. I had no prior recommendation. There was no particular player I was at that game to watch. It was just a general check. His father, Alan, was standing on his own on the far side of the pitch and I went round and introduced myself.'

Hixon approached Shearer senior about taking his son to Southampton for a schoolboy trial. His father replied that he should ask the boy himself as he was just a couple of months short of his fourteenth birthday and old enough to make up his own mind.

As the football world would see, on most occasions at least, Shearer's single-minded decision-making is one of his key characteristics and he did not hesitate in accepting Hixon's offer.

He also had trials for West Bromwich Albion, Manchester City and his beloved Newcastle United, where he spent three days. A pervasive myth that the St James' Park club snubbed him after playing him in goal is not strictly true, however.

Shearer explains in his autobiography that, on the first day of the trials, one of the coaches asked if anyone other than the one goalkeeper present fancied spending a spell between the sticks. Shearer was one of the boys who offered his services, but only spent fifteen minutes in goal.

He would soon be faced with one of the most difficult choices of his career – moving to his childhood favourites Newcastle or heading south to Southampton. Rarely one to let his heart rule his head, Shearer decided to make the 350-mile trip to Southampton and signed associate schoolboy terms with the south-coast club in August 1984.

He explained his decision in the *Daily Mirror* in 1996: 'Jack took me to The Dell and I was delighted to go there, even though I idolised Newcastle. When it was decision time, my head ruled my heart and I signed schoolboy forms for Southampton. My instincts told me that it was the right thing to do. Southampton were a smaller club and I could develop my career out of the limelight.'

In April 1986, he had to prove he was worthy of a YTS (Youth Training Scheme) contract and responded to the task magnificently in his final trial game on 3 April 1986, scoring five goals. The Southampton coaches needed no further persuading; they snapped up the young Shearer and thrust him into the frenzied world of football, a domain he would dominate in years to come.

The wheels had now been set in motion for Shearer's football career to take a major leap forward. He was also on the move in junior football, switching from Wallsend to Cramlington Juniors, a Northumberland-based club, which has helped rear renowned players such as Andy Sinton and Graham Fenton.

His innate winning mentality was a vital ingredient in all-conquering Cramlington's incredible unbeaten season at Under-16 level in 1985–86, which even saw them win the Northumberland Cup at Under-18 level against players two years older than themselves – a unique feat. In an interview with the *Daily Mirror* in 1996, manager of Cramlington at this time, Jimmy Snowdon, fondly recalled Shearer's unforgettable contribution in the final match of the season. He said: 'That final match is one that will live with me for a very long time. We were winning 4–2 with ten minutes to go, but we were under immense pressure and conceded two goals that levelled the scores with time running out. If the game had gone into extra-time, I'm sure we would have lost. They were physically much stronger than we were because of the age difference but, in the dying seconds, Shearer picked the ball up on the edge of his own box, raced the whole length of the field and won a penalty. Without hesitation he put the ball on the spot and smashed it home to win the match. He came up to me after and said that their equaliser had hurt him so much he had to do something about it. That was Alan Shearer – he could not bear losing.'

Such an insatiable thirst for success would characterise a distinguished professional career to come.

CHAPTER THREE

Saint Alan

Alan Shearer's stint at Southampton will always be massively overshadowed by his formidable feats for other clubs and country. His spell on the south coast is marginalised by most football pundits when compared to his terrific title-winning achievements at Blackburn or his heroic Euro '96 exploits for England.

But the man himself has never forgotten the priceless education in both life and football that his experience at The Dell afforded him. In an interview with Nobok for the sports company's football legends series in 2005, Shearer recalled: 'I went to Southampton at fifteen and it was a long way to go on your own, but looking back it was one of the best things that I ever did as it helped me grow up. I cleaned the boots, the dressing rooms, the toilets, and it teaches you a bit of respect and I don't think that does anyone any harm. It wasn't nice at the time, but looking back it was great for me.'

For most teenagers, leaving their friends and family and making a major career move at such a tender age would be unthinkable, but fifteen-year-old Alan Shearer relished the chance to begin his football education and, wide-eyed and full of exuberance and expectation, he joined fellow North-East trainees Tony Johnson, Barry Wilson, Neil Maddison and Adrian Ibbotson on the train south from the North-East in 1986.

The impressive manner with which Shearer dealt with this potentially traumatic upheaval served early notice of his sterling, sturdy character, according to Jack Hixon. Hixon told the *Newcastle Evening Chronicle*: 'He never flickered despite travelling to the other end of the country alone – I was unable to go with him on this particular occasion.

'He was always so self-possessed he could handle anything. It's the hallmark of a great player and a great man. It was an attraction from the first day I clapped eyes on him.'

Shearer and Maddison swiftly settled into a three-bedroom detached house owned by Maureen and Nigel Wareham, whose finances were, by their own admission, stretched to the limit by the voracious appetites of the hungry teenage pair. Mrs Wareham told the *Daily Mirror* in 1996: 'Alan and Neil were great to have around, but they cost us a fortune. We were paid £37.50 a week for each of them, but Alan would eat £50-worth of food on his own.'

On a professional level, meanwhile, Shearer was ravenous for a chance to justify Jack Hixon's judgement of his talents, but had to satisfy the stiff demands of a hard taskmaster – Southampton's youth-team coach, Dave Merrington. The straight-talking Geordie duly became, along with Hixon, one of Shearer's first football mentors.

The teenager may have left school with only one qualification to his name, but thanks to the guru-like guidance of Merrington, he would receive a tough schooling in both football and life. Merrington's ethos involved graft galore on the training field and his methods often exposed his young trainees to some unusual activities, including regular trips to the St Dismas Society, a local welfare organisation that looked after victims of alcohol and drug abuse, as well as the homeless.

Merrington explained the rationale for such visits in the *Guardian*: 'They'd see these people, homeless people or people with a drink problem, people from every walk of life. There were two ideas. First for them to give something back, these kids who had their futures in front of them. Some of the people were mad-keen football fans and I was also trying to teach the boys that they had a responsibility to the people who paid to watch them, that these were the most important people. And I also wanted them to get an idea of what could go wrong, to make them aware of the consequences.'

Merrington went on to add that his approach to nurturing young trainees was to attempt to turn them 'into a man' within two years. He recognised that a football player's career could be fleeting and that the personal skills he strived to instil in Shearer and Southampton's youngsters, such as self-belief, discipline and confidence, could be employed in other areas of their lives.

Any abuse of Merrington's regimental regime brought harsh penalties, such as punishing five-mile runs and menial chores, like sweeping the dressing-room floor. Shearer also received harsh punishment from Merrington when he inadvertently left the tap running in the boot room, causing the entire place to be flooded. He and his fellow trainees were ordered to complete 50 laps of the training pitch – in the depths of a biting cold winter. However, Shearer, whose first pay packet was a meagre £27.50 a week, responded to such an unforgiving approach in a manner reminiscent of his boyhood idol and one-time Southampton favourite, Kevin Keegan, who was renowned for his training-ground endeavours. Both would be the first to admit that they are not blessed with silky skills, but their staunch commitment to hard work and dedication in training more than compensated for any shortcomings in the natural talent department.

Before long, Southampton's first-team coach, Chris Nicholl,

recognised that the young Shearer possessed raw talent in abundance after seeing him rattle in fifty-five goals for Southampton's youth side in the South-East Counties League Division Two. Like another teenage English footballing prodigy, Wayne Rooney, Shearer was well-built and Nicholl was desperate for his immense physicality to come to the fore. He told the *Independent* in 1992: 'He already had a big backside and big thighs when we took him on, so he always had that power, but it was a raw power – there was no finesse at all. He had a touch like a bricklayer: real heavy on the ball, he was. It just wouldn't stick at his feet. I remember at The Dell we had to keep him behind to work on his touch, both in the air and on the ground, day after day.'

Meanwhile, Dave Merrington was keen to hone Shearer's raw talent for thunderous shooting. He recognised that this was a particular asset of Alan's and was keen to focus on the youngster's strengths, rather than his weaknesses. He informed his protégé that he wanted him to posses as lethal a right foot as the left foot of former Hungarian legend, Ferenc Puskás. Shearer had not heard of the ex-Real Madrid man, but listened attentively to his coach's instructions and acted upon them dutifully, staying behind for extra shooting practice after training.

It was inevitable that before long the powerfully built youth would muscle his way into the first team, and he took significant strides towards this with substitute appearances for Saints against Chelsea and Oxford during the 1987–88 campaign. Then, on 9 April 1988, at the age of seventeen years and 240 days, he powered into the history books with a sensational hat-trick on a stunning full debut against Arsenal at The Dell.

Shearer was a late call-up to Southampton's first team, owing to a late injury to striker Danny Wallace, and duly became the youngest player in the then First Division to score three goals in an unforgettable 4–2 victory over the Gunners. Two headers, the first after only five minutes, and another strike on 49 minutes thrust him into the soccer record books.

Martin Marks reported in the *Daily Mail* that Shearer proudly clutched the match ball as reward for his record-breaking efforts and quoted him as saying of his dream debut: 'It was a dream, but I've been told that I can't speak to anyone about it. My parents didn't have time to get to the game, but I've already told them what I've done.'

Another notable absentee from Shearer's breathtaking break-through was his confidant, friend and mentor, Jack Hixon. He had been to see Berwick Rangers play and heard of his protégé's astounding feats on the radio as he drove back to the North-East. But Shearer could comfort himself that another one of his nearest and dearest was watching proudly from the stands on this memorable day – his girlfriend, Lainya Arnold.

The pair had met when Shearer was on a night out with his fellow Southampton trainees, one of whom was Paul Masters, who introduced his Geordie friend to Lainya, the sister of his girlfriend, Shona. Love blossomed and Shearer soon moved out of his digs to stay with Lainya and her mother and father. A recipe for disaster for the two fledgling lovers, one might think, but Shearer reveals in his autobiography that 'we all got on famously from the word go. They must have liked me because, by the time we were eighteen, Lainya and I had set up home together with their full approval.' The couple soon signalled their commitment to a long-term relationship by buying a two-bedroomed, semi-detached house for £67,500.

Meanwhile, Southampton manager Chris Nicholl was keen to protect his prodigy from the inevitable media frenzy generated from such an explosive debut and ushered Shearer out of the back door of the club soon after the Arsenal match.

While keen to play down the precocious performance of his brilliant young player, Nicholl knew he had to act fast and ensure that

ALAN SHEARER

Shearer's long-term future lay at The Dell. Therefore, five days after his comic-book-esque heroics against the Gunners, Southampton signed up their young star on a professional contract.

A thrilled Shearer put pen to paper on a three-year deal, earning him £225 a week in the first year and an £18,000 signing-on fee spread over three years. He was unaware of it at the time, but officials at his hometown club, Newcastle, had realised the error of their ways in not capturing Shearer several years earlier and approached Southampton to sign him. Chris Nicholl explained to the *Daily Mirror* in August 1996: 'They offered him £10,000 just to sign on and normally that would have been way out of Southampton's league for a lad of just seventeen. But we knew we had something special and we were able to match Newcastle's offer.'

Ironically, eight years later, Newcastle would have to shell out considerably more than £10,000 with their record-breaking £15 million swoop for Shearer. However, Shearer has insisted that he would have snubbed a return home and stressed that he was happy on the south coast. And Southampton represented the ideal environment for the young apprentice to learn his trade without the pressures and expectations intrinsic to life at a more fashionable and more high profile club.

At the time Shearer shot to prominence, the south coast side boasted a healthy mix of youth and experience. He rose through the Saints' ranks with the likes of Tim Flowers, Neil Maddison, Jeff Kenna, Rod Wallace and his brother Danny and Francis Benali. And he was fortunate to play alongside the lavishly gifted Matt Le Tissier, a mercurial genius rated by Shearer as the most skilful player he has seen with the ball at his feet.

Then there were the seasoned campaigners from whom the enthusiastic youngster could learn – men such as the Northern Ireland centre-forward Colin Clarke, who partnered Shearer up front during his debut, the fierce-tackling midfield hard man Jimmy Case and the eccentric goalkeeper John 'Budgie' Burridge. Burridge's teachings to Shearer were particularly well absorbed by the impressionable youth. During a bout of training-ground high jinks, 'Budgie' attempted to scythe down the cocky youth with a flying tackle, but he duly hurdled over his outstretched legs. Burridge disclosed to the *Independent* in 1997: 'I shouted at him, "Never jump over the 'keeper. Go for the ball. Put your foot in." Well, I was playing for Falkirk four years later and Southampton came up for a friendly. Alan came in goal at me and gave me four stitches. He came up to me in the bar afterwards and said, "You told me to do it." I just smiled and said, "Good lad."'

Yet there was to be no meteoric rise for the young Geordie after his awesome emergence in top-flight football as he failed to net in two further appearances in the 1987–88 season. He also drew a blank the following season, in which he made ten appearances, two of them as a substitute.

Indeed, he had to wait until 24 February 1989 before he could again claim a place in Saints' first-team line-up in the 1–1 draw against Everton. The following season would see a welcome upturn in both Shearer's and Southampton's fortunes, as the Saints finished a creditable seventh in the old First Division.

Shearer weighed in with five goals in all competitions, while Le Tissier and Rodney Wallace netted fifty times between them in what many Saints fans consider to be one of their most exciting ever sides. The Geordie made his first appearance as a substitute against Crystal Palace on 16 September 1989, before he scored against QPR in a 4–1 romp.

The 1989–90 season also saw Shearer claim his first-ever goals in cup competitions when he scored twice in the 2–0 win over York City in the second round, second leg of the Littlewoods Cup on 3 October 1989. He also featured in one of Southampton's most scintillating performances of that, or any season – a 4–1 demolition of the mighty Liverpool.

In the next campaign, Shearer began to consolidate the early promise he had shown on his debut, scoring fourteen goals in all competitions in which he made a total of forty-five appearances.

Perhaps his most memorable goals came in January 1991 against Manchester United in their clashes in the fifth round of the Rumbelows Cup. Shearer finished with aplomb from an acute angle to earn Southampton a replay after a 1–1 draw at The Dell. He added two goals more as Saints bravely succumbed to a 3–2 defeat at Old Trafford in the replay.

England Under-21 recognition was his reward in the summer of 1991, when he starred in the Toulon tournament, while there was also reason to celebrate in his personal life after he married Lainya. But according to his wife-to-be, Shearer was poised to put football before marriage. In 1996 she admitted to the *Daily Mirror* that Shearer was ready to go on England's tour of Australia and New Zealand – which clashed with the date of his wedding – if he were selected. However, luckily for Lainya, he was not included in the touring party. 'He was asked in an interview afterwards what he would have done if he'd been picked to go and he replied: "I'd have gone to Australia."'

The happy couple, both of whom were just twenty at the time, tied the knot at St James' Church, Southampton, on 8 June 1991. Shearer later confessed that he had never been as nervous on the football pitch as he had on this momentous day. 'It was more nerve-racking than playing for Saints. My hand was shaking so much I had trouble putting the ring on her finger,' he was quoted as saying in the *Daily Mirror* in 1996. Neil Maddison, the fellow Geordie and Southampton team-mate with whom Shearer made the journey down from the North-East five years earlier, was best man.

Neil 'Razor' Ruddock, at that time an uncompromising defender for

Southampton, Shearer's brother-in-law Paul Masters and another friend, Lee Roddaway, were the ushers. Once the marital formalities and a family reception were over, Mr and Mrs Shearer headed off to Jamaica for a three-week honeymoon.

Shearer's next long-term commitment, or so he thought at the time, was signing a new four-year deal with Southampton in August 1991. As it turned out, his thirteen goals in forty-one appearances, making him Southampton's top finisher of the 1991–92 season, would see scores of would-be suitors swarm to The Dell to vie for his signature.

The twenty-one-year-old's coming of age as a predator supreme was confirmed with his rapier-like strike after only two minutes in Saints' 3–2 home defeat against Tottenham.

In December 1991, his eye-catching performances for Southampton had propelled him into the £1 million-plus price bracket. Speaking about Shearer's goal and overall contribution in Saints' 1–1 draw with Liverpool, the *Independent*'s Henry Winter said the youngster's value had rocketed. 'We are getting close to Gazza prices here, such is the aptitude and attitude of the Southampton striker who is the most prolific England Under-21 player ever. But unlike his fellow Geordie, Shearer possesses the temperament of Gary Lineker, the man he is strongly tipped to replace as Graham Taylor builds for USA '94.'

A full-international cap and a goal for England against France in early 1992 thrust him further into the consciousness of more glamorous clubs than Southampton. Shearer also nearly won his first professional club trophy with the Saints, who succumbed to an agonising 3–2 extra-time loss to Nottingham Forest in the final of the Zenith Data Systems Cup after goals from Matt Le Tissier and defender Kevin Moore forced the game beyond 90 minutes.

However, he was acutely aware that his lust for success was unlikely to be fulfilled on the south coast and began to entertain thoughts of progressing his career elsewhere. In his autobiography he admits that he approached Southampton supremo Ian Branfoot, who had taken over from Chris Nicholl, to ask him if he would keep him abreast of any interested parties.

Manchester United and his beloved Newcastle were among the admirers, as too were buoyant Blackburn Rovers, who had just clinched promotion to the new Premier League. Meanwhile, French champions Marseille were among the foreign posse of clubs keen to recruit Shearer. Who would have thought that that the least vaunted of this clutch of clubs would clinch the signature of the most-sought-after young striker in English football?

CHAPTER FOUR

Al of the Rovers

Bankrolled by millionaire owner Jack Walker, in 1992 Blackburn Rovers possessed the financial clout to rival any club in English football. His business, WalkerSteel, had earlier that decade been sold off to British Steel, in a takeover worth an estimated £330 million to Walker, a devoted Blackburn fan since boyhood.

After buying an initial 62 per cent stake in Blackburn in the summer of 1991 to become the club's vice-president, he set about transforming Rovers into one of the biggest clubs in England. Walker recruited ex-Liverpool legend Kenny Dalglish as manager and made significant funds available for him to attract the cream of British talent.

After last line of second para, insert: They were now perfectly primed for an assault on English football's major prizes.

However, despite boasting a proud past, which included being one of the twelve founder members of the Football League in 1875, on the face of it for any up-and-coming young player Rovers did not have the spell-binding allure of a Liverpool or a Manchester United.

ALAN SHEARER

In January 1992, the *Daily Mail*'s David Walker reported that United had registered their interest in English football's hottest prospect months before an anticipated summer transfer scramble. 'United have not tabled an offer for the twenty-one-year-old Geordie who joined Southampton from school. But the league leaders inquired about Southampton's plans for selling their prize asset and have requested to be kept informed about the situation.' Walker added: 'The Southampton hierarchy have made it clear to their Old Trafford counterparts, and other interested parties, that Shearer will not be sold until the summer.'

But according to the *Daily Mail* reporter, Blackburn had already staked their claim to snatch Shearer from their rivals' grasp earlier that season when Kenny Dalglish tabled a £3 million offer. Walker prophesised that this would 'set the scene for a British record transfer deal in the close season'.

The gloves were off and in the summer of 1992 Blackburn and Manchester United were left in a straight fight for Shearer after other clubs chasing the Geordie fell by the wayside, discouraged by the massive price required by Southampton for one of their biggest assets. But when Manchester United and their legendary manager Alex Ferguson come calling, it's usually a dead cert that they get their man.

Not in Alan Shearer's case, however. He flabbergasted Fergie by sternly rebuffing the Scot's advances and, in July 1992, opted to join Kenny Dalglish's emerging side for a fee of £3.3 million, a British transfer record at the time, which involved David Speedie heading to Southampton. Ferguson had been desperate to bolster his attacking options with a top English striker and had earmarked Shearer and Sheffield Wednesday's David Hirst as his prime targets.

He admits in his autobiography *Managing My Life* that he had 'a slight preference for Hirst' purely on the basis of his experience – the Sheffield man was twenty-four while Shearer was only twenty-one.

However, Ferguson turned his attention to the younger man when Hirst's boss, Trevor Francis, gave him 'short shrift' after he expressed an interest. Ferguson then opened initial negotiations with Mel Stein, Shearer's agent, and was given the go-ahead to approach the player himself.

However, the terse telephone conversation he had with Shearer would have been enough to turn the fiery Scot's renowned ruddy cheeks an even darker shade of crimson. 'Our talk did not last long,' he writes in his autobiography. 'I found him very hard work and quite surly. One of the first things he said to me was, "Why haven't you been interested in me before now?"'

The crafty Scot then resorted to a last-ditch ploy in a bid to persuade the stubborn Geordie to join his Reds' revolution. '"Would Kenny [Dalglish] have signed for Blackburn when he was a player?" I asked him. "I know what he'd have done if United and Blackburn had both come in for him." In answer, he snapped back at me: "I'm not interested in what Kenny would have done...it's about what I want, not Kenny."'

Interestingly, Shearer makes no mention of this conversation in his own account of the transfer in his autobiography and after his surprise move to Blackburn he has frequently denied that he had had any contact with Ferguson. He prefers to dwell on the magnetism of Blackburn, revealing that there were three key players who influenced his unexpected move to Ewood Park – manager Kenny Dalglish, his first-team coach Ray Harford and the club's cash-laden owner, Jack Walker.

In particular, Dalglish's dogged pursuit of Shearer made a telling impression on the twenty-one-year-old. While Sir Alex Ferguson favoured a telephone call in the first instance to talk to Shearer, Dalglish instigated an in-depth, face-to-face chat. Shearer and Lainya met Dalglish and his wife Marina at the Haydock Park Post Hotel by the M6 motorway. While Marina took Lainya off for a girlie outing in Southport, Dalglish set about – once his transfer target had got to grips with his broad Glaswegian accent – outlining his lofty aims for Blackburn and quizzing Shearer about his background and family life.

Such a thorough inquisition was typical of Dalglish, according to Shearer, who claimed that Mike Newell and Tim Flowers were both recruited to the club by similar means. Shearer enthused of the camaraderie and mutual respect engendered by Dalglish. He also recognised that the Scottish maestro relished the challenge of transforming Blackburn from humble beginnings into a major footballing force, having spent his career as player and manager at two of the biggest clubs in the world, Liverpool and Celtic.

Dalglish's right-hand man, Ray Harford, also had an important part to play in encouraging Shearer to galvanise the Blackburn resurgence. Indeed, in July 1992, the *Mail on Sunday*'s Bob Cass hailed Harford as 'the inspiration' behind Blackburn's coup in signing Shearer. According to Cass, Harford had hankered after Shearer ever since seeing his coruscating performances for the England Under-21 side, whom he had guided to success in the Toulon tournament the previous summer. 'Harford drew on those memories when Dalglish was reviewing possible transfer targets with him in the early spring. "Why not try for Shearer," suggested Harford.' Shearer, too, had the utmost respect for Harford's coaching abilities and was convinced that he would continue to progress under his tutelage.

The third pivotal player in this sensational transfer saga was former steel magnate Jack Walker, who was willing to lavish large portions of his estimated £500 million personal fortune on the country's finest footballing talent. Sceptics suggested that the principal reason for Shearer joining unfancied Blackburn instead of Manchester United was the lure of the filthy lucre, a suggestion he has routinely dismissed.

AL OF THE ROVERS

But wouldn't any working-class male jump at the golden chance to earn a reported £10,000 a week, the enticing terms offered in Shearer's four-year Blackburn contract? He was rightly profiting from a new 'loadsamoney' era in English football which had benefited from BskyB's £304 million deal for the television rights to the inaugural Premier League.

And to Shearer and Blackburn fans, Jack Walker did not represent a businessman looking to make a few bucks at others' expenses, as perhaps Manchester United fans viewed American tycoon Malcolm Glazer's takeover of their club in 2005. What made Walker different to the likes of Glazer was the fact that he was a Lancashire lad born and bred whose innate love for Blackburn was not in question, despite his massive wealth. Praising the late Blackburn owner in his autobiography, Shearer says: 'He is fiercely proud of his roots and that, in turn, gave him his burning desire to make Rovers a great club.'

The cumulative effect of the positive impression that Blackburn's triumvirate made on Shearer was that, following a dinner with Dalglish, Harford and his wife, the next day he agreed to the move with little hesitation.

Shearer had admitted he did not feel his hefty transfer fee was justified, but vowed not to let it affect him and made a concerted effort to prove his worth on the pitch. However, he made an indifferent start to his Ewood Park odyssey as Blackburn slumped to a 3–0 away defeat to Scottish side Hibernian in a pre-season friendly.

Nevertheless, it was on this trip north of the border that he developed a firm friendship with strike partner, Mike Newell. The pair became inseparable, living near one another in Formby, becoming inveterate golf partners and sharing lifts to and from Blackburn's training ground. Nicknamed 'Mr Angry' for his combustible temper and love of an argument, Newell proved the perfect foil for Shearer's more laidback demeanour.

The new best buddies also complemented each other on the pitch as Newell's tireless running and unselfish knockdowns were manna from heaven for Shearer. Meanwhile, winger Stuart Ripley had been snapped up from Middlesbrough for £1.2 million to provide tantalising crosses for Newell and Shearer. Veteran Gordon Cowans and the elegant Tim Sherwood were efficient in the midfield engine room, while emerging Scot Colin Hendry and gritty Irishman Kevin Moran formed a solid defensive unit. Such individuals were not, however, the collective recipe for success, according to some national journalists.

The *Independent*'s Joe Lovejoy predicted that Blackburn would finish fourteenth in the Premier League, insisting that the money spent on Shearer should have been splashed out on other areas of the side. Dispensing with the services of David Speedie, who had scored twenty-three goals in thirty-six games the previous season, and Scott Sellars, was also bad business, according to Lovejoy.

David Lacey of the *Guardian* also questioned the big-spending policy of the Premier newcomers. 'Buying players does not buy a team and no matter how many of Jack Walker's millions Kenny Dalglish spends, money alone will not bring him a blend on the field,' he declared.

The pressure was now well and truly on Blackburn and, in particular, Shearer, to perform. Yet any doubts anyone had about the costly new boy were emphatically blown away when Shearer characteristically made another devastating league debut in what was an exhilarating encounter.

He scored a glorious double as Blackburn began their Premier League campaign against Crystal Palace at Selhurst Park on 15 August 1992 with a pulsating 3–3 draw. Bryon Butler of the *Daily Telegraph* described Shearer's brilliant brace as 'two goals of luminous quality'. He wrote: 'His first was merely very good, a dambuster from just outside the penalty area, but the second was self-evidently brilliant. Shearer pursued the ball like a puppy for 30 yards towards the left, won it easily, manoeuvred it inside for another 15 yards and then whistled the ball into the low right corner from 24 yards. Speed, determination and high technique in one rich capsule.'

Suddenly, the weighty burden of his £3 million-plus price tag began to sit a little more easily on Shearer's broad shoulders. After the game, he matter-of-factly told Neil Harman of the *Daily Mail*: 'I have no control over what people pay for me. I'm wise enough to realise there will be times when people think and write that I'm not justifying all the money. I'll have to live with that. I'm not going to get carried away with the goals today, just as I won't get down on myself if I don't score for a couple of matches.'

Three days after the Crystal Palace game, Shearer struck a thunderous shot to power Blackburn to victory over Arsenal in his first home match for Rovers, prompting Colin Gibson to declare in the *Daily Telegraph* that the twenty-two-year-old's reported £12,000-a-week wages no longer seemed 'such a huge extravagance'. A penalty in Blackburn's 2–0 away win against Coventry, bringing Shearer's tally of goals to four, was by lucky coincidence despatched in front of the watching England boss, Graham Taylor. He was duly rewarded with selection to England's squad for the friendly against Spain on 9 September 1992.

Shearer celebrated becoming Blackburn's first England player since Keith Newton in 1969 by crashing in a close-range volley and adding another spot kick in a 4–1 rout of Nottingham Forest just days later.

High-flying Blackburn continued to confound the critics by winning away at championship favourites Arsenal, stretching their unbeaten run to seven games. However, despite Shearer's two goals, they then fell to their first defeat of the season when Everton triumphed 3–2 at Ewood Park.

On 3 October, they rocketed to the Premier League summit after annihilating Norwich City 7–1, usurping the previous table toppers.

Shearer and co ran riot, the gleeful Geordie helping himself to two goals while his exemplary all-round performance won plaudits from impressed members of the media. *The Times'* Clive White, for example, said: 'It was a classic Shearer performance against Norwich, full of aggressive running, selfless support and lethal finishing.'

England's new golden boy was suddenly feeling the pressure of being touted as his country's saviour following his blistering start to the season with Blackburn. He told Peter Ball of *The Times*: 'There is going to be a lot of pressure on me now. Because of what I've done at Blackburn, everyone is going to be expecting me to do it at international level, quite rightly.'

Ball also included a glowing testimony about Shearer from the benefactor behind Blackburn's barnstorming beginning in the top flight, Jack Walker. 'He is a wonderful player. He will be one of the great Blackburn players to compare with anything we have had before.'

Everything was going swimmingly for the Gosforth-born goal-grabber, who had also recently become a father to a daughter, Chloe, and suddenly all talk of his mammoth price tag was consigned to the past.

BBC football pundit and former distinguished Liverpool defender Alan Hansen was quoted by the *Mail on Sunday's* Joe Melling as saying: 'I never believed any footballer was worth £3 million until I saw Shearer playing for Blackburn.'

His partner in crime up front, Mike Newell, felt Shearer was now worth considerably more than £3 million. He told the *Mail on Sunday*: 'He was an absolute snip at the price. There is just so much to his game. Everybody knows by now that he is a great goalscorer, but he is also a very unselfish player. He always plays for the team.'

Shearer also saved Blackburn from embarrassment when he scored a last-gasp equaliser for Blackburn against Second Division Huddersfield in the Coca Cola Cup. The Lancashire side eventually secured their passage to the next round after winning 4–3 after extra-time, to progress 5–4 on aggregate. The most eagerly awaited clash of the season for Blackburn and Shearer came at the end of October, when the mighty Manchester United visited Ewood Park.

The meeting of the former flourishing market town against the city slickers had a special significance for Shearer, as he was facing for the first time the side he had snubbed in the summer.

Arguably a more rigorous examination of the Blackburn striker was dealing with the torrent of abuse likely to cascade down from the away-supporters' section. In his autobiography, he labels himself 'the most hated footballer alive in the eyes of Manchester United fans'. 'I got a sackload of mail when I left Southampton. Many of the letters were abusive and most were anonymous. They could be very unnerving, but the best place for those kind of letters was the dustbin, which is where they ended up.'

He was to be the target of venomous insults from United fans wherever he went although, typical of the character of the man, such behaviour only acted as a spur when he was playing. On this occasion against Manchester United, however, Shearer was unable to exact telling retribution against his hecklers and drew a blank, as did Blackburn, in an insipid 0–0 draw.

The Lancashire side and their leading scorer endured a lean period during the rest of the autumn and were toppled from the top of the table when Tottenham earned a 2–0 win at Ewood Park. Shearer suffered a five-match goal famine in the league, before he netted in the 1–0 win over QPR in December 1992.

In emphatic fashion, he then returned to the goal trail when he blasted two goals to help Blackburn cruise into the quarter-finals of the Coca Cola Cup after Watford were drubbed 6–1. His two goals against Leeds on Boxing Day in Blackburn were a bittersweet moment, however, as it proved to be his final full game of the season. He injured his right knee in a challenge with Leeds defender Chris Fairclough, although in the immediate aftermath of the game there was little to suggest that it would have long-term implications.

Shearer admits that he conned his way through a fitness test in order to play against Cambridge United in the Coca Cola Cup on 6 January 1993. However, his return in this match lasted just thirty minutes before he hobbled off. His injury was eventually diagnosed as a severe cruciate ligament problem and the full misery that this caused Shearer is discussed in another chapter.

Shorn of Shearer's goal-scoring prowess, Blackburn finished fourth in the Premier League – a highly creditable placing in their return to the top flight. It is academic now, but think how Blackburn's fortunes could have been so dramatically different if a fit Shearer had plundered another ten or fifteen goals to add to his season's tally of twenty-two.

Yet this encouraging beginning was to be the first stepping-stone towards eventual title glory in 1995 for Blackburn.

Characteristically, Shearer's return to action at the start of August was a goal-scoring one. Blackburn were on a pre-season tour to Ireland and he claimed two goals in a 3–0 win over Drogheda. 'It was great to be back and a tremendous feeling when that first goal went in. I have got through a lot of hard work and there is more to be done,' he told the *Daily Mail*.

Shearer was limited to substitute appearances as Blackburn commenced their Premier League campaign and scored in his side's 1–1 draw with Newcastle – his first goal for nine months.

His first start for Rovers in the 1993–94 season saw him score the only goal in Blackburn's 1–0 win over Birmingham in the Coca Cola Cup. His league comeback was 'a stunning display of aggression, pace and power', according to the Press Association, and involved him flashing a left-foot drive past Chris Woods in the Sheffield Wednesday goal to earn Blackburn a 1–1 draw on 25 September 1993. His companion up front for that match was the willowy Scot, Kevin Gallacher, while Paul Warhurst – a defender-turned-striker – had also bolstered Blackburn's attacking ranks after being signed from Sheffield Wednesday.

With this added firepower boosted by Shearer's recovery, Blackburn were bidding to launch another onslaught on the championship. Any lingering doubts about whether the rehabilitated striker could recapture his best form were banished as he slammed in eight goals in seven full matches at the start of the 1993–94 season. They were now perfectly primed for an assault on English football's major prizes.

Leeds were the opponents as he claimed his first hat-trick in Blackburn colours, but the Elland Road side clung on to force a thrilling 3–3 draw in late October. Kenny Dalglish was delighted with the phenomenal form of his No. 1 striker. 'There is even more to come from him. He has all the attributes he had before his injury and there is no problem either physically or mentally. He always makes me wonder what he's going to do, and what he can achieve in the game is up to him.'

And the dour Scot was cheered further when he snapped up the tigerish midfielder David Batty from Leeds and Shearer's former team-mate, goalkeeper Tim Flowers from Southampton, in successive weeks in the autumn of 1993. The twin signings meant that Dalglish, remarkably, had shelled out more than £20 million in transfer fees in just two years as Blackburn boss.

His vow to continue spending sent out a clear message to the rest of the Premier League that he was determined to build a side capable of competing, irrespective of Shearer's goals aplenty.

The jewel in Blackburn's crown continued to be their Geordie gem, however, whose astonishing gift for scoring goals was causing jaws to drop and opposing goalkeepers to grimace.

Southampton's Ian Branfoot, the man who sold Shearer to Blackburn, gave a ringing endorsement of his former player's talents after seeing his side succumb to a 2–0 defeat courtesy of a brace from Super Al in

November 1993. Branfoot admitted: 'I thought my centre-halves played well today, but you give Alan Shearer half a chance and he puts them away. And that was certainly £3 million-worth. If I had £3.5 million, I'd try and buy him, but he'd probably cost more than that now.'

The second of Shearer's goals was tipped to be a goal-of-the-season contender by his former team-mate Matt Le Tissier among other awestruck admirers. On 22 November 1993, John Dunhill of the *Daily Mail* said: 'The Southampton sorcerer ambled up to his old pal in the Ewood Park corridor after Blackburn's 2–0 victory, showed him the contents of a plastic carrier, and said: "See that? That's my goal of the month trophy for October. You'll be getting one of these at the end of this month."'

A rare occasion when Shearer failed to net came when Blackburn went out of the Coca Cola Cup in December 1993, losing 1–0 at Spurs. Sol Campbell, then a nineteen-year-old trainee, played up front for Ossie Ardiles' men, scored the only goal and eclipsed his more illustrious opposing number.

In the league, though, Blackburn were once again in contention in the upper echelons of the table, easing into third spot in the Premier League after Shearer struck once in a 2–0 victory over Chelsea in early December. Winning over their doubters would not be such a comfortable proposition, however, as many football devotees were not enamoured by Blackburn's prosaic style of play and the manner in which their side had been assembled.

Under the headline 'A triumph of unloved efficiency', the *Independent*'s John Culley felt that Alan Shearer's presence had proved the difference in Blackburn's 2–1 victory at Oldham. He wrote: 'They [Oldham] lost this match not because they were markedly inferior, but because Blackburn have Alan Shearer and because they have a defence which, from time to time, might as well not be there. Shearer punished them once in each half.'

AL OF THE ROVERS

Impending success for Blackburn would also receive a lukewarm response from most, added Culley. 'And yet, when they do succeed, as almost certainly they will, in collecting one of the major trophies, it is likely to bring joy to a committed minority more than to a larger impartial public.'

Blackburn still had to supplant champions Manchester United from top spot if they wanted to turn their aspirations into reality. All-conquering United were looking imperious and Blackburn needed Shearer to be on his mettle if Alex Ferguson's side's inexorable procession towards the championship was to be derailed. The straight-talking striker fired the opening salvo when, before the long-awaited confrontation, he again reiterated that he did not regret snubbing Manchester for Blackburn. Speaking in the *Mail on Sunday* on Boxing Day 1993, he said: 'I have absolutely no regrets about signing for Blackburn Rovers. Yes, I might have gone to United and won a championship medal or two, but I might not have been as content as I am at Rovers. I am very happy and convinced I made the right decision.'

Shearer and co nearly upset United, as well, but a last-minute Paul Ince strike denied the visitors victory after Kevin Gallacher had given Blackburn a 1–0 lead after 12 minutes.

As 1994 got underway, Blackburn were determined to maintain their dogged pursuit of the runaway leaders and a last-gasp winner from Shearer allowed them to see off champions Leeds 2–1 at Elland Road in late January. Meanwhile, Rovers were dumped out of the FA Cup in a fifth-round replay with Charlton Athletic, who claimed a 1–0 victory at Ewood Park. The *Independent*'s Henry Winter said of the stunning cup shock: 'Charlton's players even knew what Alan Shearer consumed before facing them – chicken and beans – following an in-depth *Match of the Day* profile on the Blackburn goalscorer. Des Lynam had even made a joke about it: "Chicken and beanz meanz goals." But not against Charlton.'

ALAN SHEARER

Yet goal machine Alan Shearer kept hitting the net with extraordinary consistency in the league and, in early February, his goal in Rovers' 2–0 win at Tottenham saw him complete the second fastest fifty-goal run in history. His phenomenal half-century was achieved in fifty-eight games; only Jimmy Greaves in the sixties boasted a better goal ratio, netting fifty times in fifty-four games.

Shearer's historic achievements aside, Blackburn were now tantalisingly within reach of Manchester United, whose lead had been cut to ten points. A 2–2 draw at Norwich in late February brought Blackburn closer still, as United players began to look anxiously over their shoulders to find the gap at the top had been closed to just six points. A 1–0 loss away to Arsenal quelled any title talk at Ewood Park, however, as lively Scottish striker Kevin Gallacher was ruled out for the rest of the season with a broken leg. Luckily, Mike Newell had recovered from a knee ligament injury sustained on Boxing Day and returned to re-form his potent strike force with Shearer.

Suddenly, what had seemed a forlorn hope a mere matter of months previously, turned into a distinct possibility when Blackburn roared right back into contention for English football's ultimate prize when Shearer's twenty-ninth and thirtieth goals of the season fired them to a 3–1 win over strugglers Swindon Town in March.

Rovers were now only three points behind United, but they blew the chance to move into top spot when they crashed 4–1 to Wimbledon. Everything now hinged on the two sides' do-or-die encounter at Ewood Park on 2 April 1994. Who else but Alan Shearer would come to the fore and reignite Blackburn's tenacious charge for the Premier League?

A header and a thunderous drive lashed past Peter Schmeichel, after he had left Gary Pallister trailing in his wake, saw Ewood Park explode with joy as United were overcome 2–0, their lead at the top once again slashed to just three points.

AL OF THE ROVERS

Legendary Scottish sports writer Hugh McIlvaney was at his lyrical best when he reflected on Shearer's instinctive finishing in the *Sunday Times* on 3 April 1994. He said: 'He is a goalscorer of the purest instincts and there was never much likelihood that he would fail to summon the nerve and technique to be influential. No one in the modern game more comprehensively qualifies for the classic definition of a great striker coined by the late Jock Stein: the kind of man who, when he cannot think of anything else to do with the ball, sticks it into the back of the net.'

However, United gained a measure of recompense for this loss by beating Blackburn to another prestigious prize just days after when their French talisman, Eric Cantona, triumphed over Shearer to win the Professional Footballers' Association Player of the Year Award.

Shearer came third while Peter Beardsley of Newcastle was the runner-up. The ultimate accolade for Shearer and Blackburn remained the championship, however, and they increased the mounting pressure on United with a 1–0 win over Aston Villa, thanks to a goal from their goal-scoring genius.

The championship rivals were now level-pegging at the top, although Manchester United had a game in hand and a superior goal difference, but a devastating 3–1 loss at Shearer's former employers Southampton and a 1–1 draw at home to QPR saw Blackburn's title bid come to a juddering halt.

While it was now looking increasingly unlikely that Blackburn would acquire a trophy, their sensational striker collected a piece of silverware in recognition of his fabulous personal feats.

An outstanding season, in which he had bludgeoned thirty-four goals – a marvellous haul only beaten by Andy Cole's forty-one contributions in all competitions – saw him earn the Football Writers' Player of the Year award ahead of Beardsley and Cantona. The Press Association quoted a jubilant Shearer as remarking: 'Ewood Park has been a great place to be in the last couple of years and with a management team like Kenny Dalglish, Ray Harford and Tony Parkes, I believe there are even more highlights to come.'

PA reporter Bill Pierce revealed that Shearer had contacted Jack Hixon, his friend, confidant and mentor, on hearing of his honour. Hixon said: 'This is a tribute to Alan's honesty and dedication as much as his skill. I am proud to be associated with him.'

Sadly for Blackburn, the fact that Shearer's striking cohorts – Messrs Newell, Gallacher and Warhurst – were indisposed towards the end of the season, finally delivered a fatal blow to their championship hopes. They slumped to a 2–1 victory at Coventry on 2 May to ensure that United would celebrate a second successive championship.

Despite their failure in the closing stages, Blackburn had shown burgeoning promise that could, with some shrewd squad strengthening from Kenny Dalglish, be fulfilled in the 1994–95 season. It was now time to unleash the SAS – aka the strike force of Alan Shearer and Chris Sutton – on opposing defences, as Blackburn prepared for their assault on the Premier League crown and a foray into Europe through the UEFA Cup.

Sutton, a former defender converted into a striker to great effect at Norwich, for whom he had scored twenty-eight goals in 1993–94, was recruited for a cool £5 million in July 1994. In turn, he became Britain's most highly paid player, earning a five-year contract worth £12,000 a week.

However, later that year, Blackburn's board demonstrated that they valued Shearer above the twenty-one-year-old young pretender by increasing his wages to an undisclosed amount. This generous gesture was greatly appreciated by Shearer, who fully expected this increment to depend on him extending his contract. Writing in his auto-biography, he said: 'There were no conditions. Blackburn merely wanted to reward me for my services. That told me a lot about the kind of club Rovers had become. I cannot think of many others who would have done that.'

Australian midfielder Robbie Slater became another Blackburn summer recruit after joining from Lens, while defender David May exited to Manchester United. However, Rovers' chief source of goals endured a torrid time in pre-season after being struck down by a mystery illness.

Speculation was rife that Shearer was suffering from the debilitating liver disease hepatitis A, but a more informed medical view confirmed that he was the victim of food poisoning, which was caused by him eating undercooked mussels on holiday in Portugal. His unfortunate choice in seafood ruled him out of Blackburn's pre-season trips to Norway and Scotland and the traditional curtain-raiser to the new season, the Charity Shield, which Rovers lost 2–0 to Manchester United.

Shearer was chomping at the bit to return for the opening game of the season, away at his former team Southampton, but received some chastening advice from Rovers' owner, Jack Walker. 'Alan has told me that he wants to play at Southampton, but I've told him: "Patience is a virtue, lad ... slow down,"' said the multi-millionaire in the *Daily Mail*.

Meanwhile, David Mullahey writing in *Agence France Presse* on 18 August 1994 believed Blackburn's hefty expenditure would reap rich dividends sooner rather than later, contrary to the belief of many, including Manchester United followers. Mullahey noted that the Old Trafford hordes had taunted Blackburn with the chant 'You'll never buy the title' as they coasted to victory in the Charity Shield match.

'But the taunt at Wembley has a hollow ring in a world of football where big spenders usually get big results, and where United have also been willing to dole out millions of pounds on a single player. Rovers' millionaire paymaster, Jack Walker, is certain to get a return on his investments. Such is its inevitability that manager Kenny Dalglish has been able to adopt a relaxed "when it comes, it comes" approach.

Mullahey also predicted that the Sutton-Shearer partnership would potentially be the England pairing for 'the next seven years'. At least he got one out of two predictions right...

Others in the media felt that Blackburn's best chance of silverware lay in cup competitions, insisting that their injury-prone squad was susceptible to the rigours of an arduous league season. Such a conviction seemed to be vindicated when Blackburn, including a fully recovered Shearer, made an undistinguished start to their Premier League campaign.

They drew 1–1 at Southampton, with Shearer on target, although he also had a penalty saved by the colourful character that is Bruce Grobbelaar. However, the SAS were on the rampage in Blackburn's next game, a 3–0 thumping of Leicester at Ewood Park. Sutton and Shearer scored a goal apiece and the former Norwich man showed he was undaunted by being in harness with someone he considered a role model when he bagged a hat-trick in Rovers' 4–0 rout of Coventry City.

Newcastle were the early pacesetters in the Premier League, with Andy Cole again scoring freely, but Blackburn climbed to third in the table in early September after Shearer's two goals helped down Everton 3–0.

But Blackburn's first incursion into Europe was an ignominious one, as their expensively assembled side crashed to an embarrassing 1–0 home defeat to Swedish part-timers Trelleborgs in the first-leg, first-round UEFA Cup-tie.

Chris Sutton knew that overturning this shock result with a win in the second leg in Sweden hinged on how he and Shearer performed against a side that included one player, Ola Severin, who was a rat exterminator by trade. On 24 September 1994 he expressed his admiration for his colleague to the *Daily Mail*. 'I see him sometimes and think "Blimey, he made that look easy". Once he gets going nobody can stop him. They said we couldn't make it as a partnership, but he's laid a few on for me, and the closest I've been to getting in his way this season is climbing on his back after he's scored. I don't think I've got under his feet. He takes everything in his stride and I'm trying to do the same.'

Shearer looked to have handed Blackburn a European lifeline when he put his side 2–1 ahead in the second round of their tie, but ten-man Trelleborgs rallied to force a 2–2 draw to send Rovers hurtling out of Europe at the first hurdle. It was a chastening experience for Rovers, but Jack Walker remained defiant and vowed to invest more money into his beloved boyhood favourites to achieve his dream of silverware. And he had words of encouragement for Shearer and Sutton. 'I've seen the signs that they are developing as a partnership. They're coming together,' he declared to the *Daily Mail* in the aftermath of Blackburn's European exit.

Despite their failings on the continent, it was business as usual for Blackburn in the league, as goals from Sutton and Shearer guaranteed the steady accumulation of points. A disappointing 4–2 loss at home to Manchester United in mid-October aside, they demonstrated their championship credentials by rocketing to pole position in late November, thanks to Shearer's hat-trick in a 4–0 demolition of QPR.

There was to be no joy for Shearer and friends in the League Cup, though, as Ian Rush's hat-trick at Ewood Park gave Liverpool a 3–1 victory and a passage into the quarter-finals of the competition. As 1994 ended, Blackburn led the men from Manchester by two points in another captivating title race.

Shearer's hat-trick in the 4–2 win over Ipswich on 3 January 1995 saw Blackburn boost their chances of glory and turned their showdown with Manchester United at the end of the month into a near championship decider. If Rovers won, they would stretch their lead over the Reds to eight points and soothe their pain at exiting the FA Cup after succumbing to Newcastle United at St James' Park.

ALAN SHEARER

Another fascinating feature of the eagerly anticipated contest would be the duel between two prolific goalscorers – Andy Cole and Alan Shearer. United had recently swooped to sign Cole from Newcastle United in a £7 million deal which involved Keith Gillespie going in the opposite direction.

Neil Harman of the *Daily Mail* voiced the view that Shearer would command a greater transfer fee in the inflated market of the mid-nineties. 'The fact that English football has found a player worth £3.7 million more than Shearer should be enough to put the price tag upon Manchester United's Andy Cole – who plays on the opposite side for the first time tomorrow – into its proper perspective. Madness is a word which springs to mind,' remarked Harman, declaring that the Blackburn man could become the country's first £10 million striker.

Neither Cole nor Shearer decided the outcome of this joust for supremacy as Eric Cantona's late headed goal reinvigorated Manchester United's quest for a third successive championship. However, Rovers were left fuming by referee Paul Durkin's decision to rule out an 89th-minute equaliser from Tim Sherwood, deeming that Shearer had fouled Roy Keane in the build-up.

A 3–1 capitulation to Tottenham in Blackburn's next game in early February compounded matters for Dalglish's men. Nerves were beginning to jangle at Ewood Park and it seemed as if the title tide was turning towards Manchester, given that Rovers had now gained only four points from as many matches.

Shearer confessed in his autobiography that the pressure of striving for Blackburn's first championship since 1914 took an immense toll on him and led to many sleepless nights. Watching or listening to Manchester United play was pure, unadulterated torture and the England man readily admits to hiding away in the corner of his house whenever United were playing and Blackburn were not.

AL OF THE ROVERS

There was nothing he could do to control United's destiny, so he concentrated his energies into doing what he does best – scoring an abundance of goals. There were two in Blackburn's 3–1 win over Arsenal on 8 March 1995, for example, to enable Shearer and co to leapfrog United at the top of the table. Later in the month, he reached a marvellous personal milestone when he notched his 100th career goal in Blackburn's match against Chelsea, and his thirtieth of the season, a game which Blackburn won 2–1. In so doing, Shearer became the first player since the predatory Jimmy Greaves in the 1960s to plunder thirty goals in consecutive seasons, putting him in contention for the European Golden Boot award. In the *Daily Mail* on 20 March 1995, an ecstatic Shearer declared: 'I'm delighted to be up there alongside someone as big as Jimmy Greaves. He set an example for everyone in how to score goals. If my name is alongside him, it's an honour and a privilege. I don't set myself any targets. I just aim to go out and enjoy my football. After suffering the injury to my right knee, that's all I set out to do.'

William Hill had installed Rovers as 4–6 favourites for the championship after their victory over Chelsea and Shearer insisted that Blackburn were enjoying their thrilling title pursuit. He said: 'There are no nerves in the dressing room. I've not noticed any anxiety. I think we're thoroughly enjoying being top with eight games to go. We're loving being up there. Manchester United are an exceptional side and I'm sure they'll push us hard. But we'll be doing our darndest to make sure we can see this through and, with a little bit of luck, we might get there.' However, Shearer and his fellow Rovers' players would not be fêted and fawned over if they were to finish as champions, according to Guy Hodgson of the *Independent*.

There was a distinct lack of style and panache on display when Blackburn disposed of Everton 2–1 at Goodison Park at the start of April, opined Hodgson, who condemned the manner of Rovers' victory which, he claimed, owed much to 'luck and naked pragmatism'.

ALAN SHEARER

Hodgson explained his and other neutrals' antipathy to Shearer and co thus: 'A lot of the aversion stems from jealousy – Jack Walker's money can buy a championship, not love – but for all their breathtaking moments, particularly at Ewood Park, there are matches like this, when Blackburn are charmless. The less-than-edifying sight of the best striker in Britain, Alan Shearer, booting the ball anywhere just to waste time summed up their play.'

Manchester United legend Paddy Crerend was equally disparaging in the *Daily Mail*. 'You would never see a United player do what Alan Shearer did at Everton last weekend. There's half a minute to go and Rovers are winning. The ball comes to him, he takes a couple of steps back and whacks it into the highest row of the stand. Kenny Dalglish did that in the last minute of a League Cup final when Liverpool were beating United. That's fine for them, but I want to be thrilled by watching adventure in my football.' And he took a further swipe at the Ewood Park men when he questioned: 'Tell me, how many people in Britain want Blackburn Rovers to win the championship? Is ITV going to offer Blackburn a contract to show all their European Cup matches?'

Perhaps Hodgson and Crerend's damning assessment was slightly unfair and, in the former Scotland defender's case, transparent evidence of a Manchester United bias.

Grinding out victories through grit and determination and by virtue of 'ugly' football, allied to a dose or two of luck, is characteristic of all potential champions. Then one has to take into account the tremendous tension pervading throughout this Blackburn side as they battled bravely to secure their first piece of major silverware since the FA Cup in 1928.

And despite this being an expensively built outfit, apart from Shearer, Sutton and one or two others, there were very few outstanding performers in this workmanlike and tenacious outfit, epitomising the final word in Blackburn's motto: 'Arte et Labore'.

There was none of the flair and free-flowing attacking football as exhibited by the Arsenal side who nonchalantly strolled through the season unbeaten in 2003–04, for instance. What Blackburn lacked in guile, they compensated with unity and team spirit. Having some of the best players in the world – in Real Madrid's case the so-called *galàcticos* of Zidane, Beckham, Raul, Ronaldo and co – is no guarantee for success.

The famous nineteenth-century rags-to-riches industrialist Andrew Carnegie summed up the importance of the team work which underpinned Blackburn's success when he said: 'Teamwork is the ability to work together towards a common vision. The ability to direct individual accomplishments towards organisational objectives. It is the fuel that allows common people to uncommon results.'

While Blackburn as a collective unit may not have won the approval of the purists, there was no doubting the universal acclaim reserved for Shearer, whose immense contribution to the Blue and Whites was rewarded with the Professional Footballers' Association Player of the Year Award, which he secured ahead of Tottenham's Jurgen Klinsmann and Matt Le Tissier of Southampton.

Collecting the award, Shearer said: 'It's a great, great honour to see my name among some of them who won it in the past. To be voted by fellow players who want to stop you playing, who want to kick you nine months of the year, is the highest accolade.' Cue eulogies from the seemingly endless pot of praise for this most magnificent of strikers. The *Guardian*'s Dave Hill said Shearer represented a throwback to a bygone era. 'The leading scorer of Blackburn Rovers, the cotton-town team on the verge of becoming English champions, resembles the very model of the classic working-class sporting hero and suits the language to match: still only twenty-four, Shearer is "upright", "clean-limbed", "well-made", everything legend demands an English centre-forward should be. And the qualities of his play are receptive to old-fashioned metaphors. There's an urge to compare his courage to a lion's and an impulse to liken his long shots at goal to the flight of cannon balls.'

ALAN SHEARER

Meanwhile, *The Times*' Rob Hughes recalled a late Blackburn fan's appreciation of their very own Roy of the Rovers. 'Robert Wright, a retired fitter, who was four when Rovers last won the title and whose stepson is John Byrom, a former Rovers player, was not keen on the fact that the millions from Jack Walker resuscitated the town's football dreams. 'It's all about money, isn't it? It's ridiculous in a town of so much unemployment, making players millionaires,' Wright reasoned. He paused, his eyes brightened and he added: 'Now there's one exception to that, this Shearer. He's a good player and a good lad. There's so many trying to injure him, but week in, week out, he's the one player that I've seen that anyone could say is worth the money.'

However, club honours were still not assured for Shearer as the 1994–95 dramatic two-horse Premier League contest took another unexpected twist when Manchester United's city rivals Manchester City resuscitated the Reds' fading championship dream with a 3–2 victory at Ewood Park.

However, a 2–1 home win over Crystal Palace rectified this mishap and put Blackburn eight points clear at the top and in reach of the prize they yearned for.

It was a bittersweet occasion for Shearer's Scottish international colleague, Kevin Gallacher, who scored the winning goal on his comeback after fifteen months out with a double fracture of his right leg, but who promptly broke his leg again.

Despite then losing 2–0 to West Ham away, Blackburn were still eight points clear of Manchester United and knew that wins from both their remaining two matches would clinch the championship.

For Shearer and his team-mates, they were about to face an extreme test of nerve and will-power as a glittering prize lay agonisingly close. 'I liken it to a major golf championship,' said Leeds manager Howard Wilkinson, whose side had overrun a nervy Manchester United to win the championship in 1992. 'You are up there on the leaderboard after three-and-three-quarter rounds. The worst thing you can do is alter your swing. You should go for important shots the way you have been doing; thinking about the consequences of the shot shouldn't affect your choice of club or shot.'

Cometh the hour cometh the man, as Alan Shearer sent 30,000 Blackburn fans into raptures with the winning goal against Newcastle at Ewood Park, as tension and nerves were replaced by relief and jubilation in the penultimate match of this tumultuous season.

Blackburn were now within a whisker of securing some silverware.

Rob Hughes in *The Times*' description of Shearer's crucial intervention was as follows: 'It was not inappropriate on this night to observe that Shearer goes in for the ball with the bravery of a soldier in action. He won it with a lunging tackle from Howey and turned it back to Batty. The little terrier miscued his shot, Peacock stretched but only half-cleared and then Le Saux beat the grounded Hottiger to chip the ball across the face of goal. There, using might and muscle to clamber all over the unfortunate Beresford, was you-know-who; the neck muscles braced, the head came down on the ball like a hammer and Shearer had scored his thirty-third goal in forty-one Premiership matches.'

The *Independent*'s Glenn Moore also borrowed Hughes' war analogy to hail Shearer's heroics. He said: 'Young and gifted, handsome and bright, brave, bold and decent. He embodies the values that were eulogised this weekend. While it is invidious to compare football to war, Shearer seems the type who would acquit himself with honour in any field of conflict.'

No prizes for guessing the worthy recipient of Blackburn's Player of the Season award. Presenting the honour to Shearer at the end of a night of unrelenting drama, was the man whose millions and vision for his club had persuaded the young Geordie to move north almost three years earlier. Walker said: 'I want to keep Alan Shearer here for next season. I think he's the making of the new Blackburn Rovers.'

Shearer's response was music to the misty-eyed Blackburn owner's ears. He wanted to stay, had never contemplated leaving and would consider extending his contract. The champagne was still on ice, however, but a win at Liverpool in Blackburn's final match of the season would seal the Premier League crown.

However, the Anfield side were determined to do no favours to their returning hero, Blackburn manager Dalglish, disproving any pre-match notions that their appetite for the battle would be diminished due to the meaningless nature of the fixture for them.

Shearer's thirty-seventh goal of the season put Blackburn within sight of their destiny; the goalscorer supreme slammed home Stuart Ripley's cross with customary aplomb from 16 yards. Blackburn's jubilation intensified after news filtered through that Manchester United were trailing 1–0 at West Ham.

Inspired by John Barnes, Liverpool threatened to spoil Blackburn's big day, however. First Barnes rammed in Mark Kennedy's cross on 64 minutes and then Jamie Rednapp's delightfully curled free-kick arrowed into the roof of Tim Flowers' net on 93 minutes to the horror of the travelling thousands.

Thankfully for Blackburn, the re-start coincided with confirmation from the bench that West Ham had held Manchester United to a 1–1 draw at Upton Park, thus rendering Blackburn's defeat academic. Kenny Dalglish and Ray Harford's ecstatic embrace on hearing the result prompted referee David Ellery to blow his whistle before time to provoke scenes of unbridled joy among Blackburn players and fans. A giant inflatable champagne bottle was tossed around by the relieved and euphoric travelling support, many of whom had had transistors clamped to their ears throughout to tune into the unfolding drama at Upton Park.

Liverpool fans, too, lapped up Blackburn's triumph, given that it had been overseen by arguably their greatest-ever player, Dalglish, and because their arch-rivals Manchester United had been denied at the final hurdle.

Liverpool's rugged defender, Neil Ruddock, Shearer's former team-mate at Southampton, led the celebrations, which involved copious amounts of beer and champagne being downed in the Anfield dressing rooms. 'I was shoved before the cameras for an interview and I don't think I was making a lot of sense when the rest of the lads pelted me with beer cans, champagne, shorts, jock straps and anything else they could lay their hands on,' Shearer recalls in his autobiography. He goes on to cite his 'most poignant moment' of the day being an emotional Jack Walker proudly holding the Premier League trophy aloft, while Kenny Dalglish sported a grin from ear to ear.

As Blackburn players and fans basked in the afterglow of their first title for eighty-one years, it is now part of folkore that Shearer celebrated his side's triumph by going home and creosoting his garden fence.

The day after arguably the greatest day in their side's history, more than 30,000 Blackburn fans packed into Ewood Park to witness a parade of the Premiership trophy by their heroes. 'When Alan Shearer took his turn to lift a cup that makes up in significance for what it lacks in aesthetic appeal, the decibel count went through the roof, to be exceeded only by the reception for Dalglish and Jack Walker,' said the *Independent*'s Dave Hadfield of the joyful occasion.

He recalls gazing, bleary-eyed, at his championship medal to confirm it was real, although was unable to focus on it properly given the intoxicating celebrations of the night before.

He was now ready to reconfirm his long-term commitment to Blackburn, convinced that the Premier League success heralded a glory-ridden era at Ewood Park. Shearer was delighted that his faith in joining Blackburn had been gloriously vindicated, insisting that he had never doubted the club's potential for greatness. He maintained that he had no desire to leave, citing the four-year contract he had signed in 1992, and admitted that he was even prepared to extend his stay at Ewood Park.

And Jack Walker pledged to retain the services of Blackburn's biggest asset in the *Daily Mail* on 13 June 1995, amid news that Italian clubs were showing an interest. He said: 'I'd like Alan to stay with Blackburn for the rest of his career. I can offer him everything here that he can get abroad. I know he's ambitious, but nobody should doubt how ambitious we are as a club. We'll be going for the league again next year. We might have to learn a bit about life in the European Cup, but I'd like us to have a real go for the FA Cup.'

However, Shearer, whose career had already embraced glorious highs and crushing lows, was well acquainted with the fact that rarely are there any certainties in football.

Imagine his dismay and disbelief when, as the ink had barely dried on his new four-year contract, his much-loved manager made the surprise announcement that he would be retiring as Blackburn boss to become the club's director of football. Ray Harford, Dalglish's No. 2, was installed as the Blackburn's new chief.

The Lancashire club tried to convey the impression that it would be business as usual, despite the unexpected managerial reshuffle and instead set about celebrating their coup of persuading Shearer to stay.

Chairman Robert Coar insisted in the *Daily Mail* on 28 June 1995: 'As far as the club is concerned, the major news of the summer is Alan's decision to sign the new contract. Just look at the transfer fees being paid for the likes of Stan Collymore and Chris Armstrong. We've re-signed for another four years the man in possession of the England centre-forward's shirt.'

Shearer admits that misgivings about the wisdom of his decision surfaced when Dalglish stepped down as manager. In his auto-biography he discloses that doubts started to ferment in his mind that Dalglish's departure could well have signalled the end of the club's good times.

AL OF THE ROVERS

While Harford was considered an excellent coach and a likeable man, he did not possess the awe-inspiring aura of Kenny Dalglish. The Scot commanded immense respect on account of his fabulous achievements during a legendary playing career with Liverpool and his enthusiasm and exhibitionism – involving brief glimpses of his genius – during training, engendered admiring glances aplenty from his players. Now his expertise would be confined to an isolated 'upstairs' role, breaking up the double act that had engineered Blackburn's successful quest for silverware the previous season.

While as a team the portents pointed to Blackburn suffering, especially as they had not spent a penny on reinforcements during the close season, Alan Shearer was determined to be as effective as ever in 1995–96.

After shrugging off a minor back injury picked up during Blackburn's pre-season tour of Scandinavia, he slipped effortlessly back into the old routine of banging in goal after goal in the Premier League.

He opened his account with a penalty in Rovers' opening game of the season, a 1–0 home win over QPR, to set the tone for another season of scintillating scoring. However, despite his two goals in Blackburn's next couple of matches against Sheffield Wednesday away and Manchester United at home, Rovers succumbed to two 2–1 defeats.

Away from the domestic scene, Blackburn had the chance to make amends for their woeful European showing the season before in the Champions League. They were paired with Spartak Moscow, Legia Warsaw and the Norwegians Rosenborg and, on paper, qualification looked eminently possible.

However, a 1–0 home loss to Spartak Moscow heightened the feeling that Shearer's Blackburn side lacked the guile to pose a threat on the European stage. Shearer was finding that well-drilled continental defences were appreciably more miserly than the often-porous rearguards in the Premier League.

But Blackburn's domestic slump was even more alarming than their

European travails, as the Ewood Park men secured only one point from their first six matches in the Premier League. An air of crisis had descended at Ewood Park, amid reports that Kenny Dalglish was pondering a future elsewhere. The phrase 'flash in the pan' was being bandied about in the media, who felt that Blackburn's perceived limitations – a lack of flair and an over-reliance on Shearer's goals – were being brutally exposed.

'Defend in numbers, soak up the pressure of the opposition, break out of defence with a long ball to wingers Stuart Ripley or Jason Wilcox – currently injured – and give the ball to England centre-forward Alan Shearer, who will score,' encapsulated Blackburn's unsophisticated and one-dimensional style, according to *Agence France Presse*.

Alan Shearer's importance to his side was self-evident after he blasted in the first of five Premier League hat-tricks in the 1995–96 season in Blackburn's 5–1 mauling of Coventry in late September. In so doing, he scored his 100th career goal for Blackburn, a milestone reached in only 133 games. *The Times*' Keith Pike said: 'It was an unremarkable treble. All three goals were scored from within the Coventry penalty area, and none required more than a sure-footed finish. It was what preceded them that confirmed Shearer's status: the awareness of others' intentions, the strength and pace to win that yard of space, the sheer bloody-minded persistence that has exasperated better defenders than Coventry's.'

His triple whammy and his partnership with Mike Newell in attack led a delighted Ray Harford to liken the dynamic duo to 'Batman and Robin'. It was a much-needed boost for both Rovers and their under-fire boss Harford, who had, the *People* claimed, been on the receiving end of 'a dressing-room tantrum' from Shearer. 'He [Shearer] blew his top after the 3–0 rout at Liverpool when boss Ray Harford blasted Mike Newell for not going over to applaud Rovers' fans. After five minutes of bickering, Shearer could take no more. He threw his boots across the room and yelled: "We've just got stuffed 3–0 and all we're talking about is waving to the crowd."'

He was infuriated further when Rosenborg defeated the English champions 2–1 in the Champions League, which again added fuel to the feeling that if you stopped Alan Shearer, you shut out Blackburn. But his two goals in each half allowed Blackburn to progress smoothly into the third round of the Coca Cola Cup after Swindon were disposed of 2–0 at Ewood Park in early October.

The mainstay of the Blackburn side also rejected Harford's offer of missing Rovers' trip to Poland, where they were due to meet Legia Warsaw in the Champions League. Harford had suggested that the striker may appreciate a break from the potentially gruelling routine of playing two games every week, but for someone who adores playing as much as Alan Shearer, this was a definite 'no–no'. 'I told him no thank you,' he said in *The Times*. 'I don't want to use the excuse, for England or the club, that I'm tired because of hard work. I've worked hard since I started playing football, the only time I'll miss any matches is when I'm injured. It's my job, the same as yours; and most people work every day.'

Even with Shearer in their side, Blackburn still slid to a third successive Champions League defeat – 1–0 – to all but extinguish their hopes of prolonging their European odyssey. For Shearer, his inability to prosper in a struggling Blackburn side on foreign shores raised question marks about his true European class, according to Watford defender David Holdsworth.

His broadside at the Blackburn hero came as Rovers prepared to face Watford in the third round of the Coca Cola Cup at Vicarage Road. Speaking to the *Daily Mail*, Holdsworth said: 'Obviously, Shearer is a quality player, the best of a very good bunch in England. But he has got a lot more learning to do on the European stage to compare with the likes of [Jürgen] Klinsmann, who's by far the best I've ever faced.'

Shearer duly answered the criticism in time-honoured style with a goal in Rovers' 2–1 victory. Blackburn then bolstered their squad with the triple signing of midfielders Lars Bohinen and Billy McKinlay and striker Graham Fenton from Aston Villa.

But despite a mini-resurgence in the league, including a 3–0 hammering of Chelsea at Ewood Park, Shearer and Blackburn were still floundering in Europe. They picked up their first point in the Champions League in a 0–0 draw with Legia Warsaw at Ewood Park at the start of November, but Shearer missed a gilt-edged chance in the last minute to open his European account. The English champs were branded European chumps as their hopes of surviving in the Champions League finally died a death.

The *Daily Mail's* Neil Harman was candid about Shearer's ineffectuality in front of goal and Blackburn's ineptitude in the European arena, writing: 'Even Alan Shearer, the most virtuous striker in England, has been unable to drag a goal from a series of defences set up to trap the myopic approach of English sides. It is fourteen games since Shearer last scored a goal against international opposition and, even if he can break that unhappy sequence against Spartak Moscow and Rosenborg in the final two games of the group, it will be utterly meaningless.'

Inevitably, reports of dissension within the Blackburn camp resurfaced, with misfiring strikers Chris Sutton and Paul Warhurst both rumoured to be unsettled as Ray Harford set about overhauling his side's championship-winning squad. Shearer was also said to be considering his future at the club, after apparently being the subject of a £10 million bid by his treasured Newcastle United.

The *Mail on Sunday's* Bob Cass reported on 5 November 1995: 'There have been moves within the last week to lure the Blackburn Rovers striker away from Ewood Park. The twenty-five-year-old England forward made a verbal agreement with the Premiership champions when he extended his contract at the start of the season that he would be allowed to move if he became disenchanted with his career at the club.'

Naturally, Shearer remained tight-lipped about the speculation, telling the *Daily Mirror*: 'I was told about the story by one of the lads, but I have heard nothing about Newcastle's interest. They are a huge club and I have always said I would like to play for them at some stage of my career. But I have a contract at Blackburn and I don't want to talk about that.'

Goals have always spoken louder than words for Alan Shearer and a tremendous hat-trick inspired Blackburn to trounce Nottingham Forest by seven goals without reply on 18 November. However, Shearer was more verbose when articulating his immense personal agony about Blackburn's pitiful displays in Europe, when Rovers travelled to Moscow to face Spartak in what was now a meaningless Champions League clash.

In a frank assessment of his side's failings on the continent, it was a case of 'From Russia with Sorrow' for the mournful frontman when he spoke to the *Daily Mirror*: 'As Ray Harford has pointed out, we're very immature in Europe. We are the babies at this level. It's all been new to us. Perhaps that's shown. The disappointment hurts. We have let ourselves down. It hurts inside us all that we know we could have done better.'

His woes worsened when Blackburn suffered a 3–0 humiliation at the hands of the rampant Russians, suffering the ill fortune of the sending-off of Scottish defender Colin Hendry and the awful embarrassment of seeing Graeme Le Saux and David Batty involved in an astonishing on-field punch-up. Blackburn saved their best for last, however, when Shearer scored his first Champions League goal – a penalty – in the 4–1 rout of Rosenborg at Ewood Park.

While Blackburn blundered consistently in Europe in 1995–96, they showed occasional flashes of their title-winning triumph form in the league and inevitably Alan Shearer was at the vanguard with a goal spree when Rovers clicked into gear. His seventh hat-trick of the season condemned West Ham to a 4–2 defeat in early December and his gleeful gaffer was bereft of superlatives to describe him: 'It's up to you fellows [the media] to find words to describe him. I'm just delighted he plays for us and not someone else.' A goal in Blackburn's 1-0 home win over Middlesbrough followed for Shearer, who was almost single-handedly salvaging the champions' season.

However, Rovers would have to do without the services of their dependable left-back, Graeme Le Saux, for the rest of the season, after he dislocated his ankle, ruptured a tendon and fractured his fibula after falling awkwardly during the match with the Teeside club. It had been a year of stupendous peaks and terrible troughs for Blackburn, but their sharp shooter's supreme form had been consistently brilliant.

And he could justifiably consider himself one of the English games greatest-ever goalscorers when he became the first man to reach 100 goals in the Premier League after he claimed the second in Blackburn's 2-1 victory over Tottenham on 30 December.

Shearer's astonishing century was achieved in just 124 games, six of which he appeared in as a substitute. His sensational scoring feat left his nearest challenger in the Premier League goal charts, Les Ferdinand, who had netted seventy-eight times, trailing in his wake. The *Sunday Times*' report of reaction to Shearer the centurion was as follows: '"He reminds me of Nat Lofthouse," his manager, Ray Harford said later, confirming the impression that Shearer has earned the right to be talked of in the same breath as some illustrious predatory predecessors. "But really I can't find words to describe him because he is just so good. He is a true role model for everybody, not just footballers, because he behaves so admirably and his 100 goals are remarkable. Don't forget he missed a whole season because of a terrible injury and he has still done this."'

As the New Year began, Shearer and Blackburn's only realistic prospect of silverware was in the FA Cup, after a miserable season in the league and an exit from the Coca Cola Cup at the hands of Leeds.

AL OF THE ROVERS

They scraped a draw at Ipswich in the third round of the FA Cup, but the replay saw them dumped out of the competition unceremoniously by the First Division side, who prevailed 1–0.

UEFA Cup qualification was now Rovers' solitary target and, with a striker of Alan Shearer's calibre, it was well within beleaguered Blackburn's reach. Bolton were on the receiving end of his fourth hat-trick of the season in early February, as Rovers cantered to a 3–1 victory at Ewood Park. His reputation as a boring and bland character also looked erroneous when he enjoyed a comic moment with a linesman during the match, mimicking the official's licking of his lips. But referee Paul Alcock did not appreciate Shearer's rare display of on-the-field humour and booked the jesting Geordie.

Shearer's face was again wreathed in smiles when his 92nd-minute winner against Tottenham at White Hart Lane allowed him to complete his fifth hat-trick of the season and Blackburn to steal a breathtaking, last-gasp 3–2 win on 16 March. He became the third Blackburn man to achieve five hat-tricks in a single season, emulating the efforts of John Southworth in 1890–91 and Andy McEvoy in 1963–64. But goals galore were not a guarantee for total happiness, Shearer told the *Independent*: 'I may have scored a few goals, but the season has not gone the way we would have wanted, and I would definitely swap all my goals for team success.'

He would also have had mixed feelings when his two assists to fellow Geordie Graham Fenton allowed Blackburn to inflict a serious blow to Newcastle's championship hopes on 8 April. Fenton's two goals in a 2–1 Blackburn triumph at Ewood Park meant that Shearer's hometown heroes' challenge for the title was beginning to wilt, making Manchester United firm favourites for a third Premier League crown in four years. Shearer then accumulated his thirty-fifth goal of the season as Blackburn hammered Nottingham Forest 5–1 at the City Ground in mid-April. Two more strikes in Blackburn's 3–2 win over Wimbledon moved him on to thirty-seven goals for the season, earning him another place in English football's history books.

Shearer the phenomenon had become the first player in England to chalk up thirty goals in three successive seasons. He had signed off his season in spectacular style, as a persistent groin injury brought an untimely end to another fabulous campaign for the country's premier striker. Not long after the 1995–96 season had ended, transfer speculation was whipped up in earnest, with Alan Shearer's name omnipresent in the newspapers. Manchester United, who had failed to lure Shearer to Old Trafford four years earlier, had once again emerged as firm favourites to persuade him to leave Ewood Park. A report in *The Times* said: 'Manchester United are understood to be close to signing Alan Shearer, the Blackburn Rovers and England forward, for a fee in excess of £10 million. Last night, a senior official at Old Trafford confirmed that the club had made a preliminary approach to Blackburn. It is understood that talks began on Tuesday evening between Tony Stephens, Shearer's agent, Martin Edwards, the United chairman, and Alex Ferguson, the manager. "The negotiations are at a difficult stage at the moment, but United are keen to sign him," said the official, before adding. "We have offered more than £10 million."'

Other European heavyweights, such as Italian giants AC Milan and Juventus, as well as Barcelona, managed by Bobby Robson, had also joined a growing queue interested in securing Shearer's services, whose value had rocketed as a result of his Euro '96 goal spree. The tone was set for a summer humming with incessant rumour and speculation about the likely destination of Blackburn's brilliant No. 9.

Jack Walker remained resolute throughout, indomitably parrying Manchester United's bids for Shearer and taking the extraordinary step of offering his leading light the player-manager's job at Ewood Park.

At the age of only twenty-five, however, Shearer did not feel ready to move into management in a role which Walker told him had the full backing of Ray Harford. He admits in his autobiography: 'With hindsight, I do not think I would have accepted his offer of the player-manager's role if I had stayed at Blackburn. It is such a tough job merely playing football at the highest level, and I do not believe it would have been possible to take on the extra responsibilities which go with running the team, even working alongside Ray [Harford].'

Walker also reportedly launched his own audacious offer in response to the Old Trafford side's dogged pursuit of his man, when he made a £4 million bid for the champions' star, Eric Cantona. The *Irish Times* reported: 'Out of the blue, and to the utter astonishment of everyone connected with United, an official bid of £4 million for the Premiership's reformed enfant terrible rolled out of one of Old Trafford's fax machines early yesterday afternoon.

'A futile act which, whether Blackburn will concede as much or not, was doomed to failure the moment it was conceived, was unquestionably the latest chapter in a simmering dispute between the two clubs over the fate of another player of great ability, Alan Shearer.'

But home was where Shearer's heart was as soon as Newcastle served notice of their desire to bring the striker back home.Blackburn had strived gamely to keep hold of Shearer, but the magnetic pull of the Magpies had proved too strong and Newcastle swooped to sign him for a world-record fee of £15 million. Shearer said of Walker: 'He's been a father figure to me. I know we will always be the best of friends. This is the way I want to leave: no animosity, no bitterness, just friendship. He battled harder than anyone can imagine to persuade me to stay. But I simply felt it was time for a fresh challenge.'

Shearer reiterated his affection for Walker when the Blackburn benefactor succumbed to throat cancer in August 2000: 'The word benefactor could have been invented for Jack Walker – he gave pride to the town of Blackburn. Jack was a kind, generous and emotional man,' were his comments in the *Daily Mirror*.

Some Blackburn fans have never forgiven Shearer for deserting the Lancashire side and the genial Geordie admits to feeling hurt by the hostile reception that awaited him when he first played at Ewood Park in a black-and-white shirt. Most reasonable Rovers' supporters recognise that he was unable to turn down the chance to play for the club he supported, however, and their side was on the wane when he opted to move.

What should never be forgotten is the lasting legacy that Alan Shearer left on Blackburn Rovers, including bequeathing the club £100,000 to fund a classroom. The generous offer paid for the 'Alan Shearer classroom', where local schoolchildren could study current affairs, history and geography under the banner of the 'Learning Through Football' programme run by former Rovers' favourite, Terry Gennoe.

Memories of his 130 goals for the club and his pivotal role in their championship triumph will also be etched forever in the hearts and minds of Blackburn fans. His place in a best-ever Blackburn XI is assured.

'I had some great times at Blackburn and so did my family and the club will always be special to me. Theirs is still one of the first results I look for,' Shearer said in 2005.

Rovers fans can also comfort themselves with the fact that Shearer won his solitary piece of club silverware while at Ewood Park. However, while his impending return to his hometown would not yield trophies, his unsurprising decision to wear the famous black and white stripes of his cherished club would furnish him with something which could be considered even more worthwhile: legendary status.

CHAPTER FIVE

Tyne of His Life

English football in the summer of 1996 was defined by two significant homecomings. Football memorably came home when Euro '96 gripped the nation's imagination; England almost repeated the momentous feats of 1966 by reaching the semi-finals of the tournament on home soil. The euphoria created by this extravaganza had barely dissipated when, at the end of July, Geordie-born Alan Shearer headed back to his Newcastle roots in one of the decade's most sensational transfers.

He swapped the North-West for the North-East and joined Newcastle from Blackburn for a then-world-record fee of £15 million. In 2004 Shearer told BBC Radio Newcastle that there were 'three big reasons' why he had opted to leave Lancashire for Tyneside.

The overriding factor in his decision, he admitted, was his yearning to fulfil a lifelong ambition of representing his hometown club. He said: 'To wear the No. 9 shirt at Newcastle, and obviously captain them for the last few years, has been everything I hoped it would be and a hell of a lot more. People have to appreciate the feeling I get running out at St James' Park, at the front, with the armband on, with the No. 9 shirt on: it does not get any bigger or better than that for me.' Then there was the irresistible prospect of working with his childhood idol, Kevin Keegan, a man whose fleeting spell on Tyneside in the early 1980s had made an indelible impact on the young Shearer. Thirdly, Keegan's Newcastle were playing an intoxicating brand of attacking football that could, and should, have swept them to the Premier League title the previous season.

Shearer was convinced that Newcastle were on the verge of something special and bound to win some silverware in the near future. The decision of where to ply his trade was initially an agonising one, however.

After discussing a move to Manchester United with Alex Ferguson, Shearer was tempted by the mouth-watering prospect of joining world-class players such as Roy Keane and Ryan Giggs. Then he held talks with Keegan, whose persuasive tongue and ebullience gave him food for thought. However, he refused to let his emotions influence his thinking.

Finally, Shearer could not resist the chance to fulfil his boyhood dreams and wear the famous black-and-white shirt of his heroes after being called by Keegan on the eve of Newcastle's departure from Heathrow to the Far East for a pre-season tour.

He was also determined that his transfer would include the guarantee that he could wear the cherished No. 9 jersey, once the property of Newcastle heroes of the past such as Jackie Milburn, Malcolm Macdonald and Hughie Gallacher. Keegan agreed, although it is understood that the then occupant of the famous No. 9 shirt, Les Ferdinand, was none too happy to relinquish it.

For Keegan, Shearer's capture represented a monumental coup. Manchester United had appeared to be front-runners for Shearer's signature throughout the summer of 1996, making a succession of failed bids for Blackburn's goal-scoring phenomenon. At the start of July, the *Mirror*'s Mike Walters believed he had gleaned irrefutable proof that Shearer was on his way to Old Trafford.

Walters asserted that Shearer had been included in a thirty-strong party for United's pre-season tour of Italy: 'I can reveal the list of passengers on British Airways flight 5060 from Manchester to Milan on 30 July includes Mr A. Shearer.' Yet, as in 1992 when he opted to move to Blackburn, Shearer rejected the allure of Old Trafford.

For a jubilant Keegan, who hailed his stunning swoop for Shearer as 'a signing for the people of Newcastle', this was sweet revenge over his bitter rival Ferguson.

The wily Scot's familiar canny mind games had infuriated Keegan near the end of the previous season, as Newcastle blew a seemingly unassailable twelve-point league at the top of the Premier League, only to capitulate within touching distance of the ultimate prize.

Fergie had mischievously suggested that Leeds players only performed to their potential against his side, after the Elland Road side had achieved a 1–0 win over Manchester United. It was widely viewed as a tacit ruse to fire Leeds up for their clash with Newcastle, sparking an astonishing tirade from Keegan, live on Sky Television. 'I'll love it if we beat them [Manchester United]... love it!' was the withering and immortal finality of Keegan's rant.

On that occasion, Ferguson prevailed as United performed the ultimate act of brinkmanship by pipping Newcastle to the title in the final throes of the championship race. Signing Shearer was the perfect tonic to the immense despondency that had descended on Tyneside in the wake of this devastating failure.

Keegan was undoubtedly motivated by the unedifying thought of Shearer and Eric Cantona in harness together for Manchester United, wreaking havoc both home and abroad. 'All the disappointment of losing the title had disappeared in that instant', remarked Keegan in his autobiography of the moment that his pursuit of England's goal king ended in glorious success.

Many felt that Keegan, who had twice enquired about Shearer since becoming manager at St James' Park in 1992, had blithely ignored the fact that Newcastle were in need of defensive bulwarks rather than forward firepower. This seemed a justified view, given that a flimsy rearguard and cavalier attacking style had proved the undoing of Keegan's side in their quest for glory. However, it did not take into account the fact that football in Newcastle is tantamount to a religion and the area's fanatical followers love to worship a footballing figurehead.

Keegan appreciated the huge significance of signing Shearer given that, like 'Supermac' Malcolm Macdonald and 'Wor' Jackie Milburn before him, he himself had enthralled a passionate public and created a thousand childhood football fantasies, including that of his prospective new signing.

Now he wanted his newly acquired centre-forward, a proud Geordie with black-and-white blood coursing through his veins, to follow in his footsteps. Keegan says in his autobiography: 'While I scoured the world for the cream, Sir John Hall [the Newcastle chairman] harboured a dream of fielding a team of Geordies in emulation of the Basques of Atletico Bilbao. I had to battle this Geordie race thing regularly, and time and again I told the chairman it was not feasible. "What could happen, though, is for Newcastle to see three or four of their youngsters come through, which would be fantastic. Alan Shearer could be a catalyst for that – there is nothing like a local hero to encourage the kids in the area to sign on at their club."'

'What about the astronomical transfer fee?' the sceptics screamed on the front and back pages of tabloid and broadsheet newspapers alike. Shearer had suddenly become the world's most expensive player, outstripping the £13.3 million Barcelona had paid to prise Brazilian superstar Ronaldo from PSV Eindhoven and the £8.5 million former British record fee Liverpool had splashed out on Stan Collymore in 1995.

Shearer's personal income was expected to soar to more than £2 million a year, including a bumper £30,000-a-week pay packet and bonuses. The *Glasgow Herald* quantified the transfer thus: 'Alan Shearer is worth his weight in gold 22.3 times over. He weighs 12st 1lb, and gold yesterday was selling at £248 per ounce. Newcastle could have bought twenty-two solid gold statues of Shearer for the price of the real thing.'

The *Mirror*, meanwhile, posed the thorny question in a front-page editorial: 'Has the world gone mad when we value a footballer at £15 million?' adding: 'It is one thousand times more than a nurse earns in a year. Alan Shearer brings pleasure to millions of soccer fans. His skills could bring his new club the success that will earn it a fortune. But that money will come from ordinary fans, many of whom cannot afford to see matches live regularly. We must value our people properly. And that means not paying our nurses too little – or our soccer stars too much.'

When set in this context, the hefty price tag looked totally obscene, but since the early nineties and the Sky television deal, English football was operating on another stratosphere to other leagues worldwide. It was not Shearer's fault that he had commanded such a fee, but he had proved more than value for money for Blackburn. As the *Guardian* reported: 'Gerry Boon, an accountant with Deloitte & Touche who has specialised in football finances, says the deal could well make sense even though it is obviously risky. "It is both a financial gamble and a sound investment," he said. "But I don't think it's way out of order." He pointed out that when Blackburn bought Shearer for £3.6 million in 1992 there were mutterings about Walker's naivety. Yet Blackburn had now made a profit of more than £11 million and they won the league in 1995.'

ALAN SHEARER

The Times pointed out that despite his burgeoning wealth, Shearer still lagged behind some of football's biggest earners. 'But he is still neither the best-paid player in England – Middlesbrough are believed to pay Fabrizzio Ravanelli a basic salary of £40,000 a week – nor is he among the ten highest earners in Europe, where Romario and Roberto Baggio reign. He also trails American sporting stars such as basketball's Shaquille O'Neal, who commanded a £60 million signing-on fee and £15 million a year.'

Although, as *The Times* went on to say, 'the so-called fat cats of industry look quite scrawny compared with Shearer: Cedric Brown, the much-criticised former British Gas chief executive, was paid £491,000 and Sir Desmond Pitcher, the United Utilities chairman, described by protesters last week as the "king of the fat cats", is paid £346,000.'

Irrespective of his untold riches, Shearer pledged to continue to live true to his working-class roots, telling the *Sunday Mirror*: 'I buy my [lottery] ticket each week using the same numbers chosen from family birthdays. My sister finds it strange that someone as well off as me should try to win the big prize, but I have told her that, if my numbers come up, the cash will go to our mum.' His wife Lainya later admitted to the *Evening Chronicle*: 'As for all the talk about the money, I can honestly say it hasn't made a great deal of difference to our lives. We didn't suddenly go out and buy lots of things.'

Newcastle had taken a huge gamble, hoping that their massive outlay on Shearer would reap rich returns in terms of glory and lucrative Champions League football. They were automatically installed as 3–1 third favourites behind Manchester United and Liverpool to lift the Premiership title. The frenzied excitement Shearer's arrival provoked on Tyneside was already proving a real money-spinner for the club in respect of revenue, however, as Newcastle shops ran out of letters to put his name on the back of replica strips.

Newcastle's bid to establish itself as a global brand through a proposed share flotation was sure to be accelerated, as were plans for a move to a 75,000-seater stadium. Its chamber of commerce believed that Shearer's presence would add to the 'feel-good factor' of the city and prove a major boon to the prosperity of the area too.

Newcastle chairman Sir John Hall defended his club's munificence, commenting: 'We have had to pay the market price. That is what we are about. We've got to make signings like this to stay in the race. We didn't win anything last year and it is imperative now that we get some silverware on the table.'

Newcastle fans did not care a jot about the financial implications of the mega-bucks deal: they were simply ecstatic. The *Daily Record* captured some of their reactions: 'Fanzine writer Steve Wraith said: "It's quite simply one of the greatest days in the club's history. It is the biggest signing since the day Kevin Keegan arrived as a player." John Regan, of the Newcastle United Independent Supporters' Association, said: "I'm still on the ceiling. It's such a high. It's Christmas come early." Supporters' club chief Kevin Miles, said: "This is the big deal of the summer, the one everybody wanted at Newcastle. Manchester United have made about six signings, but this is the one everybody is talking about."'

The day of Shearer's unveiling to the Newcastle faithful at the start of August was as joyous a Geordie homecoming as one could have expected for a local hero, even though the pouring rain seemed wholly inappropriate for such a dazzling occasion. When most football clubs parade a new acquisition, they would anticipate a small group of fanatics thronging around their ground, eager to snatch a sneaky glimpse of the signing.

Yet such is the intensity the Toon Army exude when presented with a major new recruit – as in the case of Shearer or Michael Owen in 2005 – that Newcastle are forced to turn to American-style razzmatazz to exhibit their wares. *The Times*' Peter Ball commented:

'Yesterday, the rain might have dissuaded some from attending, estimates of the crowd varying between 5,000 and 15,000, but nonetheless the event was stage-managed from start to finish, more like an American media party than an English sporting occasion. At 2pm, with the press corralled in the Leazes End stand and those lucky few supporters, guests of the sponsors, seated behind, the Newcastle directors appeared and took their seats on a temporary stage erected on the pitch, followed by Kevin Keegan, who was greeted with loud cheers, then Shearer, to still louder cheers.'

Every utterance from Shearer was greeted by huge roars from the massed ranks: 'I've always said I wanted to play for Newcastle and I can't wait for the first game to come. I think this team is good enough not only to win the Premier League, but to conquer Europe as well. The price tag is nothing at all to do with me. I don't set the price. All I can do is go out and try to do my best and, if that means I score goals, which makes me worth £15 million, that's fine.'

While a celebratory party mood prevailed on Tyneside, three other clubs in England were bemoaning their bad luck at Shearer's spectacular return home. Blackburn Rovers fans were, in football parlance, particularly gutted. *The Times* conveyed their palpable distress at losing their striking sensation. 'In Blackburn, the atmosphere around Ewood Park was more akin to a wake, with Rovers fans devastated by the loss of the man who helped propel them to Premiership success. Nigel Burton, thirty-nine, said: "I'm really shocked. He's the best player I've seen in my life and he should have been sold for £20 million. But he has messed us about. People have been handing back their season tickets."'

The club agreed to exchange Shearer shirts returned by despondent fans to the club's souvenir shop. One fan saw a silver lining: 'I am gutted by the loss, but I would have sooner cut my right leg off than see him go to Manchester United.'

Meanwhile, Blackburn's Lancashire neighbours, Manchester United, had to face up to being snubbed for the second time by Shearer, although chairman Martin Edwards bullishly claimed that any deal had foundered on Blackburn's reluctance to sell to their rivals. United goalkeeper Peter Schmeichel was more candid about Shearer's switch to Newcastle in favour of Old Trafford. 'The European Cup would have been ours if Alan had joined us instead of Newcastle – that's how good he is,' he said in the *Mirror*.

And in Sunderland there was much wailing and gnashing of teeth at their bitter rivals' big-money buy. The *Sunderland Echo* carried the headline: 'Oh No! Look Who The Mags Have Signed.'

Thankfully for Shearer, he temporarily escaped the mass hysteria created by his mega-bucks transfer by joining up with Newcastle on their pre-season tour of the Far East. Meanwhile, his first meaningful appearance in a Newcastle shirt was scheduled to be the eagerly-awaited precursor to the new season, the Charity Shield against Manchester United.

The Toon Army was getting ready to advance on Wembley, eagerly snapping up their 45,000 ticket allocation with one fan, according to the *Daily Mirror*, queuing for an astonishing fifty-seven hours to see the star attraction Shearer in action. Colin Pattinson, aged twenty, from Jarrow, said: 'I've been queuing since 11pm on Friday night, but it's all been worthwhile. I would be here even if Shearer wasn't coming, because I'm a true supporter, but I know he will be playing his heart out for the club.'

But before 'Shearmania' could invade Wembley, Shearer and co headed for Lincoln to play a friendly arranged as part of winger Darren Huckerby's £400,000 move to Newcastle. A sell-out 11,000 crowd, including 2,000 travelling Geordies, watched Shearer play a full 90 minutes and score a first-half penalty to help Newcastle to a comfortable 2–0 win.

Now it was all systems go for Newcastle's seismic showdown with Manchester United, a clash that represented both an echo of their titanic tussle for the title the season before and a keenly anticipated forerunner to their likely scrap at the Premiership summit in the campaign to come.

The Charity Shield is for many clubs an increasingly insignificant fixture, uprooting their fans for an expensive day out in London or Cardiff for an over-hyped pre-season friendly.

But in 1996, the annual hors d'oeuvre to the new season had a dash of extra spice and some vestiges of bitterness following Kevin Keegan's rant on air, Manchester United's championship success and Shearer's symbolic move to Tyneside. It promised to be a ravishing affair and Alex Ferguson was characteristically stirring things up with a sprinkling of kidology. The canny Scot was up to his old tricks when talking up his opponents' Premiership title chances. He remarked in the *Mail on Sunday*: 'There can be no doubt that Newcastle must be regarded as the favourites now they have got Shearer. Shearer got thirty-five goals for Blackburn last season and Les Ferdinand twenty-nine at Newcastle. That is more than sixty goals from just two players. Very formidable.'

Ferguson's prediction was way off the mark if the Charity Shield was to be regarded as any form of predictor for the Premiership, as United steamrollered Newcastle with contemptuous ease, mauling the hapless Geordies 4–0.

Shearer, meanwhile, was largely anonymous, starved of service and overshadowed by Manchester's Gallic genius, Eric Cantona, who swaggered around the Wembley turf with smouldering authority as if it were a stage that befitted his talents and not those of England's Euro '96 hero. 'We were hopeless, especially in the first half, but we can only get better,' a miserable Shearer lamented. 'It's early days yet, but we have got to defend as well as score goals.'

The *Independent*'s Glenn Moore asserted that Shearer might have been questioning the wisdom of his decision to choose Newcastle over the Premiership kings. He said: 'Shearer must have wondered whether letting his heart rule his head was such a wise decision. It does not matter how good he is; if he does not get the ball, he is not going to score any goals. There was much for him to ponder on the long journey home last night, not least the failure of the "dream team" partnership with Les Ferdinand. The pair looked too similar and too isolated, only linking once early in the first half when Shearer was unable to manage a clear strike after a one-two with his partner.'

Thankfully, days later, Newcastle and Shearer made amends for their Wembley horror show by beating Anderlecht of Belgium 2–1 away in a pre-season friendly. Although Shearer did not score, he provided the pass for his strike partner, Faustino Asprilla's, opening goal.

But goals at the other end continued to be the focus of Newcastle's critics as the Magpies began the league campaign with a 2–0 defeat at Everton. *The Times*' Andrew Longmore commented: 'Kevin Keegan must have been playing truant when the painful lessons from last season were being learnt. Profligate to the last, his Newcastle United side lost the title with the style of champions. So what does the man do? He puts £15 million of Sir John Hall's money down on the table and rolls the dice once more: turn those 4–3 defeats into 5–4 victories by buying the best striker in the land. "*C'est magnifique, mais ce n'est pas la guerre*," as Marshal Bosquet remarked on observing the charge of the Light Brigade.'

But Keegan would not be swayed from his propensity for relentless attacking by fielding a three-pronged strike force of Shearer, Faustino Asprilla and Les Ferdinand for Newcastle's next game with Wimbledon at St James' Park.

The trio, worth a combined £28.5 million, responded by overwhelming the Dons 2–0, with Shearer scoring his first league goal for Newcastle with a sweetly struck free-kick two minutes from time. 'It sailed out of reach of the Wimbledon goalkeeper, it brought every man, woman and child in the 36,385 audience to their feet and it lifted the heavens on a balmy Newcastle night,' said *The Times*' Rob Hughes of Shearer's magic moment. 'The North-East has known many memorable nights but, even in the history of Newcastle United, few have matched this one.' Shearer said afterwards: 'It was a great occasion for me and my family. I couldn't be more delighted but, to be honest, I'm more concerned with getting the three points than scoring. It was a big bonus to get a goal. I don't really care about the pressure.'

However, Newcastle's 2-1 loss at home to Sheffield Wednesday saw a recurrence of the defensive incohesion that threatened to undermine Shearer's inevitable goals. Jonathan Northcroft said in *Scotland on Sunday*: 'Again Alan Shearer must have felt that he was the one left holding the baby, or ten of them to be precise, dressed in black and white. The striker's display, as professional as ever, was spiced by a 13th-minute penalty, which promised so much more. From one simple cross and one high ball, however, Sheffield Wednesday were able to penetrate Shearer's team-mates. "It was Colin Hendry we should have signed from Blackburn," a wise local said.'

Discontent was rife among some of Shearer's pals, according to the *Sunday Mirror*: 'Les Ferdinand, David Ginola, Robert Lee and Faustino Asprilla – all internationals – have demanded the right to renegotiate their contracts or go on the transfer list following England skipper Shearer's world record move from Blackburn. His weekly wages at Newcastle have been put at around £30,000. But Keegan has told his rebels: no new deals.'

Newcastle's foray into Europe diverted the attention from talk of dissension back home, however, when they took on Swedish part-timers Halmstads in the UEFA Cup. Halmstads' coach, Tom Prahl, had overseen another Swedish side's – Trelleborgs – famous victory over Shearer's Blackburn two years previously and his unheralded outfit, despite including a postman, a baker and a butcher in their ranks, could point to a sensational 3–0 first-leg win over Italian giants Parma in the previous season's European Cup-Winners' Cup as proof of their pedigree.

However, Newcastle matched Parma's 4–0 second-leg win at St James' Park to all but assure their passage into the next round of the UEFA Cup and succeeded in this aim, despite a 2–1 defeat in Sweden. Shearer now faced up to a swift reacquaintance with his Blackburn team-mates and their beleaguered coach Ray Harford, and insisted that he would have no qualms in heaping more pressure on his under-fire former boss. He said: 'Ray is one of my best mates, but if I have to score the winner to beat him on Saturday, I'll do it without a second thought. Helping Newcastle get three points is all that matters, and I can't afford to think about what might happen to Ray. Anyway, I was in the same situation after I joined Blackburn and found myself lining up against my old club Southampton.'

Despite his 200 league, cup and international goals, Shearer had never scored against Rovers, but this all changed when he condemned Blackburn to a continuation of their dismal winless slump by scoring a penalty in Newcastle's 2–1 victory.

Newcastle had now leapt into third place in the league and maintained their championship challenge with a 1–0 win at Leeds in September, courtesy of you-know-who.

The sheet-metal worker's son joined some illustrious names when he moved into a £220,000 detached house on the edge of the picturesque Wynyard estate. Charles Dickens, the Duke of Wellington and Margaret Thatcher had all stayed at the luxury estate, set in 2,400 hectares of woodland, and Shearer joined his manager, chairman and fellow Newcastle striker Paul Kitson in opting to stay in the sumptuous setting.

The *Sunday Mirror* reported: '"Alan Shearer has really scored at Wynyard," said an insider. "He was able to walk into a beautiful home and just hang up his clothes. Every detail was taken care of, right down to the table being set for dinner. The homes in Wynyard village are named after poets and Alan's is called the Coleridge."'

It looked as though Shearer would have plenty of time to luxuriate in domestic bliss at the start of October after fears were raised that he would need more surgery on his troublesome groin following an operation in May. Initially, however, such concerns were allayed and he was free to help galvanise Newcastle's championship charge. He scored the only goal in his side's 1–0 win at Derby County, allowing Newcastle to occupy the Premiership summit for the first time since March during the previous season.

A trip to Hungary and a clash with Ferencváros in the UEFA Cup resulted in a 3–2 defeat, which was dogged by controversy when Shearer's late goal was chalked off for offside. Astonishingly, the official who took charge of the match confessed that he had made a mistake – by contacting the *Daily Mirror*. He told the tabloid: 'It does seem my linesman and I got it wrong,' he said. 'I'm hoping to watch a video of the match in the next few days, and I fear it will prove that we made a mistake. Everyone who has seen it says Shearer was onside when the ball was played. If the *Daily Mirror* could pass on my apologies, I'd be very grateful.'

Shearer and his team-mates shrugged off their ill fortune by leading Newcastle to one of their most comprehensive and satisfying victories in the modern era, a 5–0 humbling of Manchester United at St James' Park in late October. It cemented their position at the top of the table and emphatically underscored their championship credentials. Shearer scored once in the rout and provided an exquisite cross from which Les Ferdinand delivered a third goal with an emphatic header. It was a truly superb Man of the Match display, going some way to vindicate Shearer's choice of joining his hometown club.

The Toon Army was in dreamland, as Simon Turnbull reported in the *Independent*: 'Chants of "Shearer turned you down" had been replaced by the taunt, "What's it like to be outclassed?" The silence in the red and white pocket of St James' Park told you that last season's Double winners were not only goalless but on the suffering end of their heaviest defeat against Newcastle since 1929, when Hughie Gallacher scored a hat-trick in a 5–0 win. That the sheet-metal worker's son is much more than a goal-poacher was evident from the moment he clocked on, by taking the kick-off, to the moment he clocked off to collect the Man of the Match champagne. He never stopped grafting, whether it was toiling to slip the shackles of his one-time Blackburn colleague David May or drifting wide to prove his worth as a provider.'

Newcastle's ecstasy evaporated when it emerged that Shearer had aggravated his groin and would face up to eight weeks on the sidelines after undergoing surgery. A dejected Shearer announced: 'The pain has been getting worse in recent games and was really bad during and after the Manchester United game. Fortunately, both Newcastle and England have strength in depth and I am confident that the results will continue to be positive during my time as a spectator.'

Newcastle did not suffer too badly without their talisman, however, drubbing Ferencváros 4–0 at St James' Park to march triumphantly into the next round of the UEFA Cup.

Sky Television's football pundit Andy Gray was convinced that, despite being denuded of Shearer for several weeks, Newcastle could maintain their pursuit of the Premiership. Speaking in the *Sunday Mirror*, he said: 'I'm sticking by my tip at the start, Newcastle. I took the 5–2 odds and there's no reason to desert them. The Magpies have started well, they are hard to beat and Alan Shearer's influence is clear.' But Newcastle were rocked further when Les Ferdinand joined Shearer on the injury list after fracturing his cheekbone during a 1–1 draw with West Ham.

Trust Shearer to make a mockery of medical opinion by returning earlier than expected from his groin injury to face Chelsea in late November. And it was a goal-scoring return, too, as he netted in the 1–1 draw. He then equalled a personal best of scoring in six straight games, a feat he achieved twice while at Blackburn, by notching Newcastle's only goal in a 3–1 defeat to Middlesbrough in the Coca Cola Cup.

Arsenal deposed Newcastle from the top of the Premiership after a 2–1 win, but a 3–1 aggregate win over French club Metz in the UEFA Cup guaranteed that St James' Park would witness European football in 1997. Shearer than set his sights on notching up yet another personal milestone, when he aimed to score his eighth Premiership goal on the trot for Newcastle at Nottingham Forest.

Yet it was deemed unlikely that he would break Mark Stein's record of scoring in seven successive games for Chelsea between December 1993 and February 1994 because his goals had been sandwiched by a groin operation. In any case, Shearer failed to score in Nottingham as Newcastle drew 0–0 with Forest, a game which saw Les Ferdinand's return to action after a five-match absence.

After returning to the goal trail in Newcastle's 1–1 draw with Premiership leaders Liverpool, Shearer faced up to a return to Blackburn on Boxing Day. He was boosted by a glowing tribute by Liverpool striker, Robbie Fowler, who enthused of his England colleague in the *Northern Echo*: 'I think Alan is by far the best striker in England. Alan has got everything. He works hard for his team, scores goals and is a great all-round player.'

Shearer, meanwhile, insisted that there was no room for sentiment and no turning back as the game with his second professional club loomed, telling *Northern Echo* reporter Clive Hetherington: 'I had four tremendous years there and I'm still friendly with a lot of people, both players and management. In some ways it'll be emotional going back, but this is the move I always wanted and, in football, you can't look back.'

But Blackburn were in no mood to be charitable to their former hero, condemning Newcastle to a 1–0 defeat to extend Keegan's men's winless streak to seven matches.

TYNE OF HIS LIFE

The mercurial Magpies ended both this indifferent run of form and 1996 in majestic style by walloping Spurs 7–1 at St James' Park, with Shearer scoring twice.

On an individual level, he was also soaring to lofty heights, awarded third place in the FIFA World Footballer of the Year Award behind George Weah of AC Milan and Barcelona's 20-year-old Brazilian phenomenon, Ronaldo.

As the *Daily Telegraph* stated, Shearer lagged well behind runaway winner Ronaldo – amassing 123 votes in a poll of 120 football coaches worldwide, compared to the Brazilian's 329 – but his placing was, on balance, justified according to England manager Glenn Hoddle: 'I am delighted to see Ronaldo win the award with George Weah second,' Hoddle said. 'It seems individual flair is going out of the game but those two are recognised for just that. Alan does not have the same individual ability or score such spectacular goals but he knows what he is good at and his work for the team is exceptional. He channels so much energy into his effort for the team and offers more than those two when it comes to scoring because he can score from any range.'

Meanwhile, many observers still felt that Newcastle's most realistic hopes of claiming a trophy lay with either the FA Cup or the UEFA Cup. Yet, as the *Sunday Mirror*'s Brian McNally noted, they would have to overcome a forty-year hoodoo in their domestic cup competition when they travelled to Charlton in the third round.

'The last time Newcastle United won an FA Cup tie in London, Rocky Marciano was still the undefeated heavyweight champion of the world. Bill Haley's 'Rock Around the Clock' was the catalyst for a wave of teenage rebellion, and Hugh Gaitskell had emerged as successor to Clement Attlee as Labour leader. The year was 1956, and Jackie Milburn was the

91

ALAN SHEARER

Brylcreemed darling of FA Cup-holders Newcastle. The Cup favourites, boasting three-time Wembley winners Milburn and Bobby Mitchell, beat Fulham in a nine-goal thriller that had the headline writers confidently predicting a fourth FA Cup triumph in six years. But since that grey January afternoon, Newcastle haven't won another FA Cup-tie in London. And each passing year has only heaped the pressure on Kevin Keegan to end that dismal sequence.'

1997 could not have got off to a more unexpectedly horrific start for Newcastle, however, as Kevin Keegan sensationally resigned from his post as manager. Keegan said: 'I offered my resignation at the end of last season, but was persuaded by the board to stay. I feel I have taken the club as far as I can and that it would be in the best interests of all concerned if I resigned.'

Elaborating in his autobiography on his shock decision, he reveals that he had fallen out of love with football management, which was being constrained by financial pressures. 'It [Newcastle] was becoming a totally different organisation: suddenly the flotation had taken over everything, even the most important part of the club – the team. It was all consuming. We – and I readily acknowledge my part in it all – had created a monster which needed feeding and nurturing almost to the exclusion of all else.'

Shearer felt the pain of Keegan's departure more acutely than most, given his symbiotic bond with his idol that had developed during his childhood. 'Because of my own special feelings for Kevin,' he writes in his autobiography, 'the news hit me really hard, but once I had absorbed the shock, I knew I had to come to terms with it as quickly as possible. I reminded myself that although he was a big reason why I had moved to St James' Park in the summer, I had signed for Newcastle United not for Kevin Keegan. Life had to go on.'

TYNE OF HIS LIFE

Most Newcastle diehards could not be so philosophical, however. They had lost the man who had revitalised not only their club by promoting irresistible offensive football, but also their city. How could their saviour leave them when they were fourth in the league and still playing in two cup competitions? Grief-stricken fans gathered at St James' Park, unified in their sense of loss in scenes reminiscent of a large-scale funeral.

The Press Association captured some of their reactions: 'Drama student Victoria Rickaby, sixteen, said: "I'm upset because football and Newcastle United are my life and this is just too much to bear. How can Kevin Keegan leave us? He is God around here; he is even bigger than God. He is the life of Newcastle. People name their children after him – there are even dogs named after him." Scott Hawthorne, eighteen, added: "I can't imagine who could replace him. This is such a special job, there are very few around who could do it – probably no one better than Kevin Keegan."'

Even civic leaders felt moved to voice their shock and dismay at Keegan's decision. Newcastle's Lord Mayor, Councillor Les Russell said: 'This is a black day for Newcastle. I join hundreds of thousands of fans in deeply regretting Kevin's painful decision. I hope he will reconsider.'

British Prime Minister Tony Blair, a self-confessed Newcastle fan, also had his say: 'Kevin is very well respected, not just in the North-East but throughout the country. It just goes to show that being a football manager is a tough life.'

There was an uncanny symmetry about the appointment of Kenny Dalglish to succeed Keegan, as it mirrored the Scot's move to Liverpool in 1977 to replace his predecessor who had left for S.V. Hamburg.

And Dalglish had quit as Liverpool manager in 1990 in similar circumstances to Keegan, lamenting that the exacting demands of running a football club were ruining his life. Shearer was delighted that he could be reunited with the man who had orchestrated Blackburn's Premier League triumph in 1995.

However, many Newcastle fans were not so enamoured with Dalglish's appointment, favouring Barcelona's Bobby Robson, and fearing that their side's scintillating attacking play would now be shackled by dreary pragmatism. Shearer has insisted that Keegan and Dalglish both possessed a similar outlook to football, but just set about achieving their aims differently – the underlying similarity was that both men had an unbelievable desire to win.

To celebrate the new man's arrival, Shearer scored the winning goal in the 10th minute of extra-time in Newcastle's 2–1 win over Charlton in the FA Cup third-round replay.

Dalglish's joy was short-lived, however as, in the next round, Nottingham Forest gained a 2–1 victory over his side at St James' Park at the end of January. It was a case of Shearer to the rescue in February, when his fantastic late hat-trick allowed Newcastle to overturn a 3–1 deficit to Leicester City with 13 minutes remaining and remarkably end up 4–3 winners.

Not only was it Shearer's first hat-trick for Newcastle, but it rekindled the Magpies' hopes of catching Manchester United, who were now only five points ahead at the top of the Premiership table. 'When you come here you get entertainment, but we'd much prefer to win 1–0 or 2–1 rather than having to do it the hard way,' said Shearer of his side's thrilling victory.

Shearer's remarkable consistency in front of goal led to his father-in-law having a flutter in late February. *Sporting Life* reported: 'Alan Shearer's father-in-law has more than a family interest in the Newcastle striker's performances for the remainder of the season. He is one of the punters who backed Shearer with Hills to score against every side in the Premiership this season and the bet is still running. Shearer needs to score at Middlesbrough today and at home to Southampton, Sunderland and Nottingham Forest and away to West Ham for the bold gamblers to collect and Hills to lose a cool £350,000.'

But, just as had happened before when Shearer was at the height of his powers, injury cruelly terminated his terrific run. It was announced that he would have to undergo his second groin operation of the season, missing Newcastle's UEFA Cup quarter-final with Monaco and a number of crucial matches in the Premiership. He was striking it rich off the pitch, though, as he sealed a lucrative £1.5 million deal to promote Lucozade Sport.

A depleted Newcastle, without both Shearer and Les Ferdinand, tumbled out of Europe 4–0 on aggregate to Monaco, for whom a young, speedy striker by the name of Thierry Henry served notice of his promise. Shearer returned in early April, claiming Newcastle's equaliser in the 1–1 draw with Sunderland at St James' Park.

His outstanding efforts through a tumultuous first season for Newcastle were then rewarded with the PFA Player of the Year Award ahead of David Beckham and Ian Wright. It was the second time in three years that Shearer had won the prestigious piece of silverware, emulating the feat of Mark Hughes.

Shearer could only look on with envy when Hughes' former club Manchester United became Premiership champions for the second successive season in early May.

But he and his team-mates still had the not-inconsiderable second prize of Premiership runners-up and Champions League football to play for.

They narrowly reached their aim with a devastating 5–0 thrashing of Nottingham Forest, aided by Shearer's twenty-eighth goal of the season. Newcastle were locked on sixty-eight points with Arsenal and Liverpool, but their superior goal difference of +33, the highest in the Premiership, saw them claim the coveted second spot.

Kevin Keegan was surely gratified that his penchant for attacking abandon had left his successor with a legacy that paid off handsomely. Meanwhile, Kenny Dalglish started to lay foundations for the new season ahead by snapping up Dutch side Heerenveen's young Danish starlet, Jon Dahl Tomasson, while dispensing with the likes of David Ginola, Robbie Elliott and Lee Clark.

Tomasson ignored the advances of Ajax and Barcelona to move to St James' Park, citing his lifelong love of English football and his keenness to join up with legends such as Kenny Dalglish and Shearer. The Dane's arrival, bolstering other new additions Stuart Pearce, Temuri Ketsbaia and Alessandro Pistone and goalkeeper Shay Given, cast doubts about Les Ferdinand's future at Newcastle, but the amiable frontman was insistent that he wanted to remain and further his fruitful forward partnership with Shearer. The *Daily Mail* quoted him as saying: 'I'd love to stay at Newcastle and keep playing alongside Alan Shearer. Don't forget we were the most successful partnership in the Premier League last season as far as goals are concerned. Why should I want to walk away from that?'

However, Newcastle's affairs were being increasingly governed by monetary matters – as Kevin Keegan had found to his cost – and a £6 million bid from Tottenham for Ferdinand was too good to refuse. Geordie fans still bemoan the fact that the Shearer-Ferdinand partnership was only in existence for a matter of months given that, on their day, the pair were widely rated as almost unplayable and can be considered one of the best forward pairings in Premiership history. Newcastle initially attempted to thwart the transfer of Ferdinand when Shearer suffered a catastrophic injury, his worst yet. Sickeningly he fractured both his fibula and ruptured his ankle ligaments when the studs in his right boot caught in the turf at Goodison Park, where Everton were playing Chelsea in the pre-season Umbro tournament.

Not only was this a potentially fatal blow to Newcastle's aspirations of winning a perpetually elusive trophy, but it also engendered concerns that he may miss out on showing off his skills to a global audience for England at the 1998 World Cup.

Characteristically, as the new season loomed, he preferred to concentrate on Newcastle's chances of glory rather than on his own untimely injury misery. Speaking in the *Sunday Mirror*, he said: 'I have always maintained that my role in the team is to score goals because, after all, that is what I'm paid to do. But the performance of the team significantly outweighs that of the individual. If I were to score forty goals in the coming season and we were to win absolutely nothing, I would consider that a complete failure. But I would be happy scoring no goals if Newcastle won the Premier League.'

He even looked set for a miraculous return to action in November, just in time to join in with United's European adventure in the Champions League. Newcastle chairman Sir John Hall told BBC Radio 4: 'He's making progress. The doctors seem to think that it will be around November. He's going to see a specialist very soon and we will get more news as soon as he gives his decision.' Such hopes of an early return were soon doused, though, as an early 1998 comeback was suggested as a more realistic proposition.

Without their ace striker, Newcastle – now featuring ex-Liverpool players Ian Rush and John Barnes in their ranks – toiled both at home and abroad, exiting the Champions League at the first group stage.

There were memorable nights along the way, though, particularly a sizzling soirée which saw the Spanish football juggernaut Barcelona overcome by a marvellous hat-trick from Faustino Asprilla. Shearer could only look on helplessly as Manchester United once again indicated that their domestic hegemony was to continue inexorably, as an Andy Cole goal gave the Mighty Reds an important win at St James' Park in December. But in the *Daily Mirror*, he hammered out a message of defiance that the championship was not yet bound to end up at Old Trafford, despite the fact that Newcastle were languishing in mid-table. He said: 'Anyone who says it's Manchester United's title is a mug. It is impossible to win it in December. We certainly won't give up and I don't think the rest of the Premiership will, either. We are made of sterner stuff than that and will be working our socks off to try and stay in touch.'

Shearer's determined forward thinking was in stark contrast to the mournful, retrospective mood prevailing at St James' Park at the start of 1998. It was a year since Kevin Keegan's era of fantasy football had summarily ended, when he left both the Geordie and the national footballing public aghast at his decision to resign as Newcastle manager.

Some fans marked the unhappy anniversary by laying flowers at the Milburn Stand at St James' Park as a way of paying homage to Keegan's unforgettable contribution to Newcastle.

There was a silver lining on the horizon for those pining for Keegan's memory, however, as their other much-cherished hero was preparing to amaze and confound his loyal followers by returning to the footballing scene, several months earlier than expected. In mid-January, he took his first tentative steps back on a football field after the previous summer's horrendous injury in a private friendly against a Newcastle junior XI at the city's British Gas sports ground. He came through unscathed and was primed for a phenomenally premature reappearance in Newcastle colours at home to Bolton and, even more amazingly, installed as 7–2 favourite by some bookmakers to score the first goal.

Shearer's recovery came at a perfect time, as it coincided with the exit from St James' Park of colourful Colombian striker Faustino Asprilla to Parma, perhaps an indication that Kenny Dalglish wanted to rid the club of any last vestige of Kevin Keegan's unpredictable and often wayward attacking era.

Although he did not hit the target, Shearer did tee up Temuri Ketsbaia's last-gasp winner for Newcastle in their 2–1 success over Bolton. 'I feel very good and delighted to be back, but the win was more important,' was the Shearer verdict. 'We've not had the greatest of times recently, but there's been a lot of rubbish thrown at us from people who should know better.'

Neither he nor Newcastle could have anticipated that non-league Stevenage would then prove an indomitable stumbling block in the fourth round of the FA Cup.

They very nearly suffered a repeat of the infamous FA Cup upset of the 1971–72 season, when Malcolm Macdonald *et al* endured the ignominy of elimination from the competition at the hands of non-league Hereford, for whom Ronnie Radford scored an extraordinary long-range screamer.

Fortunately, in 1998, they did not experience the same fate, but struggled to a 1–1 draw with Stevenage away, with Shearer grabbing his first FA Cup goal of the season. The fixture had assumed an extra edge when Newcastle complained that Stevenage's stadium, Broadhall Way, which had an increased capacity of 8,000 rather than 6,600 for the tie, was not of adequate size given the visitors' anticipated huge travelling support.

Kenny Dalglish was then accused of 'Big Brother' bully-boy tactics by his opponents' chairman Victor Green after he implored Stevenage to consider switching the tie to another ground. It was an unwelcome fiasco for Newcastle and, thankfully, with two goals from Shearer, they disposed of the plucky non-leaguers 2–1 in the replay at St James' Park.

A relieved Shearer remarked afterwards: 'They would not lie down. The players did themselves proud, but they said some naughty things they should not have said having been at non-league level.'

AC Milan's Swedish striker Andreas Andersson was then unveiled as yet another forward partner for Shearer, the Swede arriving for £3 million. 'It will be terrific playing alongside Alan Shearer, who is one of the best players in Europe,' enthused Andersson, a familiar mantra of any new forward coming to Newcastle to partner a living legend.

In late January, Shearer played his first 90 minutes since returning from injury in Newcastle's 1–0 win at Aston Villa and affirmed that he was now set to recapture his electric form for club and country. But just as the going got good again, the tough and the rough set in when he was the victim of an extraordinary outburst from Leeds manager George Graham in late February.

The fiery Scot, angry that his side had five players booked to the Geordies' one, launched a verbal volley at Shearer after Leeds drew 1–1 with Newcastle in a robust encounter at St James' Park. He fumed in the *Daily Mail*: 'It was almost like an assault on Jimmy Floyd Hasselbaink by Alan Shearer at every corner. It was embarrassing. Shearer was watching the man all the time, not the ball. We should have had three or four penalties. I don't know how the referee couldn't see it – it was unbelievable.'

The *Evening Standard*'s Mick Dennis insisted that statistics showed that Shearer was unquestionably the Premier League's 'dirtiest player'. 'Kenny Dalglish, the Newcastle manager, took umbrage last week at suggestions that Mary (er, sorry, Alan) is particularly physical. Yet, according to my friends at Carling Opta, who evaluate every kick in every match in the Premiership, Shearer committed more fouls than any other player last season. He conceded 81 free-kicks in Premiership games (not including offsides) and three of the other top-five offenders were also targetmen strikers. The list reads: Shearer (81), Vieira (78), Hughes (76), Sutton (72), Ferguson (59).'

There was further scandal to ensue for Newcastle, firstly when, at the beginning of March, Shearer was alleged to have punched a drunk-and-disorderly Keith Gillespie in Dublin.

Newcastle officials thought the trip to Ireland would provide welcome rest and relaxation for their players following the gruelling rigours of the football season. Instead, undesirable drunken shenanigans resulted, including some bizarre frolicking with traffic cones, one of which Belgian defender Phillipe Albert adopted as a makeshift hat.

It is then claimed that inside a Dublin nightspot, Newcastle's Northern Ireland winger started flicking bottle tops at Shearer to which, former Magpies midfielder David Batty alleged in his autobiography, the irate Geordie said: 'Do that one more time and I'll give you a good hiding.' Batty added: 'We ran out to see Gillespie spark out in the gutter. There was blood everywhere. Allegedly, Keith had taken a swing as the two made their way towards the rear of the pub and Al had turned and decked him.'

Newcastle temporarily escaped the unsavoury headlines by making news for all the right reasons when they reached the FA Cup semi-finals for the first time in twenty-four years after a 3–1 win over Barnsley. Yet another shameful controversy bedevilled them just a week later, however, when Newcastle chairman Freddy Shepherd and vice-chairman Douglas Hall contrived to drag the proud club's name through the mud once again.

The pair were ensnared in a tabloid sting which provoked them to make a series of incredible criticisms about Novocastrian women being 'dogs' and Kevin Keegan's lack of trophy success after spending £60 million and Alan Shearer's clean-cut, 'boring' image, attaching the soubriquet 'Mary Poppins' to him. Outraged Newcastle fans implored the disgraced duo to quit immediately, which they duly did, and Sir John Hall resumed his role as chairman. Shearer, meanwhile, maintained a dignified vow of silence about the scandalous revelations about Shepherd and Hall. He only makes a fleeting mention of the embarrassing episode in his autobiography, saying: 'The only thing I had to say about the matter was that I knew the two directors personally and there were no bigger Newcastle fans anywhere.'

Shearer also stuck up for his manager during the Magpies malaise, reiterating his belief that Dalglish could steer Newcastle to the silverware the Geordie public coveted. He said in the *Sunday Mirror*: 'I'd much prefer it if we had won something at Newcastle. I always said it might take two or three years to do that. But we *will* win something. You can't do anything about injuries, and we have had our fair share of them this season. I honestly believe that, given a full-strength side, we would have been challenging for everything this season, including the European Cup. But anyone who questions Kenny Dalglish is crazy. He has a proven track record and the success will come. He has done the job to the best of his ability, but he can't control injuries.'

Yet Shearer's passionate defence of his manager could not disguise the fact that Newcastle were perilously close to losing their Premiership status, fears of which intensified when bottom club Crystal Palace came away with a precious 2–1 victory from St James' Park in mid-March. Shearer smashed in a 25-yard free-kick after 75 minutes, his first goal in six games, but it was to be in vain. The *Sunday Mirror* suggested that the unthinkable could happen if Newcastle were relegated – Shearer would lead a mass exodus out of St James' Park: 'The £15 million England superstar is believed to have a clause in his contract ensuring he can go if Newcastle lose their Premier League status. A Newcastle source said last night: "Alan is happy enough here at the moment, but where he is next season will depend on which division the club is in."'

The *Daily Mail*'s John Richardson reckoned that Newcastle would resort to installing Shearer as their manager in a bid to prevent him from walking away from his lifelong love. He wrote: 'It is understood there is considerable support within the dressing room for Shearer to take over the managerial reigns one day.'

Ironically, the promise of stepping into management was used as a carrot to try to keep him at Ewood Park when Newcastle first made overtures for him in the summer of 1996. 'Undoubtedly, Shearer would love to be in charge of the Toon Army if Dalglish ever moved on and after the current problems have vanished,' continued Richardson.

Yet the Geordie hero showed that he was very much committed to his playing days by firing Newcastle into the FA Cup final and a confrontation with Arsenal after a 1–0 semi-final victory over Sheffield United. Shearer met a perfect cross from the left by John Barnes with a powerful downward header, which Sheffield United goalkeeper Alan Kelly somehow managed to stop entering the net. But the England captain was not to be denied, smashing home the loose ball to spark hysterical celebrations among Newcastle's massive travelling support. Fittingly, watching the latest occupant of the Newcastle No. 9 shirt fashion another Wembley trip for the Geordies was the man whose goals propelled the Magpies into the FA Cup final twenty-four years earlier – SuperMac, Malcolm Macdonald.

Veteran left-back Stuart Pearce, who believed his days of Wembley glory were long behind him, led the chorus of approval for Shearer's seminal role in his side's victory. He said: 'We know that we owe this trip largely to Alan Shearer. Having someone like that in the side is the big difference. Any club in the world would want a player like that.'

But the league was still regarded as Newcastle's bread and butter as they strived gamely to extricate themselves from their precarious position in the pits of the Premiership. A 3–1 defeat at Arsenal did not do much to inspire confidence in their chances of survival, nor did it bode well for the forthcoming FA Cup final.

With impeccable timing, Shearer then scored a last-ditch winner for Newcastle in a 2–1 win over fellow strugglers Barnsley, proving his uncanny ability for match-winning flair to bail his side out of impending adversity. Kenny Dalglish heaped lavish praise on his priceless forward: 'It was a fantastic leap by Alan – certainly a lot higher than I ever managed in my playing days. I don't know how he does it, but I was certainly grateful when I saw his header go in. It said a lot for his fitness that he was still going strong so late in the game and was able to get up and put so much power into the header.'

Newcastle were also galvanised by the appointment of Newcastle

ALAN SHEARER

Breweries managing director, Alastair Wilson, to spearhead a new public relations' drive in his role as the club's communications director. It was a move designed to eradicate the memory of the sleazy allegations that had stained the club's proud name in recent times and to inject new life into flagging merchandise sales.

On the pitch, Newcastle travelled to Old Trafford in what was a formidable barrier to their desperate bid to preserve their top-flight status. History suggested an ominous outcome for the Magpies, as they had not won at Manchester United since 1972.

As ever for Shearer, meeting Manchester United meant that he would have to run a gauntlet of hate as hails of invective inevitably rained down from baying Red's fans, aggrieved at his audacity to turn his back twice on Alex Ferguson's men.

Team-mate Stuart Pearce, no stranger to verbal attacks from hostile supporters over the years, had every confidence in Shearer's ability to rise above the taunts and the tirades. He told the *Daily Mail*: 'It will be water off a duck's back as far as Alan is concerned. Whenever I get booed by opposition fans it only makes me more determined to sicken them.'

Shearer survived the heckling and Newcastle battled bravely to a valuable point in a hard-fought 1–1 draw, which not only pushed the Geordies closer to safety but also almost certainly spelt a ruinous end for Manchester United's championship challenge.

This was a campaign of wildly fluctuating fortunes for the striker, however, and, in late April, he received perhaps the harshest condemnation of his professional career, one that made a mockery of his newly acquired 'Mary Poppins' tag. During Newcastle's 0–0 draw at Leicester, he appeared to kick Foxes' midfielder Neil Lennon in the face when the pair were jostling for possession. Shearer maintained that such an incident, as unsavoury as it looked on television replays, was not born of malicious intent, but many newspapers, who dedicated an avalanche of coverage to the event – and Leicester manager Martin

O'Neill – thought otherwise and lambasted him for his actions, which went unpunished by referee Martin Bodenham. O'Neill fumed: 'Of course it was deliberate. I don't care if he was in an enraged mood or not. Rules are rules – they should be the same for anyone. I don't care if you are Alan Shearer or the Pope, you don't do something like that. It's not in the game and he should have been sent off.'

Suddenly, players such as former Newcastle team-mate David Ginola joined an anti-Shearer lobby and lashed out at what was perceived to be his overly-aggressive style of play; the Newcastle No. 9 was also slapped with a misconduct charge by the Football Association. Shearer questioned the video evidence and could not believe what was being said about him in the press.

Naturally, many people rallied to his cause, including team-mate Andreas Andersson, who told the *Northern Echo*: 'There are a lot of players in our team who want to win games and Alan is one of them. He is competitive and he wants to win badly. I think Alan will emerge as one of the best players in the World Cup this summer.'

Gordon Taylor, chief executive of the Professional Footballers' Association, believed Shearer was the victim of a witch-hunt. The *Daily Mail* suggested that Shearer's muscularity often pushed the boundaries of foul play. Nigel Clarke and John Richardson wrote: 'Shearer is ruthless, not evil. There is a big difference. He is also a very special player, but one who at times runs out of control.'

Clarke and Richardson also noted that Shearer's actions were born of both self-protection – explained by his injury-plagued past – and his frustration at Newcastle's faltering league campaign. They said: 'Constant weeks on the treatment table – three groin operations, serious knee ligament damage and a nine-month absence after a horrific ankle injury – have taught him that it is sometimes necessary to get your retaliation in first. It is called self-protection and Shearer now knows more than most the value of looking after himself.'

Shearer made no excuses about his physical approach when he spoke to the *Daily Mail* at the launch of his autobiography. He said: 'It's a case of fending for yourself. If that entails a bit of pushing and shoving, then so be it. No one just sits back and allows you to score. You've got to be a bit streetwise.'

Much to Shearer's relief, the Football Association returned a 'not guilty' verdict on allegations that he had deliberately kicked Lennon in the face – just four days before the FA Cup final.

He appeared before a three-man FA commission in Sheffield and it is believed that a second television camera angle of the incident, which had not been witnessed before, was vital in determining the outcome. Shearer said afterwards: 'I am delighted to have cleared my name and can now look forward to Saturday's Cup final and the countdown to the World Cup. I am pleased to put the record straight and, in doing so, clear my name. I was always confident that I would.'

Further delight ensued for the plagued striker, as Newcastle managed to haul themselves to safety in the Premiership through precious wins, such as the 3–1 home defeat of Chelsea. Then, as FA Cup fever intensified in Newcastle, members of the Toon Army displayed their affection for Shearer through a striking tribute to their hero. About twenty-five imaginative Newcastle fans draped a 29ft by 17ft shirt, for which they paid £1,000, on the 65-foot statue, the Angel of the North. The BBC News website reported: 'In a daring dawn raid, a giant-sized replica of the striker's No. 9 shirt was draped across the chest of the statue on the A1 at Gateshead. The shirt stayed up for 20 minutes until police arrived at the scene, having got there as a result of a combination of fishing line, rubber balls and catapults wielded by around twenty-five people, who managed to redesign Anthony Gormley's metal creation radically.'

Shearer was now well and truly up for the cup, free from the worries about his blemished reputation and the injuries that had beset him. 'This will be my first major final and I am determined to enjoy it to the full', he said. 'I am feeling strong and fit and mentally far fresher than I normally would at this stage of the season. We want to bring the cup home to Tyneside for our fans. They have been tremendous, and hopefully the pubs of Newcastle will be hosting a giant celebration on Saturday night.'

Shearer and Newcastle could have predicted that the footballing gods would conspire against them from the moment that their team coach failed to start due to a flat battery. The final was to end in bitter disappointment, however, for Shearer and the Newcastle legions that flocked to Wembley, as Arsenal coasted to a comfortable 2–0 victory, thanks to goals from talented young French striker Nicolas Anelka.

Sadly Shearer made little impact on the game, although his left-foot shot hit a post in the second half and he again attracted unwelcome headlines when he was lucky not to have been sent off for clattering Tony Adams, a fierce challenge which earned him a booking.

Kevin Keegan slated his former team's predictable tactics and failure to maximise the talents of their main man. He said in the *Daily Mirror*: 'Playing balls over the top for Shearer to run onto is not playing to his strengths. He gets most of his goals in the penalty area, but there didn't seem to be anyone around to provide the right service. I just couldn't see where they were expecting it to come from.'

He and his team Shearer and Newcastle could console themselves with the fact that they would enter the European Cup-Winners' Cup, given that Arsenal had been crowned Premiership champions. The end of the season witnessed the habitual flurry of comings and goings and persistent transfer talk, much of which centred on the Geordie ace.

Newcastle snapped up Greek midfielder George Georgiadis from Panathinaikos for £500,000 in mid-May, while Real Madrid and Juventus led the hunt for Shearer. Newcastle chief executive Freddie Fletcher insisted that the England captain was not for sale and that he was an intrinsic part of the Magpies' long-term strategy.

ALAN SHEARER

Shearer's place in Football League history was also assured when he was chosen as one of '100 League Legends' containing a veritable 'who's who' of British soccer. He was one of the Premiership players named in the illustrious list, joining Tony Adams, Paul Gascoigne, Ryan Giggs, Peter Schmeichel, Dennis Bergkamp and Eric Cantona in a venture designed to commemorate the Football League's inception in 1888.

Following the World Cup in France, Kenny Dalglish recruited a member of the triumphant French squad for his Newcastle side – forward Stéphane Guivarc'h. And guess what? Yes, he trotted out the habitual platitudes for Newcastle's No. 9. 'I am very happy to be at Newcastle and look forward to playing with Alan,' he declared in the *Journal*. 'But this is my first season and I will be playing around the man wearing the No. 9 shirt. My job is to help him as much as possible.'

New-look Newcastle, galvanised by new signings, including Dietmar Hamann from Bayern Munich and Peruvian midfielder Nolberto Solano, warmed up for the new season by thumping Irish side Bray Wanderers 6–0 in Dublin, with Shearer scoring a hat-trick. It was clear that Shearer's appetite for goals was undiminished, although he was surprisingly ranked below Michael Owen by the bookmakers to be leading Premiership goalscorer, with his England colleague rated at 3–1 to top the goal charts.

A sheepish Freddy Shepherd was reinstalled as Newcastle chairman just months after his and Douglas Hall's inconsiderate comments had whipped up a storm of controversy. Suitably chastened by the furore subsequently created in Newcastle, Shepherd admitted to the *Sunday Mirror* that he had miscalculated Shearer's worth to the club. 'I think we misjudged just how important Alan was to Kenny's plans and to the morale of the rest of the team. We learned a painful lesson about just how important a player and a leader Alan Shearer is to Newcastle United. Our experience last season tells us that Shearer is irreplaceable. We want to build a team to challenge the best in

Europe – and I can assure Newcastle fans that Alan Shearer is a vital part of those plans.'

Newcastle made a stuttering start to the 1998–99 league campaign, stumbling to a 0–0 draw with newly promoted Charlton in their opening fixture at St James' Park. As his team prepared to face multi-cultural Chelsea – with whom Newcastle drew 1–1 – Shearer suggested that the changing face of English football was being scarred by a massive influx of foreigners. 'The problem you face is when you bring in a lot of foreigners who are of the same ability as English players,' he said. 'I'm sure that will stifle the growth of young players and that could be a problem for the English league in years to come.'

Kenny Dalglish's turmoil-riddled, eighteen-month spell at the helm of Newcastle was then abruptly ended when he was sacked. Shearer was left reeling at the shock announcement, writing later that Dalglish's departure made him feel just as bad as he had felt following Kevin Keegan's abrupt exit from St James' Park.

In Dalglish's stead came a totally different character in Ruud Gullit; a controversial character who would, sadly for Shearer and his proud football institution, do little to reverse their ailing fortunes.

CHAPTER SIX

England Excellence

'When I was growing up in the streets of Newcastle,
my strongest aim was to play for my country. I cannot describe
the feeling I get when I play and score for England.'
ALAN SHEARER, TALKING TO THE *DAILY MIRROR* IN 1997.

The famous English literary figure of the eighteenth century, Dr Samuel Johnson, once said that patriotism is the last refuge of a scoundrel. If you believe this, then Alan Shearer's 'Mary Poppins' nickname is a serious misnomer.

Between 1992 and 2000, his selfless devotion to his country was self-evident as goals in abundance and a myriad of marvellous performances saw him acclaimed as one of England's best-ever strikers. Shearer's England story also countenanced both injury and an inexplicable and seemingly never-ending goal drought that would have conspired to crush men of less resilient character.

But there was to be no rapid rise through the England ranks for

Shearer, as he never represented his country at schoolboy level, and finally donned a white shirt for the first time when he turned out for the Under-17s in February 1988. Typically, as has become his trademark on debuts, he scored in a 2–1 win over the Republic of Ireland with a near-post header as Southampton coach Dave Merrington, and the man that unearthed his talents, Jack Hixon, looked on in the company of Shearer's proud mother and father. Shearer then bypassed the Under-18 age group at international level before, at the age of twenty, appearing as an England Under-21 substitute against Poland at White Hart Lane.

His full Under-21 debut proved far more memorable, however, as he scored twice against the Republic of Ireland in Cork in November 1990. His second goal, in the 51st minute, saw Shearer pick the ball up on the halfway line and crash home an unstoppable shot from the edge of the area. Peter Ball in *The Times* described the youngster's performance as 'outstanding'.

The manager of the England Under-21s, Lawrie McMenemy – who signed Shearer for Southampton – was also left purring at the devastating debut, according to Ball. 'He's strong; I've seen him play against experienced internationals and shrug them off. We saw his finishing ability for the goals and that was a lovely ball for [Ian] Olney to score which showed another side of his game,' McMenemy enthused.

If this goal-scoring cameo had only offered a brief, yet tantalising, glimpse of Shearer's youthful promise, the summer of 1991 witnessed the making of a maestro. He was selected for the England Under-21 squad for the Toulon tournament in France, which had, since its inception in 1972, proved a fertile breeding talent for emerging European stars.

Over the years, this annual festival of football has showcased the talents of World Cup stars of the future, such as France's Zinedine

ENGLAND EXCELLENCE

Zidane, Laurent Blanc and Didier Deschamps, as well as initiating the likes of young England lions David Beckham, Robbie Fowler and Kieron Dyer into the rigours of international football. Shearer has acknowledged that this platform provided him with an invaluable football education and, in turn, he rewarded the French football public with some sterling performances and some unforgettable goals. He scored both England's goals in their opening game, a 2–1 victory over Senegal, which led to the Mexicans meting out some harsh punishment to the young English prodigy in his country's next game.

In a stormy encounter, four players were red-carded – three Mexicans, along with Shearer's Southampton team-mate Jason Dodd. It was, Shearer later recalled, the worst behaviour he had ever seen on a football field.

Revenge was to be sweet for a bruised-and-battered but unbowed England, as Shearer netted a hat-trick in a 6–0 romp. He then claimed the winning goal in a 2–1 win over the Soviet Union in the semi-finals and then repeated the feat as hosts France were disposed of 1–0.

Not only did Shearer garner two personal trophies – one for being the tournament's best player and another for being the top goalscorer with seven goals in four games – but, perhaps more importantly, his reputation had been appreciably enhanced. Two more goals in October 1991 to help England overcome Turkey Under-21s 2–0, bolstered a mounting media campaign calling for the young Shearer to be thrust forward for selection to his country's senior side.

His then England Under-21 record haul of thirteen goals in eleven games – in 2005 he shared this honour with Charlton Athletic's Francis Jeffers – certainly made a compelling case for a swift promotion up the ranks. However, it was not until February 1992 that he achieved every wide-eyed English schoolboy's dream – playing for his country at Wembley.

Shearer and his sumptuously gifted, but enigmatic, Southampton team-mate, Matt Le Tissier, were called up to the England squad to play France in a friendly and competed for striking berths with Arsenal's Ian Wright and David Hirst of Sheffield Wednesday. Shearer positively relished his forthcoming baptism in a white shirt, telling *The Times*: 'I love playing against foreign teams with sweepers where you have to go hunting for the ball. I know I am capable of playing for England and I will work hard to keep my place.'

England were building towards the forthcoming European Championships in Sweden in the knowledge that one of their greatest-ever strikers, Gary Lineker, was nearing the end of his illustrious career. Controversially, Lineker was relegated to the bench for the game – and was reported to be none too pleased about it, as he was determinedly chasing Bobby Charlton's England record goal haul of forty-nine.

Meanwhile, his heir apparent, Alan Shearer, was paired with Hirst against their Gallic rivals, who were hotly tipped to be in contention for the summer's European prize. The French, coached by the legendary midfield maestro Michel Platini, were resurgent after they had failed to qualify for the World Cup finals in 1990. 'Les Bleus' were unbeaten in nineteen matches and included household names in their ranks, such as the prolific marksman Jean-Pierre Papin, as well as the maverick genius, Eric Cantona, whose English odyssey had just begun at Leeds United.

Their clash with England promised to be a fascinating precursor to the two countries' scheduled match in the forthcoming European Championships. As it transpired, however, a lacklustre French team failed to impress, while an England striking legend was born.

Alan Shearer was to reinforce the growing belief that he, more than any other of his striking rivals, deserved to assume the mantle of the thirty-one-year-old Lineker by netting in a 2–0 win over the French. His first England goal exemplified, like many of the twenty-nine that followed, a truly instinctive finish born of deadly decisiveness in the penalty area. Nigel Clough's floated corner was nodded down by Ian Wright into the path of Shearer, who swivelled and tucked in his first England goal with some aplomb.

He then teed up a second for substitute Lineker, his forty-seventh for England, and was rewarded for his efforts with a Man of the Match award of two American Airlines tickets, which he generously gave to his sister Karen.

Shearer's night to remember easily eclipsed anything he had achieved in football up until this point, including his hat-trick heroics on his Southampton debut four years previously. He gushed in the *Evening Standard*: 'It was the greatest night of my life. I didn't want it to end. It has all come so quickly for me. I half wish it would slow down a bit so I can enjoy it. When I scored I couldn't wait to get my hands up in the air. I've never had a feeling like that in my life before. They talk about replacing Gary Lineker, but how can you replace a player like that? No one will ever take his place in my book.'

The fact that his opening bow in the international arena was on the hallowed turf of Wembley fulfilled another childhood fantasy for Shearer, as he admitted to *thefa.com* website. 'To represent your country is the dream of any footballer. The fact it was at Wembley made it extra special. Wembley will always be special for footballers, certainly when I was growing up that was where everything happened.'

England manager Graham Taylor was satisfied at seeing his faith in Shearer repaid handsomely. He told the *Guardian*: 'He's played extremely well up front. I wouldn't think he could have had a better debut. Shearer's responsibility is to snap up opportunities in the six-yard box. We know he can do that.'

Despite making such an impressive initial impact in the cut and thrust of international football, Shearer's next outing in an England shirt was in the B team against Czechoslovakia in Prague in March. The twenty-one-year-old was philosophical about his 'demotion', however. 'I'm just pleased to be involved. I'm only twenty-one years old and I've got to look and learn,' he said prior to the match.

Graham Taylor explained the perceived relegation in *The Times*: 'He has played fifty-four games on the trot,' Taylor said. 'And he has a big game coming up [the Zenith Data Systems Cup final at Wembley for Southampton]. I like to bear things like that in mind.'

Shearer partnered his club colleague Matt Le Tissier and Arsenal's Alan Smith in attack for the game, in which he was substituted without scoring. A month later, he was restored to the England first team and reunited with Gary Lineker in Moscow against the Commonwealth of Independent States (CIS). However, Shearer was replaced by Nigel Clough, while Lineker edged ever nearer Bobby Charlton's goal-scoring record by scoring his forty-eighth international goal in a thrilling 2–2 draw.

Failure to get picked for England's next two friendlies, against Brazil and Hungary, coupled with feverish competition for places up front, left the new boy uncertain of his place on the plane to Sweden for Euro '92.

As a torturous, sleepless night of worry and doubt awaited him on the eve of manager Graham Taylor's announcement of his squad for the forthcoming tournament, Shearer confesses in his autobiography that he decided enough was enough – he had to know if he was in or not.

Spurred on by one of the England coaches of the era, the flame-haired World Cup winner Alan Ball, he audaciously opted to confront Taylor and quiz him on whether or not he would be included in the travelling party. Taylor responded gruffly that Shearer would have to play the waiting game like every other prospective pick. However, the Geordie reckons that his cheek made a telling impression. 'I believe Graham respected me for what I did,' wrote Shearer. 'I think he saw it as an act of a confident young man who was forthright enough to go looking for the answer to an awkward question.'

Whether or not such a bold move swayed Taylor's thoughts is a moot point, but the following day Shearer was to celebrate the news he yearned to hear – he was included in England's Euro '92 squad.

The scene was set for England to take Sweden by storm, as Gary Lineker eyed a prize-winning swansong and the prospect of superseding Bobby Charlton as England's greatest-ever goalscorer, while Shearer relished the chance to stake his claim as the ready-made replacement.

Yet what followed was another hugely dispiriting and insipid England European campaign, during which the anti-Graham Taylor hate campaign gathered momentum. Shearer was not picked for England's opener, a drab goalless draw with Denmark, but started up front with Lineker in the second group game against France. Once again, England failed to sparkle and score – although Shearer came closest to netting with a spectacular diving header, which missed the target – as they endured a disappointing deadlock with France. Two points from two games meant that England had to defeat hosts Sweden in a do-or-die decider.

Shearer sat on the bench kicking his heels in frustration while David Platt fired his side into an early lead. But two Swedish goals, including a delightful solo effort from Tomas Brolin, crushed England hopes and proved an unhappy farewell for Gary Lineker, who was controversially hauled off by Taylor. Shearer had been primed to replace the Tottenham man, but Arsenal's Alan Smith was preferred.

The image of Lineker disconsolately trudging off and flinging away his captain's armband in disgust is an indelible one and also hammered several nails into the coffin of the beleaguered Taylor. 'Swedes 2 Turnips 1' was the savage headline in one tabloid newspaper in the aftermath of the match and condemned Taylor to being horribly saddled with the unforgiving label of 'Turnip head'.

He had become renowned as a proponent of the unsophisticated long-ball game and was later lampooned as a foul-mouthed buffoon on a Channel 4 documentary tracing the 1994 World Cup qualifying campaign, which gave rise to the immortal catchphrase, 'Do I not like that'.

However, Shearer has hailed Taylor as a man of great integrity and self-belief who did not deserve to be the focus of cruel media jokes and jibes. While Taylor was enduring his own personal hell, Shearer was suffering frustrations of his own, after a cruciate ligament injury in December 1992 shattered his hopes of cementing his position as Lineker's successor.

He played in the World Cup qualifying matches against Norway and Turkey, scoring with a diving header in a 4–0 trouncing of Turkey. Shearer described his second goal as 'a precious moment' and defended his fledgling partnership with Arsenal's Ian Wright when he spoke to the *Guardian*. 'That might shut a few people up,' he said. 'We've had a few people sniping at us, saying that the partnership wouldn't work. But he [Wright] was unlucky not to score and he set up my goal very well'.

He also later revealed to the *Daily Mirror* in February 1997 that he had requested the presence of a lucky charm to aid his performance – his mother-in-law Jenny Arnold. He explained: 'She came to see me play on my England debut – and I scored. But I didn't score in the next four games, so when we played Turkey at Wembley, I told my wife, Lainya, to bring her mum along. And guess what? I scored again!'

However, serious injury halted Shearer's progress, and it was another eleven months before he was surprisingly, and somewhat controversially, drafted into the starting line-up for the vital trip away to Holland in Rotterdam.

ENGLAND EXCELLENCE

Some sections of the English media questioned Taylor's decision to include the Blackburn man after his long lay-off from action given that, although his prodigious goal-scoring powers were clearly undiminished – he had scored four goals in his first full three games for Blackburn in the 1993–94 season – he had not yet achieved 100 per cent fitness.

Holland's Dennis Bergkamp felt Shearer's return would be a welcome fillip for England and a severe threat to the Dutch's progress, however. He said in the *Daily Mail*: 'Shearer is the man who can really make it difficult for us. He has speed and strength, which are the requirements of all good strikers, and we know how much England have missed him.'

But Shearer was unable to impose himself on the Dutch defence, cutting a frustrated figure up front for much of the game, as Holland earned a highly-controversial 2–0 win to deliver a shattering blow to England's World Cup 1994 qualifying hopes. The game hinged on the German referee Karl Josef Assenmacher's failure to brandish the red card to Dutch defender Ronald Koeman after he hauled down David Platt when he was clean through on goal.

To England's amazement, Koeman was not sent off and then, to compound matters, curled in a cute free-kick, a delightful effort, which was supplemented by a goal from Dennis Bergkamp.

England now had only faint hopes of World Cup qualification, as they had to score at least seven goals away to minnows San Marino while relying on Poland to down the Dutch; a not insurmountable task with a striker of the calibre of Alan Shearer leading the line. However, Shearer was ruled out of the goal chase due to a back injury and England's 7–1 win was rendered academic as Holland secured three points in Poland to progress to USA '94 at the Three Lions' expense.

Days later, the much-maligned Taylor's three-year England reign ended when he was sacked. Shearer showed his sympathy for and gratitude to the unfortunate Taylor by calling him up on hearing the announcement.

However, he was a confirmed admirer of Taylor's successor, Terry Venables, whose unstinting faith in his No. 1 striker would prove crucial over the ensuing years. Acknowledged as a shrewd tactician, Venables was hailed as a saviour for English football, but his masterplan contained a radical new system that would coincide with a startling goal drought for Shearer.

The ex-Tottenham and Barcelona chief Venables believed it was time to eschew tradition and dispense with England's favoured 4-4-2 formation, in a bid to make his country a less predictable proposition. He employed the 4-3-2-1 'Christmas Tree' formation, which involved a lone striker being supported by two deep-lying attacking midfielders. The theory was that it would ensure England was not overrun in midfield by quality continental opposition.

And on paper, with Shearer as a forward totem supported by the cunning of a Peter Beardsley or the lung-busting, late penalty-box surges of a David Platt, the new system offered exciting possibilities. Indeed, the early signs suggested that the Christmas Tree would bear plentiful gifts for both Shearer and England.

In Venables' second game in charge, England cruised to a 5–0 victory over Greece at Wembley in May 1994 and Shearer was on the scoresheet. Mulling over the perceived merits of the 'tree tactics', Hugh McIlvaney wrote in the *Sunday Times* that there had been rumours that 'Shearer's profound, almost obsessional commitment to scoring goals caused him to be resentful when all his arduous foraging, all the unselfish running that drags defenders away from the areas they are meant to police, provided others with the glory of applying the killer blows.' McIlvaney went on to report that Venables had been so disturbed by mutterings in the media that England's style of play did not suit Shearer's goal cravings that he sat down with the striker and confronted him on the issue.

'Terrific' was the answer, a reassuring one from someone the manager recognises as 'an honest boy, one I'd count on to express his feelings directly', added McIlvaney.

Significantly, when Venables decided to pair Shearer with Teddy Sheringham in his fourth game in charge, the Blackburn man notched both goals in a 2–0 home win over the United States.

However, it was a bittersweet occasion for Shearer, as he had to have a lump removed from the side of his temple after colliding with American defender Alexi Lalas. 'Alan Shearer pulled them hither and thither with a display of his voluminous all-round abilities,' wrote the *Independent*'s Ian Ridley of Shearer's ceaseless tormenting of the American defence. 'There may be several strikers pressing for an England place, but it will be a hot day in Hull before Shearer's is under scrutiny.'

The *Observer*'s Patrick Barclay was also glowing in his assessment of Shearer's worth to both Venables and England: 'Alan Shearer has come to mean as much to the Venables regime as Paul Gascoigne once did to Graham Taylor's, the difference being the reliable character of the Blackburn centre-forward, who seems destined to move onward and upward, driven by attributes significantly including the capacity to learn, until he is acknowledged as the best in the world. Marco Van Basten, the last centre-forward to achieve such status, would have been proud of the goals Shearer put past the Americans. The second especially, a header steered against the grain of Graeme Le Saux's cross, bore the hallmark of high class.'

Fulsome praise such as this proved the fateful kiss of death for Shearer's England career, as he was about to face a barren goal-scoring spell that would have ended the careers of strikers of lesser ability and mental strength. Inexplicably, he would not score another international goal until Euro '96, despite netting with stunning regularity with Blackburn.

The 'Christmas Tree' formation was cited as one factor that

contributed to Shearer's goalless run as he struggled to adapt to being bereft of forward support. He has since admitted that while he did not blame the Christmas Tree formation totally for him losing his goal touch prior to Euro '96, he did find it a lonely experience. However, Venables did not always persist with the new tactics, often introducing a second striker to partner Shearer during the pre-Euro '96 period.

Not even partnerships with such luminous talents as Matt Le Tissier, Stan Collymore, Les Ferdinand and Teddy Sheringham could help Shearer break his own interminable 'duck'. Perhaps it was a combination of a proliferation of forward partners, the experimentation of different styles and systems and the lack of competitive edge for England in the build-up to Euro '96 that contributed to his persistent woes in front of goal.

It is true testament to the man that, during such torrid times, his belief in his own ability never wavered and he consistently insisted that the goals would flow freely at some point. He cited a time at Southampton when he also drew a blank for an extended period. 'I once went seventeen games for Southampton without getting a goal,' the *Sunday Mirror* quoted him as saying in October 1995. 'My confidence has not been affected by not scoring for England for so long.'

Naturally, some sections of the media began to express their doubts about Shearer's continued presence in the England team while he continued to misfire and opposing supporters began to revel in the goal machine's incredible malfunctioning. Ken Montgomery, writing in the *Sunday Mirror* on 15 October 1995, offered a more reasoned and colourful analysis of Shearer's plight following England's flat goalless draw with Norway in Oslo. He said: 'Terry Venables must come up fast with the right fodder for Alan Shearer – or he'll reduce England's thoroughbred striker to an emaciated, goal-starved and totally disillusioned international donkey.'

Montgomery asserted that Shearer was beginning to become

Alan Shearer had an impressive start to his professional football career when he scored a hat-trick on his Southampton debut against Arsenal.

When he moved to Blackburn Rovers, the goal scoring continued and in 1995 he got his hands on his first, and only, piece of silverware when his side won the Premiership.

After his Premier League success, Alan was named PFA Player of the Year.

Shearer's England career started in 1992 against France.

With over sixty full caps and thirty international goals, Alan was an obvious choice to receive the captain's arm band.

In 1996, the Geordie lad returned to his Tyneside roots when manager Kevin Keegan (*pictured below*, *right*) signed the player to his dream club, Newcastle United.

Shearer's trademark one-arm-aloft goal-scoring salute.

Top: Shearer and fellow Geordie hero, Paul Gascoigne, celebrate scoring in England's World Cup qualifying match against Moldova.

Bottom: Shearer's former club manager, Kevin Keegan, became the England manager in 1999. He is seen here presenting the England star with a commemorative shirt to mark his fiftieth appearance for the national side.

'cheesed off' at England's lack of ammunition and ambition and he reported that Norway defender and Blackburn team-mate Henning Berg also understood his predicament. 'Alan Shearer is not to blame for the fact that he hasn't scored for his country in more than a year. He needs support – and he isn't getting it,' Berg said.

But Venables maintained that he believed in the system of play and declared that two strikers could get just as isolated as one. Shearer's predecessor as England's chief plunderer of goals, Gary Lineker, also offered his encouragement and support for the beleaguered striker.

In France's *Agence Presse* on 7 September 1995, he said: 'All strikers go through patches like this. But it's when you find out if they're made of the right stuff. They either go into their shells and succumb to the pressure, or it makes them all the more determined to succeed and put things right. I'm sure Alan is in the latter category.'

Germany's world-class goalscorer Jürgen Klinsmann also identified with Shearer's sadness, telling the *Daily Mirror*: 'It's such a difficult situation and it will be getting to Alan. It will be working its way into his brain and he needs a goal urgently. Any goal will do. It doesn't matter how it goes in as long as it crosses the line.'

If only the cynics had known then that a scintillating summer and a glorious goal haul awaited England's central striker in 1996. Shearer was conscious that Liverpool's Robbie Fowler and Stan Collymore were doing their utmost to dislodge him from his seemingly intractable place in England's forward line. 'I'm no mug and I know exactly who is snapping at my heels, but as long as I continue to contribute to England's positive results, I am not too concerned,' he told the *Independent* in March 1996.

Shearer was also buoyed by Venables' unbreakable confidence in him and, as Euro '96 loomed, was provided with the assurance that if he were fit, he and Teddy Sheringham would be England's goal-getting double act. Venables later remarked during Euro '96: 'He did not let it [his goal drought] worry him. He never snatched at chances or began shooting from silly angles. He just kept working, knowing that the goals would come.'

In 2005, Shearer hailed his partnership with Sheringham as his most pleasurable for England and the statistics validate this view. In fifteen games together, they shared eighteen goals – an average of 1.2 goals a game, the best return of any of his England double acts. Sheringham and Shearer, England's very own SAS, had an uncanny understanding of each other's playing styles and dovetailed beautifully.

While cerebral 'Sheri' was more often than not the creator, Shearer was the executioner in chief, punishing the opposition with his famed deadly accuracy.

'Teddy was my best England strike partner,' said Shearer in the *Mirror* in 2005. 'You can't explain how a partnership like that developed. It just happened. Sometimes two players find their styles just complement each other. That is what happened to us. It wasn't about the work we did on the training ground, we just understood each other's game and the runs we'd make.'

Sheringham echoed his old pal's sentiments, adding: 'He was a fantastic partner. We complemented each other's styles. The manager at the time, Terry Venables, saw that and he stuck with us. We were very comfortable together as a partnership. But we didn't quite win anything. We were very close to winning the European Championships in 1996. That would have been fantastic, but not quite.'

However, Shearer's participation in England's biggest sporting event since the 1966 World Cup looked in jeopardy when he was beset by a persistent groin injury in late March. Fortunately, his enforced absence did not persist and he appeared as a substitute in England's final Euro '96 warm-up game on home turf – a 3–0 victory over Hungary on 18 May.

He had soothed concerns about his fitness, but doubts still remained about his scoreless stint and it was clearly preying on the predator's mind, according to the *Daily Mirror*'s Nigel Clarke: 'While at Bisham Abbey last week preparing for the match against Hungary, Shearer walked in to be interviewed like a man on his way to the gallows. When it was all over he breathed a sigh of relief and said: "That's the first time nobody has asked about my scoring record with England." He was told: "That will come next week." Shearer grinned, but the message has hit home.'

Then it was time to for Shearer and England to embark on a hugely controversial three-game tour in the Far East. Many questioned Terry Venables' logic in hauling his players halfway across the world so near to a major tournament, although such a contentious move was also applauded in some quarters, as it allowed the team to escape the simmering Euro '96 hype and the expectation that was brewing back home. However, what happened at the tail-end of the trip sparked an even greater public outcry.

After England had laboured to beat a Hong Kong Golden Select XI 1–0, self-confessed hedonists in the England ranks, such as Paul Gascoigne, Teddy Sheringham and Steve McManaman, decided to take turns in the 'dentist's chair' in a nightspot called China Jump Club. The problem was, there were no teeth examined; instead, copious amounts of alcohol had to be downed by the person strapped into the chair.

Shearer, meanwhile, was elsewhere with Blackburn goalkeeper Tim Flowers and representatives from his football kit firm, Umbro, according to his account of the embarrassing episode in his autobiography. He defended his team-mates' alcohol-fuelled antics, claiming that it was all 'good, harmless fun' and insisted that everyone involved in the boozy night out had not broken the 2am hotel curfew.

However, the damage was done as pictures of half-cut and half-dressed England players were splashed all over the tabloids back home and worse was to follow when the touring party jetted home: yet more drink and yet more adverse publicity after several televisions were smashed on the Cathay Pacific flight back to England.

England's hopes of emulating the legends of 1966 looked as though they had been extinguished before the tournament had even begun, as a press-player silence broke out. However, rather than implode under the mass of media hatred which threatened to ruin their European dream, England developed a siege mentality and were galvanised.

And with Alan Shearer leading the line, the Three Lions knew they had a chance. Winners of every major international competition are spearheaded by a prolific striker – Maradona for Argentina in 1986 and Romario for Brazil in 1994 in World Cups, for example – and Shearer knew he had to deliver in similar fashion.

Ex-England striker Trevor Francis echoed the sentiments of fans nationwide when he mused in the *Daily Mirror*: 'Alan Shearer must come of age as an international striker over the next twenty-one days – or we can forget about being the hosts with the most in Euro '96. Can he finally pull on an England shirt without smothering the killer instinct that's made him the Premiership's deadliest finisher over the past three seasons?'

Brazilian legend Pelé also supported calls for England to be more positive and furnish Shearer with a partner to fire England to victory: 'The formation they will play against Switzerland has only one striker and I feel sorry for Alan Shearer. For his club he scores lots of goals and plays well, but in the national team he looks a different player and no one supports him. That's when people turn round and ask why he isn't scoring. I'm from a different school of thought. In my book you have to play for the win.'

Meanwhile, as he prepared to embark on his European adventure, Shearer received a welcome fillip from 1966 World Cup-winning hero, Geoff Hurst. Hurst told the *People*: 'Alan Shearer fills me with hope for England, even though he hasn't scored in twelve internationals. Unusually for me, I really believe he means it when he says he's not at all concerned by his lack of goals for his country. And there are not many forwards I'll say that about.'

Switzerland, England's opening opponents in Euro '96, were a workmanlike, but unspectacular outfit and, on paper, looked the ideal opposition for Shearer to end months of goalless misery. However, uneasiness and tremendous tension filled the air as England struggled to assert their authority over the stubborn Swiss.

Who else but Alan Shearer would then answer his country's call and score for the first time in 1,087 minutes of play, or fourteen international matches? After 23 minutes, he latched onto a Paul Ince through-ball and hammered home an emphatic goal that obliterated the weight of expectations on both his and England's shoulders and exorcised any shred of self-doubt that may have been lingering in his mind. The *Mail on Sunday's* Joe Melling enthused that Shearer 'reacted with the cold-eyed aplomb of a trained assassin in bludgeoning a shot of immense power', while the *Observer's* Amy Lawrence said: 'He hit the ball as if his life depended on it and then glanced to the heavens with relief.' Shearer later said that it had been the most important goal of his career and one that may well have saved his England place.

Yet England could not capitalise on the springboard of Shearer's seminal goal, as the Swiss proved obdurate opponents and snatched a late equaliser from Kubilay Turkyilmaz's penalty after Stuart Pearce was alleged to have handled the ball in the penalty area.

Sadly, Shearer's sledgehammer-like shot and Man of the Match performance was largely shrouded in the match postmortems after most pundits focused on England's less-than-convincing start to the tournament that failed to feed a frenzied nation's insatiable appetite for goals and impressive performances. But Shearer pointed out that past history proved that one unsatisfactory result did not preclude ultimate success. He told the *Daily Mirror*: 'It's certainly not all doom and gloom. We haven't started as well as we'd hoped, but we've got the chance to have a bit of a rest now and start to work on a few things. We've still got two more games to play. After all, back in 1966, England drew their first game against Uruguay and we all know what happened after that.'

Next up for Shearer and England was a clash with the 'Auld Enemy' Scotland, buoyed by a heroic Braveheart display in their fortuitous 0–0 draw against much-fancied Holland. A personal battle to savour amid the frenzy and fervour would be Shearer's confrontation with his Blackburn team-mate, Colin Hendry, a defender who was the very epitome of Scottish grit and passion.

Once again, England looked anything but fluent against the indomitable Scots in a cagey first half. But once again, it was Super Al to the rescue.

In the 53rd minute, Gary Neville's sumptuous right-wing cross was met with a glorious header from Shearer to spark bedlam among white-shirted legions in the cauldron of Wembley.

Scotland were not to be subdued totally, however, and England had to survive some nervy moments, including Gary McAllister's missed penalty and a bullet header from Gordon Durie, which David Seaman clawed away superbly.

Another Geordie genius, Paul Gascoigne, would then apply the *coup de grâce* to England's vanquishing of their old foe when he flicked the ball over Colin Hendry's head with his left foot and then crashed home an exquisite right-foot volley. Cue wild celebrations, which saw a prostrate Gazza gulp down the contents of a drinks bottle which was squirted into his face – a comic parody of England's pre-tournament antics.

Shearer was understandably delighted at scoring his second goal of the tournament. 'I am pleased for myself, not for anyone else. And I've always had faith in my ability. I got behind everyone and timed my run to perfection. I could get onto the end of those crosses all day,' he remarked of his vital goal in the *Sunday Mirror*.

Terry Venables was thrilled that Shearer's patience during his barren run had been rewarded, enthusing in the *Guardian*: 'Alan Shearer has kept his head clear and remained confident right through this difficult period. He knows that if you start panicking, you begin hitting shots from bad angles and making wrong decisions. He's never done that. Now he looks good and hungry.'

This victory saw mass hysteria and hype engulf a country, which was now well and truly enveloped by football fever, the likes of which had not been witnessed since the halcyon World Cup-winning year of 1966. Comedians David Baddiel and Frank Skinner had heightened the reawakening of patriotic fervour with the release of their unforgettable anthem 'Football's Coming Home' and Shearer and his fellow Three Lions restored a heady feeling of national pride and feel-good factor to England.

Nevertheless, England had still not met a team of genuine quality and their next match with Holland represented a formidable examination of their tournament-winning credentials, as the Dutch drew heavily on a crop of exciting young players from the 1995 European Cup-winners Ajax.

However, rampant England confounded all expectations by crushing the Dutch masters with a cannonade of goals – two of them delivered by a superb Alan Shearer – in what was one of his country's most devastating displays, full of pace, panache, passion and abundant skill.

When England fans reflect on Shearer's magnificent career for the Three Lions, most of them will call the exhilarating 4–1 victory his greatest game in a white shirt. His first goal was a penalty after 23 minutes and was despatched with supreme confidence past Edwin van der Sar in the Holland goal. His second, and England's third, is etched in the memory, as it involved scintillating interplay between Paul

Gascoigne and Teddy Sheringham – who claimed two goals in the rout – which was rounded off by a thunderous drive by Shearer.

Shearer believed the sensational thrashing of one of Europe's heavyweights would make England an intimidating prospect for any side. 'Hopefully the fear factor will come into it. We can impose our game on others and let the other teams worry about us,' he said.

England now progressed to a quarter-final clash with Spain, but there was to be no repeat of the swashbuckling, goal-laden victory over Holland. Instead, Shearer and co were lucky to stay on level terms with a technically adept and well-organised Spanish side, who took England to extra-time and penalties.

However, Shearer could have spared his country the additional burden of extra-time when he uncharacteristically scooped his shot over the bar from three yards after 73 minutes. As Glenn Moore observed in the *Independent*, when penalty-kick drama ensued: 'England were favourites from the moment Shearer marched off to take the first kick.'

While some English footballers have habitually fluffed their penalties under extreme pressure, Shearer has always claimed to relish taking penalties, seeing it as an opportunity to add to his goal tally.

Yet even this ice-cool and unflappable Geordie is not immune to the singular stresses and strains engendered by the penalty-kick phenomenon. He told the *Newcastle Journal* in May 2000: 'There are not many times when I get nervous, but I do a little bit with penalties. There's a lot more pressure standing there with thousands of people watching you in the stadium and at home on television. It's that stop-start situation where all eyes are on you.' He goes on to reveal in his autobiography that he first honed his peerless penalty-kick prowess at the tender age of fifteen, scoring from 12 yards to help Cramlington Juniors win the Northumberland FA Junior Cup in 1986.

However, ten years later, there were far more people than one man and his dog praying that Shearer could succeed from the spot – the eyes of a nervous nation were transfixed upon him.

As expected, however, Shearer successfully slotted past Zubizarreta with his customary coolness, while the fist-clinching passion of Stuart Pearce and David Seaman's penalty-saving heroics ensured that England's European hopes were kept alive. England could certainly have hoped for any other opponent than arch-rivals Germany, who could boast an imposing hegemony in their clashes over the years – with the notable exception of 1966 – in the semi-finals. Who could forget the devastating defeat in Turin six years earlier when the Germans held their nerve in a tension-filled penalty shoot-out to proceed to the World Cup final of 1990? However, the country was convinced that England had the beating of a German side that was widely regarded as being inferior to their formidable sides of the past.

Such bullish confidence was owed in part to the fact that one Alan Shearer, who had already struck four times in the tournament, was spearheading England's challenge. The *Mirror*'s columnist Trevor Francis tipped England's chief destroyer to emulate the World Cup-winning heroics of Geoff Hurst thirty years previously: 'Now just watch Shearer carve out his own piece of history by toppling the tournament favourites tonight and extending his lead as top scorer with another match-winner on Sunday. Then brace yourself for the reaction across the continent as he becomes one of the three most wanted men in Europe. Strikers will always be the hottest property in football and Shearer is now up there with Jürgen Klinsmann and Davor Suker as the best in the business.'

Wembley was bubbling with expectation as a roaring, flag-waving 76,862 crowd created an atmosphere to rival the carnival scenes in 1966. Comedians Baddiel and Skinner were there, lending their voices to lusty, joyously uplifting verses of their anthem 'Football's Coming Home', which reverberated around the rafters of the Venue of Legends.

The appetite-whetting hors d'oeuvre promised a feast of football laced with lashings of drama and tension and England expected Shearer and co to deliver in style.

Looking oddly unrecognisable in their change strip of grey, an emotionally-charged England seized the initiative almost immediately when, after only three minutes, Shearer darted into the box and sent a stooping header beyond Köpke in the German goal after Tony Adams had flicked on a Paul Gascoigne corner. Joy unconfined erupted in the Wembley stands as an ecstatic Shearer wheeled away after scoring what could have become one of the most significant goals of his England career.

But a well-crafted second-half equaliser from Stefan Kuntz made for a nail-biting finale which, as fate cruelly decreed, would culminate in a replay of the World Cup 1990 semi-final. The ever-dependable Shearer was successful as always from the spot, but Gareth Southgate's woeful effort sent England tumbling out 6–5 on penalties as Euro '96's eventual winners Germany progressed to a final showdown with the Czech Republic.

Nevertheless, England's reputation as a world footballing force and Shearer's standing as a predator supreme had been emphatically reconfirmed when he ended as the tournament's top goalscorer with five goals – the first Englishman ever to top the European Championship goal charts. 'Shearer's stock is rising with every goal. His transfer value is now £15 million and his reward for any move abroad would be a £30,000-a-week salary,' claimed the *Daily Mirror*'s Harry Harris, while British Prime Minister John Major added his own rich praise, commenting: 'In Alan Shearer, I believe we have the most complete centre-forward in the world.'

England's agonising European exit was matched by Terry Venables' departure as coach of his country. Venables had announced that he would relinquish control of the national team in January, claiming he wanted to concentrate his energies on the legal battles he was fighting.

ENGLAND EXCELLENCE

But some insiders claimed that the chirpy Cockney had been enraged by the Football Association's failure to offer him a contract up to the 1998 World Cup in France. Shearer was devastated that the man who had been fiercely loyal to him through his bleak and barren goalless spell was stepping down from the most prestigious managerial role in English football after masterminding the glorious revival of his country's fortunes.

On the verge of tears, he said: 'Personally, and I think I am speaking on behalf of everybody, I believe it is a crying shame that Terry Venables has been allowed to leave. He is second to none with his knowledge of football and tactics. I am sure he has got his reasons for leaving and the FA have theirs.'

His disappointment was soon assuaged when, in September, Venables' replacement, Glenn Hoddle, bestowed on him arguably the greatest personal honour a footballer can aspire to – the captaincy of his country – for England's opening World Cup 1998 qualifying fixture away to Moldova.

The *Independent*'s Glenn Moore summed up Shearer's whirlwind few months perfectly: 'After all those years when we thought Roy of the Rovers was a fictional character, it turns out he really does exist. He is twenty-six, lives in Newcastle and answers to the name Alan Shearer. Having being crowned leading goalscorer in the European Championship and become the world's most expensive player [following his sensational post-Euro '96 move to Newcastle], Shearer yesterday added the title of England captain to his roll of honours. Truly a *Boy's Own* story.'

Hoddle had admired Shearer from afar – he had never met his new captain in person – but summoned him to his room at England's Burnham Beeches Hotel prior to their flight to Moldova in September 1996. Hoddle's discussions with people who knew the Geordie more intimately than him, such as his former manager at Blackburn Ray Harford, had convinced him that Shearer was leadership material.

ALAN SHEARER

Now it was a case of gauging whether the man himself wanted the job. In the *Independent*, Hoddle said of Shearer's appointment: 'I spoke to Alan, he seemed up for it, he wanted the job. In four days it is obviously difficult to come to 100 per cent conclusions. He knows how to conduct himself both on and off the pitch, fellow pros respect him and he understands the team situation even though he is a goalscorer, which is a rare quality to have. A captain needs to be unselfish and keep a cool head in the heat of the moment. I think he can and he will also have the respect of referees, which is important.'

Shearer claims that Hoddle gave him three games in which to prove his captaincy capabilities and dispel any lingering doubts that his prolific goal-scoring would be compromised.

However, as Gary Lineker had proved, captaining England did not necessarily curtail the goals. Shearer's response to the honour was therefore emphatic. 'I'm obviously delighted, I won't change and I don't see why it should affect my goal-scoring. I will be a leader on and off the pitch. I always hoped he'd ask me and there was no way I would turn it down.'

The new captain had been chosen ahead of more experienced players than him, men like David Platt, Tony Adams and Stuart Pearce. However, Platt's England place no longer looked assured under Hoddle, while the tub-thumping, passion, pugnacity and patriotism of the likes of Adams and Pearce did not mirror the former Tottenham ace's more calm and measured managerial style.

Shearer was not inclined to making inspirational speeches *à la* Henry V at Agincourt, preferring to lead by example and provide an excellent role model for England's up-and-coming talents, like David Beckham. He had watched and learnt from captains such as Jimmy Case at Southampton, and possessed leadership pedigree after captaining both the England Under-21s and Blackburn. 'A shiver went down my spine that day, 1 September 1996, when they played the national anthem before the kick-off, Shearer recalled in his autobiography of the unspeakably proud moment when he puffed out his chest and led England out for the first time.

His experience was enhanced when he scored the third goal in England's comfortable 3–0 victory and, after the match, he received a kiss on the cheek from Paul Gascoigne! 'It was a great feeling to captain my country and even better to score a goal and lead the team to victory in the manager's first game,' Shearer said, admitting that he feared his joyous day was set to be ruined when he skied a shot over the bar from only a few yards out.

Captaining England in their next match against Poland at Wembley represented the pinnacle of Shearer's career. With his wife and mother in attendance, he proved that he was thriving on the responsibility of leading his country by scoring twice in England's 2–1 victory.

The *Sunday Times*' Joy Lovejoy voiced the opinion that Shearer's continued prosperity on the back of his Euro '96 excellence gave credence to the view that the Newcastle man 'may well be the best striker in the world just now'.

Glenn Hoddle, meanwhile, believed that Shearer matched Gary Lineker's deadliness in front of goal and was superior to his forward predecessor with the quality of his strikes. 'He's got a great temperament and he is single-minded when it comes to goal-scoring. He's quite similar to Gary Lineker – though he scores more spectacular goals.' Hoddle added: 'After Euro '96 he knows he can score against the best defenders in Europe and that has given him the confidence to take it onto the world level. With the levelling of standards, that is where games are won and lost at international level. If he is on the pitch you have a chance. He works hard, he is a leader.'

However, Shearer had to wait until the spring of 1997 before he could wear the captain's armband again, as a groin injury ruled him out of England's trip to Georgia in November 1996.

Tony Adams deputised for the convalescing captain and led England to a 2–0 victory to maintain their 100 per cent World Cup qualifying record. Any fears that Shearer had about his captain's reign being over were quelled when Glenn Hoddle stuck by his pledge to give the Geordie three games in which to prove his leadership credentials in England's forthcoming match against Italy. The *Daily Mirror* reported: 'Abroad they look to Platini, to Maradona, that sort of player. Not necessarily the best captain for 90 minutes, but someone who commands respect from everyone in the world, including referees, which is a big advantage,' says Hoddle. 'There is no doubt that Shearer now falls into that class. Only Ronaldo and George Weah match his current standing.'

Italy's coach Cesare Maldini knew that his son Paolo would be presented with a stern test of his defensive qualities by the reinstated England captain: 'He is one of the best strikers in the world and it is his strength that is going to be a problem for us. Although the English game has changed enormously in recent seasons, we cannot afford to simply defend and try to contain Shearer, because that would be a recipe for disaster.'

Meanwhile, Shearer insisted that his combative, aggressive playing style would not infect his captaincy. He said: 'If you've seen me shouting and bawling at linesmen and having a go at other players, it is just because I so badly want to win. Everyone is entitled to an opinion, but I've done nothing to change the way I play or how I am and my relationship with players has never changed either.'

As the big match loomed, England's manager of the future, then Sampdoria boss Sven-Goran Eriksson, hinted that Shearer would struggle to score as freely in Italy. He said in the *People*: 'To score thirty goals every season in the Premiership you have to be very special. Shearer's always capable of scoring goals and not many players carry that threat. Those kinds of players are like gold in your team, but for me it would be very interesting to see him playing in

ENGLAND EXCELLENCE

Italy or Spain against some of the best defenders in the world. I'm sure he could do it, but Italian defenders get closer to opponents and they do the same in Spain.'

But after shrugging off a back injury and despite being partnered by former Southampton team-mate Matt Le Tissier up front, Shearer was unable to inspire England to glory over the ever-cautious Italians, who prevailed 1–0 courtesy of a Gianfranco Zola goal.

Italy now looked to be in pole position to qualify automatically for the World Cup, leaving England potentially in second place and fighting for their passage to the world's greatest sporting event through the play-offs. 'It's going to be extremely difficult,' Shearer admitted afterwards. 'They've got an edge, of course. They have got a game in hand, but both of us still have got to go to Poland and it's far from over.'

A groin operation sidelined Shearer for several months and his next England appearance was in the home World Cup qualifying match against Georgia on 30 April.

Shearer and Sheringham were back in harness and Glenn Hoddle was hopeful that the strike duo would recapture their bountiful alliance of Euro '96. They did not disappoint, scoring a goal apiece – created by each other – as England powered to a 2–0 victory to maintain their bid to pip Italy to World Cup qualification. 'In Alan Shearer, and the resumption of his fruitful partnership with Teddy Sheringham, England have a scoring potential to compare with the Lineker-Beardsley combination under Bobby Robson,' was the verdict of the *Guardian*'s David Lacey. Glenn Hoddle added: 'Teddy's mind is quick and he and Alan linked up well even in the early part of the game. You always sensed something was going to come from that.'

However, soon members of the media were looking towards England's next match, a far more daunting prospect away to Poland, and whipped up the frenzied debate on whether Shearer's fellow Newcastle-born friend, Paul Gascoigne, should play.

ALAN SHEARER

The troubled genius had suffered injury on the field at Rangers in Scotland and trauma in his personal life, but on the evidence of the poverty of England's midfield display against Georgia, the press pack hounded Hoddle to keep faith with his prodigal son.

Hoddle heeded such pleas and Gazza started in Katowice on 31 May – but once again he was overshadowed by the deadly Shearer-Sheringham axis. Rock-steady Teddy and Captain Fantastic both scored as England set up a winner-takes-all clash of the titans with Italy later that year.

Shearer, who uncharacteristically missed a penalty in the match, had now scored ten goals in as many internationals, consigning unhappy memories of his two-year goal drought to the dim and distant past. 'In Shearer and Sheringham, England have a pair who can make and take chances against anybody. With those two up front they can certainly win in Rome', insisted Poland coach, Antoni Piechniczek, in *The Times*.

Glenn Hoddle, meanwhile, believed Shearer and Sheringham's propitious partnership was swiftly making them the most feared forward pairing in world football.

The bitter disappointment of England's loss to Italy had been blown away, after they had subsequently earned three victories and plundered seven goals in the process, and now everyone in the Three Lions' camp was relishing the gladiatorial-type conflict in Rome. 'After a bad result against the Italians', said Shearer, 'we're back in it now. It looks like it will go all the way to Rome like we always thought it would.'

Shearer and England also achieved an historic first in their win in Poland – the match was the inaugural major broadcast of Britain's newest television station, Channel 5. The favourable outcome for England supporters was manna from heaven for the channel's football commentator, the wildly enthusiastic Jonathan Pearce, whose effervescent commentary featured a ecstatic roar of 'Shearreeerrrrr!' when the great man scored his goal.

Win-or-bust World Cup qualification was put on the backburner for the summer when England travelled across the English channel to take part in Le Tournoi de France – a four-team tournament involving Italy, Brazil and hosts France. Arranged by French legend Michel Platini as a rehearsal for the following year's World Cup, it also afforded England or Italy the opportunity to earn an early psychological advantage ahead of October's titanic clash. It also presented Shearer with the ideal stage on which to advance the burgeoning belief that he was among the world's élite strikers. He had the chance to measure himself against a glittering array of forward talent, such as Romario, Djorkaeff and Del Piero. Shearer was rested for England's first game of the French friendly tournament, but his country nevertheless impressively overcame the Italians 2–0. Hoddle explained his decision not to play his star striker as a desire to keep him under wraps for when the two countries met in February. In addition, Shearer's groin injury prevented him from playing at full throttle.

Next up were World Cup hosts France, for whom Shearer would add that extra 'je ne sais quoi', according to Arsenal's Gallic gaffer, Arsène Wenger. 'We are well organised defensively, but as host nation at the World Cup we will be under pressure to attack and score. We don't score enough goals. We need a centre-forward who can score regularly. With that type of player the balance would be correct. Jacquet is using this tournament to find that balance. If Alan Shearer, for instance, were French, we would have a marvellous team', said Wenger in the *Evening Standard*.

England duly earned a notable scalp for a team who had only lost once in thirty-five matches, thanks to Shearer's eleventh goal in as many internationals. Buoyed by their success, England approached their final game against Brazil full of zeal, bringing Shearer into direct opposition with the latest Samba star – Ronaldo.

The pair had encountered each other before – at the 1996 World Football of the Year award – won by Ronaldo, while Shearer achieved third place – and the England star was full of admiration for his Brazilian counterpart. He told the *Daily Mail*: 'I can relate to the kind of pressures he's facing, because it's not easy to be up there, leading the line, with everyone looking for you all the time. The goalscorer's life can be a great one, but it's not adulation all the time.'

The heavyweight contest never lived up to the hype, however, and it was a World Cup hero of the past, Romario, who settled the game in the bewitching Brazilians' favour. Shearer's reputation had, however, still been appreciably enhanced by his appearance at the festival of football, with Brazilian legends past and present acutely aware of his enormous importance to England. Speaking in the *Daily Mirror*, Pelé said: 'I also believe England must make better use of Alan Shearer. He is a great goalscorer and his strength is remarkable. But he must get the right kind of service. It's no good putting over so many crosses without some kind of purpose or direction. They have to get him into the areas where being so strong will be useful.'

The industrious Dunga, captain of Brazil's 1994 World Cup-winning side, added: 'We knew that if you stop Shearer, you stop England. But whether he's got what it takes is the huge question Shearer must answer next year.' What a difference a couple of months can make as, after suffering horrendous injuries in a pre-season friendly with Newcastle in late July, England would be cruelly deprived of their talisman against Italy. 'There were encouraging signs in Le Tournoi that Ian Wright could play instinctively with Paul Scholes and Teddy Sheringham, but these were a series of friendlies, albeit encouraging ones for Hoddle. All of that optimism has been blown away by one devastating twist of Shearer's ankle,' was one lament in the press from the *Daily Mail*'s Neil Harman.

Glenn Hoddle was now faced with the king-sized headache of who would replace Shearer up front for the autumn showdown in Rome. His dilemma would be who to choose from the quintet of Robbie

Fowler, Stan Collymore, Ian Wright, Les Ferdinand and Andy Cole, with Teddy Sheringham an immovable object in the other striking berth.

The irrepressible Ian Wright emerged as the overwhelming favourite, despite being the oldest of the contenders at thirty-three. Shearer, meanwhile, was insistent that he would overcome his latest injury setback and return to lead England's line in the World Cup. While on the sidelines, he vowed to be his country's chief cheerleader. 'I've spoken to Glenn and John Gorman and told them that I'm coming to the next two matches,' he commented to the *Daily Mirror* in August 1997. 'I want to show that I'm backing them all the way, and it can also do me a power of good. I want to come back and find that England are in the World Cup finals and Newcastle are challenging for honours.'

England cruised to a comfortable 4–0 win over Moldova in their first match of the 1997–98 season minus Shearer, who afterwards said that he would watch the drama unfold in Rome from the comfort of his own living room. He said in the *Journal*: 'Like millions of football supporters around the country, I will be watching on television – cheering the lads on and mentally kicking every ball and making every tackle. I am confident that we will all be on our feet cheering by the end of the game – me too, ankle or no ankle!'

In fact, Shearer actually observed the nerve-shredding action from a far-flung location. He recalled in the *Observer* in May 1998: 'I was in Barbados at the time. I had just had my plaster removed and the only way I could follow the game was by telephone. The original plan was to keep ringing home to keep in touch with the score, but the game was so tight I ended up listening to the whole of the second half, with my dad doing a running commentary. As a commentator, he definitely makes a better sheet-metal worker. I nearly hit the roof when Wrighty hit the post, but I had every confidence in the lads, really, especially when I came home and watched a tape of the game.'

Shearer's optimism proved well founded as England achieved automatic qualification for the following year's World Cup with a magnificent and heroic display in a 0–0 draw with the Italians. Glenn Moore of the *Independent* insisted a fit-again Alan Shearer could shoot England to international football's most-coveted prize. He said: 'If Alan Shearer is fit – Ian Wright, though keen and brave, was an unconvincing replacement – and if Gascoigne, Ince, Adams and David Seaman stay fit, England will be serious contenders. On present form, only Brazil, who have inflicted two of England's three defeats in thirty-seven games and four years, need be feared.'

The irresistible lure of representing his country in the global arena undoubtedly proved a massive spur to the sidelined striker throughout his lengthy lay-off. While representing sponsors Umbro in Marseille in December, he said: 'I've got a hell of a big incentive to go for in the World Cup. I have over thirty caps and scored sixteen goals. I've done all right, but I'm hoping there is a lot more to come.'

As is his wont, rather than extend his stay in France to encompass the World Cup draw, Shearer returned home to plunge himself back into his rehabilitation programme. He and England were also cheered by being handed a very satisfactory World Cup group – they were paired with Romania, Colombia and Tunisia in Group G – and immediately installed as joint third favourites with Italy and Germany for the trophy.

An intriguing aspect of the draw for Shearer was that he would confront his Newcastle team-mate, Tino Asprilla, when England tackled the Colombians. He commented: 'It should be fun possibly coming up against Tino – it's just about impossible knowing what he's going to do. So I don't know whether I can pass on any useful information to Glenn Hoddle about him.' The Newcastle *Evening Chronicle* offered patriotic Geordie fans the choice of two songs in honour of Asprilla and Shearer: 'If patriotism wins the day, you're going to have to lustily sing "We hate

ENGLAND EXCELLENCE

Tino and we hate Tino, We hate Tino and we hate Tino, We hate Tino and we hate Tino, We are the Tino-haters" as well as "One Alan Shearer, there's only one Alan Shearer".

The amazing alacrity of Shearer's recovery from injury at the start of the 1998 fuelled hopes that he would face Chile at Wembley in England's first game of the year. He was duly recalled to the squad to face the Chileans in February, but this was viewed as a symbolic gesture from Glenn Hoddle, who declared that Shearer would make his full international comeback against Switzerland in March.

Michael Owen and Dion Dublin were the unlikely little-and-large combination paired up front in Hoddle's experimental line-up, which succumbed to a surprise 2–0 defeat to the South Americans – despite the introduction of Shearer on 63 minutes. The Newcastle *Journal* reported of his arrival on the pitch, in place of Teddy Sheringham: 'Shearer's introduction was warmly applauded by the 65,000 crowd and though he failed to crown his international comeback with a goal, the £15 million man was prominent during England's best spell.'

Hoddle revealed that though the hosts struggled badly during the first half, he was never tempted to throw his prize asset into the fray too early. He said: 'Alan was always going to get half an hour. That was always the plan. He has not played too many games for Newcastle recently and is still not 100 per cent fit. The last thing I wanted was for him to play too long and risk an injury. That would have been a big mistake.'

Shearer, meanwhile, insisted that England would, after being jolted out of their World Cup reverie and coming back to earth with a bone-shuddering bump, be on their mettle for the summer soccer showpiece. One of the few agreeable aspects for him and England to emerge from the chastening defeat to the South Americans was Michael Owen's electrifying debut for his country. 'I cannot remember a better debut by an eighteen-year-old than that,' enthused Shearer in the *Daily Mail.* 'He's done his own thing and he's not frightened by it. I didn't have to talk to him in the match or say anything much to him.'

Shearer returned to the starting line-up in tandem with Owen up front for the away game to Switzerland in March, a game which ended in a 1–1 draw, with Paul Merson scoring for England. In April, he and Teddy Sheringham re-formed their prodigious SAS partnership to great effect as England achieved a rather flattering 3–0 win over Portugal at Wembley.

Shearer, who was at his brilliant best, netted twice with a trademark header and a stunning volley, and Sheringham scored once to serve notice of England's World Cup credentials. 'It's been a long time since I scored my last England goal,' said a delighted Shearer after the match. 'It had all been gloom and doom in some quarters after our last couple of results. But we kept our heads high and came up with the goods.'

Glenn Hoddle predicted that his captain colossus would be the vital ingredient in England's quest for World Cup glory. 'I think he's back to his very sharpest,' Hoddle said. 'I just hope he stays injury-free. If we can create chances, we've got someone who can put the ball in the net and, if you look around world football, there aren't many teams who have such a player. We're very thankful we have him. If you look through the history of the World Cup, the team that wins always has someone who will score five or more goals, and he did that in Euro '96.'

Making light of Glenn Hoddle's unorthodox use of faith healer Eileen Drewery in attempting to make England successful, the *Daily Mirror* led with the headline: 'Shearer is God (Will Someone Please Let Glenn and Eileen Know).'

Another renowned spiritualist and erstwhile spoon bender, Uri Geller, also hailed Alan Shearer – the silent assassin. He told the *Daily Mirror*: 'I have always admired Alan Shearer's wonderful calmness under pressure, but his second goal was a supreme example of the clinical, confident artist at work. If you were to sit beside him at a dinner party, you would never believe what damage he can do to an opponent. That is because he is a quiet type of man, but under that calm exterior is a steely determination and will to win.'

A revitalised Alan Shearer was now, after silencing his critics and demonstrating that he was one of the most accomplished strikers in the game, quite simply on top of the world as he looked forward optimistically to conquering the world. 'It wasn't until the Portugal game that everyone thought I was back to my best, but even before that I was feeling good and strong. It just took that game to convince people,' said Shearer in the *Mail on Sunday*. 'I think we [England] have a great chance of winning the World Cup. I really do believe that with the players we have got.'

Ex-England and West Ham legend Trevor Brooking was eager for his country to play to Shearer's strengths by pairing him with a recognised striker. Brooking told the *Evening Standard*: 'At twenty-seven, he enters the World Cup as a world-class striker who should be at the peak of his career. In Euro '96 he showed the class, composure and determination required to score at the highest level. He is ambitious and desperately wants success this summer. However, I believe he will struggle to fulfil his dreams if he is asked to battle up front without a recognised striking partner.' The *Daily Mail* shared Brooking's concerns: 'Glenn Hoddle used an evocative phrase last week to describe his Christian faith by saying that life is a film, God is the director and we are all merely playing our parts. By the same logic, if England – The Movie is to be a success, then it is a bit worrying that after our leading man, Alan Shearer, there is a scarcity of candidates to play best supporting actor.'

His popularity among young English males was at his zenith, and that was official according to the *Los Angeles Times*: 'In England, where baseball is regarded as nothing more than a bastardized version of cricket and Kasey Keller is a more famous American than Shaquille O'Neal, a poll recently was taken of that country's male sports fans. Of fans ages twenty to thirty-four, 95 per cent said they would prefer watching England striker Alan Shearer score a goal in the World Cup to making love with a supermodel. Ah, youth, sighed amused male fans thirty-five and older. Among that demographic group, with their lives more in balance and their priorities in order, 60 percent opted for Shearer in the back of the net over super shenanigans in the bedroom.'

Shearer was also having to deal with a barrage of brickbats as well as bouquets as his aggressive approach, fuelled by a season of frustration with Newcastle and injury, was a cause for concern for some. Under new, stringent FIFA directives, World Cup referees would be told to brandish a red card for tackles from behind, such as the robust challenge Shearer had made on Arsenal's Tony Adams in the 1998 FA Cup final.

Indeed, the referee who presided over this match, Paul Durkin, joined up with England to educate Shearer and co about the new rules. Meanwhile, on the pitch, England looked anything like being among the contenders for the World Cup as the normally deadly combination of Shearer and Sheringham squandered a number of chances in the 0–0 draw with Saudi Arabia at Wembley.

Even more worryingly, Hoddle had handpicked the Saudis for the home warm-up because he thought they would replicate the challenge likely to be presented by Tunisia, England's first opponents in the World Cup. Shearer warned that England would have to improve drastically if they were to have any hope of becoming the best in the world: 'We are entitled to an off day, but the Saudis were similar opposition to what we will face in our first game – and we will have to do better to beat Tunisia. And what Saturday emphasised is that there will certainly be no mugs in the World Cup.'

Nevertheless, despite this stuttering draw, Saudi Arabia's Brazilian coach, Nelson Alberto Perreira, backed England and their captain to push his countrymen close for the capture of football's ultimate prize. He said: 'When you look at the Brazilian side you have to admit that the chances are they will win again,' said Perreira. 'However, it will be tougher in Europe than it was in the USA. The time of the matches and the weather will not be to their advantage. It will be a tough test and a more competitive tournament as a result. But England have a team of great players and if the likes of [Paul] Gascoigne, [David] Beckham and [Alan] Shearer are on form and fit they will be very difficult to stop.'

Shearer and England then flew out to La Manga to fine-tune their preparations for the World Cup with games against Morocco and Belgium. He was rested for both games, the first of which witnessed the unearthing of potentially both his future forward accomplice at the World Cup and his successor as chief source of goals for England. England won 1–0 against the North Africans, thanks to a goal from boy wonder Michael Owen, who became his country's youngest scorer at the age of eighteen years and 164 days old, beating the previous record set by Tommy Lawton, who was nineteen years and six days when he scored a penalty against Wales in Cardiff on 22 October 1938.

Devoid of his killer instinct, England then laboured to a goalless draw with Belgium, who finally prevailed 4–3 on penalties. England's ability to rise to the occasion when they faced the intensity of competitive action and challenge World Cup heavyweights such as Brazil was again called into question. The *Daily Mail*'s Graham Hunter reflected on England's recent indifferent form, musing: 'Goals have been rare, the defence has relied on a great deal of poor finishing in front of goal by the opposition and, if Alan Shearer has not provided a killer touch, England are very susceptible to drawing winnable games. Hoddle, however, has a good track record and deserves the benefit of the doubt when he tells you things which seem at odds with the performance in front of your eyes.'

ALAN SHEARER

Now it was time for Glenn Hoddle to wield the axe and prune his World Cup squad down to twenty-two players who, barring a repeat of his nightmarish injuries of the past, would be captained by Alan Shearer. While Shearer was duly included for the trip to France, supplementing Les Ferdinand, Teddy Sheringham and Michael Owen as England's other strikers, all the talk was of Glenn Hoddle's controversial decision to exclude wayward genius Paul Gascoigne from his travelling party.

The fallen idol – the one England player with prior World Cup experience, having illuminated Italia '90 with his jinking brilliance and lachrymose commitment to the cause – had failed to convince Hoddle of his fitness, form and mental stability. Hoddle had no misgivings about his other Geordie jewel in the crown, Alan Shearer, however, and admitted that he had been 'protecting him' after keeping him out of England's friendlies. He told the *Sunday Mirror*: 'There are certain players in each camp who can win matches for you. Like Salas of Chile, Del Piero of Italy and, of course, Ronaldo of Brazil. Shearer is the man who can do that for us. To win the World Cup, you must score consistently and Shearer has proved he can do that at this level. This is the sharpest Alan Shearer I have ever seen. Better even than he was before his injury. Sharper, leaner and more eager.'

Football pundits underscored Hoddle's conviction that Shearer would, as he had done at Euro '96, spectacularly rise to the occasion and produce the goods for England. ITV's voice of football, Brian Moore, who was due to hang up his microphone after the tournament, was confident of roaring out his trademark throaty growl to acclaim an England victory, thanks to their strength up front, underpinned by a revitalised Shearer. Quoted in the *People*, he said: 'Brian Clough used to say that a major injury can be a blessing in disguise to a player if it happens at the right time and I believe that's what's happened with Alan Shearer. Having missed the season until January, he won't be as tired as many of the players on show this month. Yet, having got a few games under his belt, he won't be lacking match practice, so it's the best of both worlds. Alan will be desperate to succeed and that's got to be dangerous for any defence.'

The *Independent*'s Ian Ridley also felt that Shearer shouldered the burden of an expectant nation. He said: 'If England are to have any chance of progressing a long way in the competition, then much rests on Shearer's contribution; as was seen at Euro '96 when he scored five goals. Such a tally would be welcome again in his quest for the Golden Boot and, as long as his muscular style is not negated, he should prove himself one of the top five strikers in the world, provided he receives some decent crosses to make use of his exceptional heading. His captaincy, exemplary rather than noisy, will also be crucial.'

Yet far from buckling under the weight of expectation, Shearer appeared to be relaxed and calm and was eagerly anticipating the prospect of entering the maelstrom of the World Cup – his biggest test for England yet. The *Daily Mirror*'s Harry Harris and John Dillon reported of his final press conference before England tackled Tunisia: 'He swaggered in wearing flip-flops, shorts and a blue-and-white hooped Pirates of Penzance-style England T-shirt. Shearer swaggering around the World Cup is precisely what we all want to see. It means goals ... and Shearer lives for goals. Smiling and tanned, Shearer accepts the burden of 40 million frenzied English souls today as easily as he would receive a short, kickabout pass in training.'

Beneath the cool exterior, though, was a fierce determination to succeed, mirroring his manager's steely self-belief. Shearer told the *Mirror*: 'Glenn pulled us into a meeting before we came out and said: "Look, we're going to win this thing." That impressed all of us. There's no point in entering a competition unless you believe you can win it. Now the rest is up to us. He believes we can win it and so do the players. I've not known anyone be so positive to us as a group before.'

Shearer was not the only focal point of the intense media glare, as his strike partner in waiting, Michael Owen, was facing a feverish press pack in a manner not too dissimilar to his more established colleague. The *Independent* said: 'Michael Owen shares the same agent as Alan Shearer, Tony Stephens, and the same deadpan, no-chance-of-a-racy-comment demeanour of the Newcastle striker when he meets the press. Cold and clinical, he could be facing an opposition goalkeeper instead of a thicket of tape recorders.'

Owen would have to wait before he could be unleashed onto the world's defences as the established SAS partnership of Shearer and Sheringham was preferred for England's opening Group G game against Tunisia. And it was Shearer who led the way, just as he had done two years earlier, scoring with a header after 42 minutes to give England the lead, an advantage doubled by the inspired Paul Scholes in the second half.

For Shearer, it was one step towards fulfillment of an ambitious personal mission: to be crowned as the World Cup's top goalscorer, emulating his predecessor Gary Lineker in 1986 and the likes of Italy's Toto Schillaci in 1990 and Paolo Rossi in 1982. 'All my goals are special, but this one meant such a lot,' he says in his autobiography of his contribution against the Tunisians. 'To score in the World Cup finals was another personal milestone reached. Now I was on the way to that coveted Golden Boot award.'

Merriment and music, in the form of a trumpeter playing the theme from *The Great Escape*, accompanied Shearer and England throughout their victory and, sadly, many Three Lions' fans spent the night like Steve McQueen, locked up after violence spilt out onto the streets of Marseille.

England and Shearer approached their next group game with Romania in buoyant mood, convinced that they could match anything, bar perhaps only Brazilian brilliance, served up in the tournament so far. The Romanians presented a not-insignificant test, however, as the talismanic Gheorghe Hagi orchestrated their eye-catching, pretty passing game, while razor-sharp striker Adrian Ilie could trouble any defence. They took the lead through Viorel Moldovan, prompting England to unchain Michael Owen from his shackles – in place of the disappointing Teddy Sheringham – to immediate effect.

Owen levelled matters, fully justifying the clamour from the English press and public for his youthful exuberance and scorching pace to be employed as England's trump card. Shortly afterwards, Shearer's former Newcastle manager, Kevin Keegan, in his position as co-commentator for ITV, uttered the immortal, and in hindsight overweening words that 'there is only one team going to win this now'.

It was the fateful kiss of death, because as the match moved into stoppage time, Chelsea defender Dan Petrescu took advantage of defensive uncertainty from Graeme Le Saux and stole in to secure Romania's last-gasp victory. Shearer was able to avoid post-match recriminations, however, as he was ordered to take a random drugs test.

More irritating for Shearer was his paucity of goal-scoring opportunities in the tournament thus far. 'It's very frustrating. I've only had one chance in two games – and I scored from that', he said at the time.

A draw for England against Colombia would secure their passage to the second round and Glenn Hoddle opted to reward Michael Owen for his impressive performance against Romania with a starting spot alongside Alan Shearer in attack, with Teddy Sheringham dropping to the bench. Another emerging English talent, David Beckham, had also performed creditably after coming on as a substitute against Romania, and was deployed to England's midfield to add guile. He responded with a brilliant curling free-kick, following Darren Anderton's opener, to sweep the Three Lions to a convincing 2–0 victory over the Colombians.

Lying in wait for England in the second round were old foes

Argentina who, twelve years earlier, thanks to Diego Maradona's intervention with both controversial hand and mesmerising left boot, prevailed in the stifling heat of Mexico. At the time, Shearer had been on holiday with his family in Portugal, and admits that initially he thought Maradona's infamous 'hand of God' goal was legitimate.

If Shearer could forge as productive a strike force with Owen as he had with Teddy Sheringham at Euro '96, England knew they had an excellent chance to progress.

As ever when questions were being asked about him, Shearer was apt to answer them, equalising Gabriel Batistuta's penalty with his own decisive effort from 12 yards after ten breathless and action-packed minutes in St Etienne. Enter Michael Owen, who put England 2–1 up with a dazzling piece of virtuosity: he embarked on a magical, mazy solo run which culminated in a sublime angled finish past Argentina's despairing goalkeeper, Carlos Roa. But just before half-time, the Argentinians roared back onto level terms when midfielder Javier Zanetti scored after a superbly worked free-kick to end a pulsating first 45 minutes.

The South Americans were buoyed further after England were reduced to ten men early in the second half when David Beckham petulantly flicked his boot at Diego Simeone, who collapsed in a heap.

England now needed a performance of Herculean proportions to survive the onslaught and overcome the eleven men of Argentina, and required Shearer to plough a lone furrow up front and in the channels, hassling and harrying his opposing defenders, a duty he performed assiduously. England could even have claimed victory if Shearer's leap, which prefaced Sol Campbell's disallowed goal, had not been deemed a foul on Argentina's goalkeeper Roa.

Shearer subsequently branded referee Kim Nielsen a disgrace after this decision and his failure to award a penalty to England when defender Jose Chamot appeared to handle inside the box after attempting to clear a Paul Merson cross. Instead, a stoic defensive display was needed to keep a rampant Argentina at bay, as they swarmed forward incessantly, but could not penetrate England's well-disciplined rearguard, which even featured Shearer at right-back, as wave upon wave of South American pressure threatened to bear fruit.

Extra-time arrived and there was a depressing sense of inevitability that this absorbing, epic encounter would be decided by every England fan's worst nightmare – the dreaded penalty shoot-out. Shearer later admitted that, as the match went on, he could not foresee a happy ending for England.

And those worst fears were realised when England's World Cup dreams foundered on a missed penalty from his Newcastle team-mate David Batty after he himself had earlier succeeded from the spot as Argentina won the shoot-out duel 4–3. He could be proud that he had stood strong and been a pillar of strength for his team-mates during unbearable pressure and tension. Michael Owen, for example, sought solace in Captain Marvel when faced with the daunting prospect of football's equivalent to the interminable march to death row, the Green Mile. Shearer later revealed in the *Evening Standard*: 'He walked up to me and asked, "What shall I do?" I told him: "Do what you effing normally do and put the ball in the net." I knew he would score – and he did.'

The devastation and sense of injustice among England players was palpable, surpassing even the depths of dejection reached when they suffered the same cruel fate at the hands of Germany at Euro '96.

World Cup elimination was a bitter pill for Shearer to swallow on a personal level, as he had entered the tournament bristling with confidence that he could emerge as its top scorer. He ended with two goals in four games and, while this return did not merit a place in the World Cup history books, it did at least prove that Shearer could mix it with the world's best.

Perhaps if he and Michael Owen been allowed to develop their partnership together, he would have plundered more goals and England could have advanced to the latter stages of the competition. But 'ifs' and 'maybes' could not soothe Shearer's gut-wrenching misery – he reveals in his autobiography that he sat motionless in the dressing room for hours after England's agonising World Cup exit.

'No England player returned from France last week feeling lower than the captain,' suggested *Sunday Mirror* columnist, Barry Venison. 'There are two reasons. The first is that, as someone who takes great pride in representing his country, our World Cup exit is something Alan will find hard to accept. Having shared an England dressing room with him I know that from experience. The second reason is personal. He'll be very disappointed that he didn't have the chance to show the world what Alan Shearer is all about. That's goals. Even though he scored two in four games, it won't have satisfied him.'

Meanwhile, Oliver Holt of *The Times* rated Shearer's World Cup thus: 'Never looked like challenging for the Golden Boot, but still had a fine World Cup. Role changed when Owen started alongside him and he proved that he could be provider and goalscorer. Worked hard and unselfishly and did enough to suggest he is still a big threat.'

In the end, it was a Zinedine Zidane-inspired France who claimed the World Cup honours on home soil after earlier being denounced as a punchless side without a Shearer-esque forward figure to supply the cutting edge.

It took a while for the distraught Shearer's wounds to heal and many a sleepless night ensued as painful thoughts of what might have been were replayed time and time again in his mind. Thankfully, the end of a World Cup is soon followed by the swift transition into qualification for another major competition – the European Championships.

England had been grouped together with Sweden, Bulgaria, Luxembourg and Poland, so qualification for the forthcoming European showdown in Holland and Belgium looked eminently possible. First, however, they had to cope with the furore caused by the publication of Glenn Hoddle's controversial World Cup memoirs, including his no-holds-barred revelation of his decision to axe Paul Gascoigne from the squad, which allegedly angered senior players such as Shearer for betraying their trust.

The *Sunday Mirror* reported: 'England captain Alan Shearer is spearheading a players' move to take unprecedented action against Glenn Hoddle. Shearer will be the players' spokesman when he meets England coach Hoddle tonight and asks for an explanation for the controversial revelations in his World Cup memoirs. Numerous telephone calls have been made between key England stars, who are appalled at the treatment of Paul Gascoigne in Hoddle's book.'

This article was in contrast to other reports suggesting that Shearer was unworried by Hoddle's brutal openness in print. The *Journal*, for instance, quoted him as saying: 'I have been amazed by some of the comments made over the past week in connection with Glenn Hoddle's new book. I was given a copy of it yesterday and have read all the extracts relating to me, as well as several other bits that caught my eye as I went along. It seemed fairly straightforward to me and I did not feel that any of my confidences had been broken.'

One senior player who did object to Hoddle's unexpurgated account of the World Cup was Tony Adams, whose riposte included a stinging attack on the England coach and Shearer himself in his own autobiography, *Addicted*. Adams insisted that, for one, Hoddle had made a serious error of judgement by ignoring his leadership qualities and installing Shearer as captain for the World Cup.

Although Shearer refused to be drawn into a war of words with Adams, he was clearly displeased that distractions had detracted from England's forthcoming European campaign on which he urged his country to focus. He said in the *Evening Standard*: 'I haven't spoken to Tony, but he would say that because he's Tony Adams and you have to look after your own interests and that of the team. There's a lot of things been said, a lot of rubbish written, but if people don't like me being captain, that's fine. I won't hold any grudges. I just feel it's a shame that there's only two days to go before what is a big match and we've only just started talking about the football. Everyone is entitled to their opinions and if they want to put it in a book, then that's their style. I haven't got a problem with that.'

Hoddle, meanwhile, insisted that he would persist with the Shearer-Sheringham duo for England's opening European qualification game away to Sweden. 'The understanding between Alan and Teddy is probably ahead of the understanding between young Michael and Alan,' said Hoddle in the *Mail on Sunday*. 'Whether Michael and Alan can gel together remains to be seen. Getting the two of them to gel together and getting the best out of them is the test for the coaching staff and for the players themselves. Developing a partnership takes time.'

However, he had a rapid change of heart as Owen's eye-catching early season form, including a hat-trick in Liverpool's 4–1 rout of Shearer's Newcastle at St James' Park, made his case for a start in Sweden irresistible. Hoddle said, on current form, Owen had supplanted Shearer as the country's in-form finisher, while the *Mirror* felt that the youngster's sustained brilliance could help the old master recapture the mantle he had held for so long. 'Shearer is too sensible for jealousy. He's the kind of skipper who's happy to see any goals go in for England, even if they're scored by David Seaman. And surely a bit of friendly rivalry can harm nobody but opposing defences. The hope is that the stuttering Shearer will be spurred into reclaiming his lost crown and that England will cash in against Sweden.'

Shearer has stressed that he did not mind that Owen had grabbed the limelight, which had once shone so brilliantly upon him, insisting that he relished adjusting his game to suit the Liverpool youngster's blistering pace and eye for goal.

Yet England made a demoralising start along the long and winding road to Holland and Belgium when they slumped to a 2–1 defeat away to Sweden, indicating that they were suffering a lingering post-World Cup hangover.

Shearer gave England a dream start, scoring after 76 seconds from a free-kick from the edge of the penalty area that hit the outstretched left hand of goalkeeper Magnus Hedman and ricocheted into the corner of the net off the inside of the far post. But a sterling Swedish display yielded two goals courtesy of Shearer's Newcastle colleague Andreas Andersson and Johan Mjallby, condemning England to a lacklustre loss, which was compounded by Paul Ince being sent off and the referee's failure to award a penalty when the Three Lions' captain appeared to some to have been tripped in the area in stoppage time.

The damning headline that heralded England's horrible failure under Graham Taylor's tutelage in Euro '92 – Swedes 2 Turnips 1 – was predictably wheeled out again in some tabloids in the wake of this damaging blow to England's Euro 2000 qualification aspirations.

England and Hoddle were rightly vilified for failure to reproduce the same bulldog spirit and passion that had characterised their heroic defeat to Argentina a few months earlier, although Shearer was exempt from such fierce criticism. The Newcastle *Evening Chronicle* rallied round their local hero: 'At least our Geordie boy, who keeps his head when all others around him are losing theirs, came out of the shambles with total dignity. He proved, despite Tony Adams' cutting words, that he is indeed a leader of men and he proved that Michael Owen's wondrous talent won't overshadow the old hand. Shearer can walk tall, but Hoddle must feel small.'

A furious Shearer blamed England's ignominious defeat on the hullabaloo that had been whipped up before the game by what had turned out to be the contoversial writings of Hoddle and Adams. He fumed in the *Mirror*: 'I don't think all the crap that went on before the game helped. I mean all the stuff about books, the things that were said and all the bad publicity. It didn't affect me because I have got a thick skin, but it could have affected others. One thing is sure – it didn't help.'

As the pressure increased on Hoddle, the self-confessed committed Christian was praying that Michael Owen and Shearer could flourish together in attack and propel England to a morale-boosting victory over Bulgaria at Wembley in October. Sadly, the pair could not sparkle, their twin attacking threats blunted by the indomitable Bulgarians, who deservedly held on to claim a point in a 0–0 draw.

Shearer was eager that the boo-boys who vented their frustrations raucously at the final whistle gained some perspective of the situation. 'Only two games ago, people were saying that with a bit of luck we could have won the World Cup. The players are still motivated by Glenn, there's absolutely no doubt about that,' he said. 'The manager has got the players' backing 100 per cent.'

England could now take no pity on one of the weakest countries in world football, Luxembourg, in what had become a must-win match for under-fire Hoddle and his beleaguered players. But they laboured to an unconvincing 3–0 victory over one of the world's supposed whipping boys – achieved thanks to goals from a Shearer penalty, Owen and Gareth Southgate's first for his country – which failed to dispel growing doubts over Hoddle's management.

While his country won few plaudits for their dire display, Shearer could comfort himself with the fact that he had achieved a pleasing personal milestone. His goal propelled him into England's all-time top-ten goal-scoring chart with twenty-two goals, nudging him ahead of his idol Kevin Keegan and Mick Channon. Yet his rock-solid captaincy and unshakeable confidence in his country had been tested to the limit by the hammering the team had taken in the press, although Hoddle's treatment was infinitely worse. In the wake of the match, it seemed that some sections of the press were launching a concerted attack to hound Hoddle out, as headlines such as 'Quit now Hod!', 'Hoddle fights for survival' and 'We've Hod enough' dominated tabloid newspaper back pages.

The Arsenal manager, Arsène Wenger, a committed Anglophile, emerged as favourite to succeed Hoddle, according to some newspapers. Even Tony Banks, then sports minister, weighed into the debate when interviewed on Radio 4's *Today* programme, hitting out at the 'impossible, ridiculous expectations' that England followers had for the national team and its coach.

To compound matters, the *Sun* reported that Shearer had become embroiled in a dressing-room spat with Hoddle after the Luxembourg game. The alleged bust-up occurred when Hoddle reportedly asked his players why their recent performances had been so woeful, to which Shearer was said to have replied: 'Have you ever thought it might be you?'

Hoddle vehemently denounced the damning speculation as 'a vicious lie', while Shearer added: 'The story is nonsense. There was a discussion in the dressing room after the game, but I'm not prepared to say what was said. I believe that dressing-room conversations are, and should remain, private. But I never used the words that appeared on the front page of the newspaper today.'

Yet the storm of controversy was perpetuated when Talk Radio host Danny Baker claimed on the 'Baker and Kelly' show that his co-host, Danny Kelly, had been informed by one of his friends, an unnamed England player, that one of the team had recorded Shearer and Hoddle's alleged feud on tape. Baker said: 'It has now been put on a recordable mini-disc, so there's probably a few copies around. Apparently there's a lot more on it than the Shearer thing. As soon as

Glenn Hoddle leaves the room, there are a lot more vindictive comments and lots of laughing going on.'

Hoddle and the FA challenged anyone who knew of the tape's existence to come forward – although Gareth Southgate, writing in his column for the *Evening Standard*, denied that such a recording had been made or listened to. He said: 'The only tape we were having to listen to was Ian Wright's rap music.'

Eventually, the normally intransigent newspaper the *Sun* sheepishly conceded that no such conversation had taken place between Hoddle and Shearer and apologised for any embarrassment that the report may have caused the pair. A relieved Shearer, who still would not disclose exactly what had been uttered in the dressing room, said: 'I am delighted that this matter has been settled amicably and quickly. There was no row and no revolt. There was simply a frank exchange of views about the team's performance.'

Meanwhile, back on the pitch, Shearer missed England's next game – a friendly with the Czech Republic at Wembley in December – with a strained hamstring. In his absence – and that of Michael Owen – Dion Dublin and Ian Wright were paired together up front and goals from Darren Anderton and Paul Merson gave England a welcome 2–0 victory.

The New Year saw Glenn Hoddle involved in another scandal and this time it had terminal implications for his job. He had given an interview to *The Times* and when asked what he had done wrong in a former life to deserve his current trials and tribulations, he replied: 'There are millions of people who would swap with me. You and I have been physically given two hands and two legs and half-decent brains. Some people have not been born like that for a reason. The karma is working from another lifetime. I have nothing to hide about that. It is not only people with disabilities. What you sow, you have to reap.' His breathtaking honesty, or naivety according to some hacks – who branded his views 'Hoddle's twaddle' – sparked a public outcry.

ENGLAND EXCELLENCE

The *Independent*'s Nick Townsend questioned the gaffer's gaffe: 'Why was it necessary to get involved in discussions about the hereafter, when his philosophy about 4-4-2 and the role of Alan Shearer are of principal concern to football followers, who tend to regard a theological debate as being more about wing-backs than prayer?'

It was inevitable that Hoddle's controversial views would lead to his dismissal, which the former Tottenham hero revealed had been followed by calls of sympathy from among others, Alan Shearer. The loyal captain touches on Hoddle's sacking briefly in his autobiography, but refuses to condemn him for his comments about the disabled. He says: 'Now I do not have a view on this complex subject, but if I did, I would prefer to keep my thoughts private. I thought it was sad that a man of his ability should be forced to quit a job he loved for non-football reasons. I had a lot to thank him for. He gave me the single greatest honour I have achieved in football – the captaincy of England – and I will always be grateful to him for that.'

Soon afterwards, Howard Wilkinson was installed as Hoddle's replacement in a caretaker role and his old-fashioned, down-to-earth managerial approach, which had seen him labelled 'Sergeant Wilko' while he managed Leeds United, saw a *joie de vivre* return to Shearer and his England team-mates. But Shearer rebuffed claims that he would be instrumental in helping to fill the England manager's vacancy in the long term. He said: 'I've never been asked the question about who should come in as manager. If it came along now, I wouldn't know what I'd say. I am a footballer, not an FA councillor, not a manager. We don't get paid to make those decisions.' But he added that he embraced his own leadership position wholeheartedly after being named as captain for England's friendly with world champions France at Wembley: 'I would love to stay on as captain. I've been named as captain for this game; Howard told me on Sunday night when we got together. It's always a great honour for me. It's the greatest honour that's happened to me.'

Yet Shearer could not inspire England to victory as he and strike partner Michael Owen were outshone by French striker Nicolas Anelka of Arsenal, who scored twice for the dominant French in an impressive 2-0 victory. Soon after this humbling defeat, Shearer's former Newcastle manager, Kevin Keegan, was unveiled as England manager – but only for four months. Then manager of Fulham, Keegan insisted he would fulfil his sixteen-month contract with the London club.

While there was widespread scepticism in the media about the short-term nature of the appointment, many believed that the charismatic Keegan would imbue England with a renewed zeal and ensure his players played the adventurous, attacking football that had characterised his Newcastle sides. His morale-boosting, Messianic impact would also, it was felt, have a favourable impact on Shearer, who had worshipped King Kevin since his formative years.

Shearer welcomed being reunited with the man who signed him for Newcastle, commenting in the *Daily Mail*: 'Everyone knows what his qualities are. His enthusiasm is infectious and rubs off on everyone.'

The Times said that Keegan's initial press conference as England manager was stirring and inspirational, and boded well for the future of Shearer: 'His dynamism spread across the room at a London hotel, infusing his audience with new optimism about England's chances of qualifying for the Euro 2000 finals in Holland and Belgium. He gave a beguiling vision of his England: an England in which every player would be encouraged to roar the national anthem, an England that would attack at every opportunity, an England with Alan Shearer retained as captain, a re-creation of the brief alliance that they forged in Newcastle.'

As promised, England's new saviour retained Shearer as captain and included him in his first squad for the European Championship qualifier for the home game with Poland in March. More surprisingly, there was also a recall for Shearer's former Blackburn team-mate, Chris Sutton. Keegan knew Shearer's cutting edge would be vital in his gung-ho, all-out attacking policy. 'I know Alan Shearer and I know he's good enough. I know he's a great player, and I hope he'll prove it to people time and time again,' said Keegan in the *Sunday Times* prior to the Poland game. 'That's what drives people like Alan on – and people like me. Some of us need criticism sometimes. We don't like it, but it makes us think, "Hold on, what am I going to do about it?" Some players phone journalists and say, "Hey, this is wrong,"; others think, "I'll make him write something different next time by my performance on the pitch." Alan falls into that category. He doesn't say much, does he?'

Keegan had spoken of 'lighting the blue touch-paper, sitting back and seeing what happens' when he announced that Andy Cole would form a new attacking unit with Shearer, but it was Paul Scholes who provided the spark for England and eclipsed those much-vaunted strikers with a sensational hat-trick to sweep England to an impressive 3–1 victory.

Before the match, an England forward legend of the past, Jimmy Greaves, had opined that Shearer's days as England's first-choice forward should be numbered. The England captain's failure to score would have done little to change his mind, although Newcastle midfielder Rob Lee gave his team-mate a ringing endorsement, telling *The Times*: 'Neither Alan nor Andy will be totally happy because they always want to score, but everybody else will think that they did very well. Alan is still the top man. They created goals and held the ball up very well. Andy was exceptional at holding it up.'

Keegan also proved that he was willing to emulate Hoddle's penchant for recruiting unorthodox aides to assist his side when he enlisted the help of Watt Nicoll, a Scottish personal motivation guru with no discernible knowledge of football. Nicoll was not familiar with any of the England players apart from David Beckham, but was invited to speak with them and then give his assessments of Keegan's squad. 'Though initially so hazy on detail that he did not know Shearer was captain, Nicoll has quickly analysed the foibles and personalities of the team. Shearer is "a prima donna who has grown into the captain's role", reported the *Daily Mail* of Nicoll's first session with the England players. 'Some tried to be unkind, saying that Alan Shearer spent a session laughing at me. Well, I think he was laughing with me, which is rather different. Those who don't understand like to ridicule but, remember, to date I haven't worked with one football team that hasn't gone out and won as a result', reflected Nicoll in the *Evening Standard*.

If he had analysed Keegan, Nicoll would no doubt have concluded that he was a man prone to changes of heart and a passionate person who responded to his intuition, as was evidenced by his decision to stay on as England manager in April 1999. The staunch patriot could not resist the chance to continue his country's fortunes, a fact he confirmed after England drew 1–1 in a friendly in Hungary, with Shearer netting with a 21st-minute penalty. Unsurprisingly, Shearer was thrilled at Keegan's long-term ambitions and gave a flattering appraisal of his new boss.

'It's great news for England. He's enthusiastic and no one has a bad word to say about him and the performances prove that. He listens to players. He's a players' manager. He's on their wavelength; not a tremendous amount of tactics go into it. He likes his players to go out and play. But you want to play for him because of his attitude and enthusiasm. Keegan has this aura about him with the public. He wants to help everyone. He signs autographs, laughs, does the right thing. He's never down in front of the players.'

Yet Keegan's harmonious honeymoon period at the helm of the Three Lions was unceremoniously ended when England stumbled to a 0–0 draw with Sweden in the crucial European Championship qualifier in June. Shearer, winning his fiftieth cap, struggled, as did England as a whole, in a deflating performance made all the worse by Paul Scholes becoming the first man to be sent off for his country at Wembley. It was now odds-on that England would have to procure a place in the following year's championships through the lottery of the play-offs. A 1–1 draw in Bulgaria did little to alter this view.

Shearer did at least score, though. It was his first England goal in open play for a year, but he was fortunate not to have been shown the red card for elbowing Rossen Kirilov in the face. Dutch master, Johan Cruyff, was a disgruntled onlooker, slating the disjointedness of England's play and their inability to carve out decent chances for Shearer and Robbie Fowler. He said in the *Daily Mail*: 'You must have had twenty-five crosses and only one of them was any good. That is not an acceptable average. If a team does not put in good crosses then it doesn't score goals. Even the best strikers in the world need to be given the right sort of ball if they are going to find the net.'

The bright new dawn that seemed to have been heralded when Keegan arrived in a blaze of glory had now been replaced by a murky malaise, at the centre of which was a demoralised Alan Shearer.

As England approached their final two European championship qualifiers at home to Luxembourg and away to Poland, the *Evening Standard*'s Michael Hart believed Keegan would need to exercise his legendary motivational skills to lift the morale of his flagging forward. 'Although the twenty-nine-year-old England captain is clearly not the formidable force he once was, his name is still the first on the England coach's team sheet. In terms of experience and international pedigree, he is unrivalled among current England marksmen, yet there is no doubt that a catalogue of serious injuries and the latest upheaval at Newcastle have dulled Shearer's edge, if not his appetite for the game.'

Shearer suffered further when former Football Association chief executive, Graham Kelly, took a swipe at him in his book, *Sweet FA*. The Newcastle *Evening Chronicle* reported that Kelly had accused Shearer of threatening to boycott the World Cup in France if he faced FA charges for his high-profile incident with Leicester's Neil Lennon. According to the newspaper, Kelly claimed in his book that Glenn

Hoddle had made a similar threat, infuriating the former FA chief: 'It was childish behaviour for the England captain to threaten to give up the job of leading his country. It lacked the maturity I had come to expect from him. The FA went ahead with proceedings to charge Shearer over the incident at Filbert Street on 29 April last year and Alan backed down over his threat.' The case was eventually found not proven and Shearer went to France. Kelly added: 'Shearer also warned me that I could drive him out of the country altogether. The inference was that he would not only refuse to play in France, but would also leave Newcastle for a club abroad. Shearer is a good captain when things are going well, but if he is not getting the service you can tell from his body language that he is not the most inspirational player to lead a side.'

In the face of adversity, however, Shearer tends to flourish, and he did so again by returning triumphantly to the scoresheet with a welcome hat-trick in England's 6–0 demolition of minnows Luxembourg. This was just a rehearsal for the main event however, as they then travelled to Poland in a game they couldn't afford to lose. A win for England would secure a play-off place, a draw would mean they would have to rely on Sweden beating the Poles at home, while a loss was simply unthinkable.

The critical clash brought to mind memorable meetings between England and Poland in the past, including the unforgettable night at Wembley in 1973 when the Three Lions failed to convert an inordinate number of chances thanks to the unorthodox heroics of Polish goalkeeper Jan Tomaszewski. England would need their embattled skipper to be at his best and Shearer said he was ready to silence his critics. 'This season, there have been some seriously untrue accusations against me,' said Shearer. 'There are two sides to every story. I choose to be professional and it's a shame that other people don't. There will be a time for me to tell my side of the story, but this isn't the right time... the book [Graham Kelly's] has been released at this time to cause maximum damage to me and maximum disruption to an England side which is focusing on such an important game.'

The barrage of criticism he had recently endured would not overly affect him, he insisted: 'You just have to be focused, to have belief in your own ability and to be 100 per cent committed. My belief in myself has never wavered.'

He was also fortunate that, as with Graham Taylor, Terry Venables and Glenn Hoddle previously, he had a manager who had never lost faith in him. Keegan said that performances such as Shearer's hat-trick against Luxembourg made him the cornerstone of his side: 'He's a very special guy. It's not blind faith I have in him, though, because there will come a day if I'm England manager for a long time when I will have to leave Alan Shearer out. But I know that is nowhere near happening at the moment, and he proved that on Saturday. I saw afterwards a guy who felt he had proved something again, but the more he's tested, the more likely he is to come out and make people eat their words.'

But neither Shearer nor the rest of the England team could score in Poland in a 0–0 stalemate, in which David Batty became the eighth player to be sent off for his country, that left the Three Lions perilously close to failing to reach the European Championships. The *Mail on Sunday*'s Joe Melling urged Keegan to drop 'a totally ineffectual Shearer, both as player and captain' and believed that he could no longer be considered an automatic choice. Melling said:

> The realisation that the Shearer of old would have blitzed the hugely physical Poles with his strength and pace served only to enhance the sadness of a former England great deluding himself he is the player he once was. For the first time in fifty-three England appearances, even the fans who had worshipped at Shearer's shrine abandoned their faith and

hurled abuse. Shearer was understandably shaken. But he remains publicly bullish. 'I don't think there is any doubt that we have the quality to do well,' he told me while attempting to ignore the background hecklers in the Legia Warsaw stadium. 'If we get through, we all believe we can do a damned good job in the finals. When you look at our squad, there's no way we should find ourselves in this position.' Behind that stone-faced facade lies enormous dignity and massive pride. Those closest to Shearer would not be surprised if he chose to jump before he is pushed and called time on his international career should England fail to make Euro 2000.

Thankfully for Shearer and England, they were given a second chance to secure a place in Euro 2000 after Sweden beat Poland 2–0 in October. They would now face a play-off tie against either Turkey, Scotland or Ukraine over two legs, home and away. They celebrated the Swedes' win by beating Belgium 2–1 at the Stadium of Light in Sunderland, with Shearer again firing a riposte to his doubters with his twenty-eighth goal in fifty-four internationals.

It was then somewhat predictable that England would find Scotland barring their passage to the European Championships. There were wry smiles in both the English and Scottish camps when their respective countries were paired together in a meeting, which was billed as 'The Match of the Millennium'.

As the showdown approached, Andy Cole's frustrations at being overlooked in favour of Shearer for England throughout the 1990s were spilled out in his new autobiography. The combustible Cole claimed he couldn't care less if he never played for England again, annoyed that 'Golden boy', 'teacher's pet' or 'favourite son' as he labelled Shearer could not be shifted from the prime striking spot. The Newcastle *Evening Chronicle* believed Cole had 'done himself no favours by griping about it', insisting that he had never replicated his stunning scoring feats in English football on the international stage where he had looked 'a mere mortal'. 'Shearer, on the other hand, was top scorer in the European Championships of 1996, topped the Premier League goal-scoring list more than once, and was in the frame behind Ronaldo for World Player of the Year. That isn't preferential treatment, it's fact', said the *Chronicle*'s John Gibson.

Newcastle manager Bobby Robson was similarly disdainful of Cole's criticism of his No. 1 striker, telling the *Daily Mirror*: 'He should stick to playing football and driving his Ferrari, because those are probably the two things he does best. Cole has made his bed and now he has to lie in it. Personally, I treat what Cole says with absolute disdain, as it is exactly how such poorly judged words should be treated and I would expect others to do the same.'

But Kevin Keegan believed Cole's formidable form for Manchester United meant that he could not be jettisoned purely on the basis of a handful of ill-advised comments. He also revealed that Shearer had been the pillar of professionalism when asked for his thoughts on whether Cole's outburst bothered him. Keegan said: 'You don't always like to read stuff where one player is talking about another. I spoke to Andy when I saw him and, while I didn't think it was particularly nasty, when you're talking about somebody you might be playing with at a national level, it's a bit worrying. I also spoke to Alan Shearer so he knew what was on my mind and his response was better than anything I could have expected. He said that to leave Andy out of an England squad would be ridiculous considering the way he was playing. Those are my thoughts entirely.'

Off-the-field spats may have briefly interrupted the hype and anticipation that was steadily brewing as the first leg at Hampden Park approached, but soon all thoughts were firmly fixed on the oldest international in the world, England versus Scotland.

ALAN SHEARER

For Alan Shearer, it meant him setting aside club friendliness for national rivalry with Newcastle team-mate and Scotland striker, Kevin Gallacher. Shearer told the *News of the World* that the forthcoming blood-and-thunder encounter was on everyone's minds at Newcastle with bragging rights on offer: 'It's the only thing everybody in the dressing room has been talking about since the draw was made. We have a big tartan contingent at Newcastle – Kevin, Duncan Ferguson, Stephen Glass and reserve-team coach Tommy Craig – and the banter has been flying. It has all been good, light-hearted fun, though sometimes it is hard to make out what the Jocks are talking about! Only joking – having worked with Kenny Dalglish for so long, I'm quite fluent in Glaswegian!'

But it was Paul Scholes rather than Shearer, who was partnered by Michael Owen in attack with his chief critic Andy Cole a substitute, who silenced the Hampden Roar with two goals in an efficient England win in the first leg of the play-off in Glasgow.

Shearer was in a buoyant mood after England had all but achieved qualification for the European Championships, attributing much of the feel-good factor to Kevin Keegan. 'The spirit in the camp is fantastic, and I don't think it could be any better to be honest. We're all rolling in the same direction, which is hopefully qualifying for the European Championships – and it's really good to see', he said. 'Kevin Keegan is a figurehead and goes out of his way to have a good relationship with everyone and that's very important as a manager, because you will then get the best out of your players. He makes a special case to give the players what they ask for; he gets on with everyone and treats everyone with respect.' On hearing of Shearer's comments, Keegan joked that he was 'a creep'.

England's optimism was very nearly obliterated when a nervy display from Shearer and co and a battling performance from Scotland saw the gallant Scots win 1–0 at Wembley in the second leg.

ENGLAND EXCELLENCE

The shapeless performance from Keegan's men aroused renewed questions in the media about his tactical nous. Keegan responded by saying that he had the capacity to be ruthless in his selection including, if need be, doing what he had never previously done – axing Alan Shearer. Keegan said in the *Sunday Express*: 'Everybody knows what I think about Alan Shearer. I still regard him as the best striker we've got. But we've got three friendlies from now until the finals, so I might well have to say to him and Michael Owen, "I need to look at something different." I have to do that because they could get injured. I need to have looked at another combination. The Shearer-Owen partnership has got a lot of potential, but so far it hasn't really hit off. And maybe I will have to look at a different approach with just one right up with someone else dropping off, like Yorke does for Manchester United or Bergkamp with Holland.'

He was hardly encouraged by the European Championships draw in December, which saw England plunged into a very difficult Group A alongside Portugal, Germany and Romania.

The main talking point was that through a similar quirk of fate to the one that thrust Scotland into England's path in the play-offs, another old foe, Germany, would again pose a significant hurdle to the Three Lions' European ambitions. Shearer said: 'When I first saw it I thought, that's a difficult draw. But having looked at the rest of them there isn't an easy team in the competition. There have been some very tough draws, but we've got to play Germany again and it will be interesting.'

As 2000 began, Shearer set his sights firmly on securing a major piece of silverware as England captain, although it is often forgotten that he led his country to victory in Le Tournoi, the World Cup rehearsal in 1997. His battle cry in the *Sun* was as follows: 'It is a massive year for English football. My burning ambition has always been to lift a major trophy for England and is this going to be our year? I thought we were going to do it in the World Cup and before that in Euro '96, but the luck was against us. That is what we will need, a bit of luck. I will go to the finals expecting to win it, believing we can – and praying that we do. It is about time we put England back on the map.'

Yet UEFA effectively wrote off England's chances in the forthcoming tournament in an unfavourable critique on its website, suggesting that Shearer's presence could hinder their quest for European glory.

UEFA bosses claimed that a place in the semi-finals was the best England could hope for when the finals kicked off in Holland and Belgium in June, despite Keegan's declaration that his team could emerge victorious. The UEFA website said: 'The main problem facing Keegan is the advancing age and loss of top-class form of several of his players, such as goalkeeper David Seaman, midfielder Paul Ince and Alan Shearer, the imbalance on the left side of the team and Shearer's lack of understanding with either Michael Owen or Andy Cole, his two most obvious attacking partners. He is loathe to drop Shearer – but it could be an answer to one of his problems.'

England had a chance not only to disprove such a theory but also to avenge their shattering World Cup defeat to Argentina eighteen months earlier in an appetising friendly against the South Americans at Wembley in February. There was the usual whir of speculation in the press about who would partner Shearer for the game, with Sunderland's prolific striker Kevin Phillips leading the list of contenders. Shearer had had fifteen different forward partners during his career and Phillips had mounted a compelling case to form a potentially highly fruitful Tyne-Wear combination against the Argentinians by scoring more than twenty goals for Sunderland by February.

The pair's partnership had shown signs of promise when they played together in England's friendlies against Hungary and Belgium at the tail-end of 1999, and Keegan was expected to offer them another chance to excel against the South Americans. But Phillips was clearly in awe of his illustrious potential strike partner, enthusing in the *Daily Mirror*: 'Nobody can knock what Alan Shearer has done. He's on my shortlist for Player of the Year. Just six months ago, people were saying he was finished, yet he's got twenty-five goals for his club and country. He's just incredible and I take my hat off to him... I know everyone is going to compare us, but we are totally different people and players. I have only been in the Premiership for ten minutes. Maybe in five or six years I may be able to say that I have matched him.'

Yet it was Leicester's bustling forward, Emile Heskey, who was chosen above Phillips for the coveted striking berth alongside Shearer. Many observers believed this was a wise choice, as Heskey's imposing presence mirrored that of Shearer's Newcastle forward colleague, Duncan Ferguson. Ferguson and Shearer had begun to blossom together at St James' Park, with the former's aerial strength creating a wealth of chances for the latter.

Keegan explained his decision to opt for Heskey in favour of Phillips by saying: 'I've got to see what Emile Heskey can do with Alan Shearer. I have seen Kevin Phillips and I thought it [the partnership] worked well at times and it will get better given another chance.' Heskey was thrilled to have the chance to stake his claim for a place alongside Shearer, commenting: 'I enjoyed playing alongside him in the Scotland game and it was a big boost when Kevin Keegan put me on when he obviously had Andy Cole on the bench. I thought I did reasonably well. Alan Shearer is the No. 1 striker at the moment and I see things in his game that I can take into mine as well.'

Shearer, meanwhile, turned his thoughts towards his eagerly awaited match-up with highly acclaimed Argentinian striker, Gabriel Batistuta. The Newcastle *Journal* billed the contest of sorts as: 'the pragmatic and down-to-earth Geordie against the richly talented and flamboyant South American. In short, two master craftsmen at work,' adding: 'Such was the admiration with which Shearer spoke of his rival in the picturesque setting of Burnham Beeches yesterday that in another age it could almost have been Leonardo da Vinci extolling the virtues of Michaelangelo. "He is powerful, he is big, he is strong, he's quick, he scores goals, he's a huge name around the world," said Shearer, in deference to the Argentinian star. "He has scored goals in one of the toughest leagues on a regular basis. You cannot do anything but admire him. He has done it on the world stage as well. He will be a big threat."

Shearer dismissed suggestions that England would be gunning for revenge for their depressing losses to Argentina in the World Cup finals of 1986 and 1998, preferring to perceive the game as mere preparation for Euro 2000. England turned in a battling performance, but were unable to break down the stubborn South Americans in a game that ended 0–0.

Shearer said that he and his players had hoped to win as a tribute to England legend, the flying winger Sir Stanley Matthews, who had passed away on the eve of the game. He said: 'We wanted to put on a good performance for Sir Stanley Matthews. Our sympathies go out to his friends and family. It was a shame we couldn't get a win for him. I think we merited a win. We were really on top in the first half and one or two chances were flying around and that was the time to punish them.'

No one could have expected Shearer's next utterance while on England duty...

CHAPTER SEVEN

Farewell to the Three Lions

Alan Shearer's colossal contribution to his country's cause has spawned endless debates about his placing in the pantheon of great England strikers. In 2005, thirty goals in sixty-three internationals ranked him in the top-ten list of England goalscorers of all time. His inspirational captaincy – he captained his country 31 times, winning 16 games – and uncanny knack of scoring in crucial matches ensured he stamped his name indelibly in the history books of the England football team.

But perhaps the true level of his England excellence can be best judged by the repeated and often-vociferous calls for him to reverse his decision to retire somewhat prematurely at the age of twenty-nine. It is difficult to think of an England footballer who has been as frequently implored to step out of international retirement. Perhaps Sweden's pleas for Henrik Larsson to return prior to Euro 2004, which were ultimately answered, provide an example on the same scale. In Shearer's case, impassioned entreaties continued even up until the 2004 World Cup – some four years after he last wore the coveted white shirt. His sustained brilliance in the Premiership made the 'Shearer for England debate' an omnipresent topic every time Sven-Goran Eriksson was due to select a squad.

It was following England's 0–0 draw with Argentina at Wembley in February 2000 that Shearer delivered the devastating news that sent shockwaves around the football world – he planned to retire from international football at the end of Euro 2000. He revealed that he had told Kevin Keegan of his plans twenty-four hours before England played Argentina. In a statement, Shearer said:

> After a huge amount of thought, I have decided to retire from international football. I would like to play, if selected, in Euro 2000 and then bow out so that the manager has time to plan effectively for the 2002 World Cup. I have spoken to both Bobby Robson and Kevin Keegan and they understand my reasoning. I want everyone to understand that I am not walking away from a challenge. I am hugely patriotic and my time as England captain has made me incredibly proud. However, I realise that if I want to give Newcastle value for money in the remaining four years of my contract with them, I will need to pace myself a bit more than I am able to do at the moment. I am not saying that I would never play for England again – if there was an injury crisis or a real need for me to help out, I would always be honoured to answer the call. However, football is about planning for the future and, hopefully, my decision today will help England become even more successful in the coming years.

He later confessed that the fact that his wife Lainya – the first person he informed of his impending international retirement – was expecting the couple's third child had influenced his thinking.

FAREWELL TO THE THREE LIONS

A bemused and dejected England manager, Kevin Keegan, admitted that he had attempted to change Shearer's mind, but conceded that he had ultimately been forced to respect his decision. 'Of course I was very sad and I tried to persuade him to change his mind,' Keegan said. 'But I know that what makes Alan Shearer special is that he is his own man and his record speaks for itself. A total of twenty-eight goals in fifty-seven games for his country has been a tremendous achievement and, who knows, the best could be yet to come at Euro 2000.'

The Football Association's executive director David Davies insisted in the *Sunday Mirror* that Shearer would be eager to end his illustrious international career on a high note. He said: 'The Alan Shearer I've got to know over the last few years will not end his career as a lame duck. Knowing him, he will end it with a bang at Euro 2000. Alan will leave a huge gap to fill. Only six people in history have scored more international goals for England than him. But knowing Alan, this decision won't have been taken without a lot of thought. You never get the timing right with decisions like this, whatever you do. For a top sports professional, knowing the right moment can be very difficult.'

William Hill bookmakers endorsed Davies' view by installing Shearer as 7–1 to be top scorer at Euro 2000, quoting England at 10–1 to win the tournament.

Newcastle chairman Freddy Shepherd and manager Bobby Robson were as shocked as everyone else at their striker's staggering announcement, but understandably welcomed it for selfish reasons. Shepherd said: 'We didn't know anything about it and are still coming to terms with the enormity of his decision. But from a selfish point of view, it's certainly of benefit to Newcastle. Alan has four years of his contract left at Newcastle United and we know he still has a great deal to give this club.'

Robson added: 'This is a decision made entirely by Alan and he had made that decision in the best interests of himself. We support him in whatever decision he makes. He has served England wonderfully and magnificently and he wishes to move on from international football while he is still at the top of his form, and Newcastle United will benefit from that.'

Opinions on whether Shearer's decision was in the best interests of his country were divided among the media. The *Observer*'s Paul Wilson was understandably worried that Shearer's boots would not be adequately filled. He said: 'Shearer's England retirement is not good news, and most England supporters will hope he fills his boots in Belgium and Holland this summer. For there are fitness questions over Michael Owen and Fowler, Heskey is not a noted goalscorer, Cole does not appear to have impressed Keegan and Phillips, so far, looks slightly out of his depth.'

But other journalists felt that while Shearer was still capable of scoring almost at will in the Premiership, he found the international arena a less fertile and more demanding proposition. The *Sunday Times*' Joe Lovejoy, for instance, said: 'Shearer remains a major player in the Premiership, where he scored again for Newcastle yesterday, but there is a world of difference between Sheffield Wednesday and Brazil, who are next on England's agenda, and recent matches have shown Shearer, stripped of his speed off the mark, to be a diminishing force. Like Gary Lineker, who made a similar announcement before the finals of the 1992 European championship, he is the best judge of his own form and fitness, and if he feels it is time to go, we can be sure it is.'

Jack Hixon, the man who had unearthed Shearer at the age of thirteen, said: 'Whenever Alan Shearer decides something, you can guarantee it will be logical. You can serve two masters, but you can only do it for so long.'

Terry Venables was dismayed that Shearer would not be able to cement his position as arguably England's greatest-ever forward. He said in his column in the *News of the World*: 'Shearer was – and still is – the greatest England goalscorer of them all. I just hope he's making the right decision to quit. When I was England manager, it staggered me that some people felt he wasn't good enough, that aspects of his game weren't up to scratch. For me, Alan was above reproach, a striker who had all the attributes necessary for survival in the modern game. You can name England stars of the past with fabulous records, but it's far tougher, far more demanding, far, far more difficult to come out on top these days and maintain some balance in your life. Denis Law was that type of striker, a real demon, and the highest compliment I can pay Alan is to say that he comes from the same magnificent class as the Scot.'

Television pundits were also invited to have their say on football's massive talking point of early 2000. BBC's *Match of the Day* pundit Alan Hansen felt that the barracking England fans who had subjected Shearer to boos during the 1–0 loss to Scotland in late 1999 could have prompted him to contemplate calling time on his international career. He told the *Mirror*: 'There has never been a top-class striker with such a record who has had so many doubters. The press and media you can put up with, but once your own supporters – the England fans – start doubting you, you've got a problem. Maybe he's had a look at that and decided to get out at the top. The timing is the strange bit. Really he should have waited until after Euro 2000, but he is a very single-minded man.'

As a player who called a halt to his own glittering England career in similar circumstances before Euro '92, Gary Lineker understood more than most about Shearer's acceptance that his injury-ravaged body would not allow him to continue until the 2002 World Cup. Lineker said: 'He knows his body better than anyone else. I did the same thing in 1991 because I didn't think I could get to the World Cup in 1994. I think it's a bit premature, because he's not yet thirty whereas I was thirty-two when I made my announcement, but he is saying he will be thirty-two by the time of the next big tournament and he wants to go out now while he's at the top.'

Once the initial shock, and subsequent frenzied debate about Shearer's forthcoming international retirement, had subsided, England's focus swiftly switched to their next friendly match – at home against Brazil.

It would be another chance for Shearer and his team-mates to ascertain their position in football's global world order as, although the Brazilians did not quite possess the stars of old, they were still unrivalled in soccer's glamour stakes for imagination and technical excellence.

England went on to obtain a creditable 1–1 draw against the Brazilians with Michael Owen displaying a piece of sublime skill that the South Americans would have been proud of, when he bamboozled Zé Roberto with a subtle drag-back before firing home. Shearer believed that he and Owen had played their best game together since Argentina in the 1998 World Cup, although Kevin Keegan insisted that his influential Geordie captain had never expressed a preference for his forward partner.

However, there was a growing belief that, as in the case of the Peter Beardsley-Gary Lineker alliance, which took time to gel in the 1980s, the Shearer and Owen union could eventually prosper. But, as had happened with the recent emergence of Emile Heskey, Robbie Fowler's goal, added to Shearer's header, clouded the issue yet further when England cruised to a 2–0 victory over the Ukraine in their final home friendly match before Euro 2000.

Then there was Kevin Phillips, a particular favourite of the ever-opinionated ex-Nottingham Forest manager, Brian Clough. The Newcastle *Journal* reported him saying: 'I'd throw Phillips in with Alan Shearer. He's a natural and he can dip his bread at any level. I met him up at Sunderland. He smiled and called me "Mr Clough", which shows he's got some brains!'

And the Nottingham Forest legend was convinced that Shearer would play a major role in the championships. He added: 'He is smiling again – which is good news – and he knows how lucky he is to have beaten all those injuries – unlike another great goalscorer who was never the same after getting injured at twenty-seven – and his movement is good. For his size, he's good. He jumps as high as Tommy Lawton.'

As the nation geared up for a feast of football that was Euro 2000, Three Lions' fans' appetites for the beautiful game were whetted by *Match of the Day* magazine's compilation of the greatest goals scored for England.

Shearer took fourth spot in the list for his thunderous drive in England's 4–1 thrashing of Holland in Euro '96, with Michael Owen's mazy dribble and wonder goal against Argentina in the 1998 World Cup finishing in first place.

In its own focus on Shearer, the *Mirror* suggested his best England goal had been his long-range volley against Portugal in April 1998, while his outstanding performance in England's massacre of Holland two years earlier was said to be his most impressive display.

Yet Shearer looked in danger of missing the chance to net more spectacular strikes when he limped off in England's final pre-tournament friendly in Malta with a knee injury.

England struggled to a 2–1 win in Valetta, yet this lacklustre performance, coupled with Shearer's injury woes, at least offered some encouragement, given that it echoed the indifferent form of the Three Lions and the fitness of their key striker prior to the euphoric Euro '96 campaign.

For some observers, fit or not, Shearer's form, and indeed combative style, was yet again called into question and he was made the scapegoat for the dispiriting England performance. The *Mirror* suggested that Shearer had been 'bitterly disappointing' and 'sluggish', pointing out that he had now gone six games without scoring. And it focused on the rumpus he had been involved in with Malta defender Darren Debono, whose nose was broken. Debono fumed in the *Mirror*: 'Shearer should have been sent off, but he was not even booked. It was a deliberate elbow and the referee should have stopped the game. Shearer said sorry, but it was too late and it was the worst injury I've had from a foul. A cross came in and I was before him for the ball, but when I went for it he gave me the elbow. He pushed me out with his elbow. It is not what I expect from an England captain.'

For his part, Shearer insisted that he had not acted maliciously, although his critics seized on the chance to compare the unsavoury incident to the allegations that he deliberately kicked Leicester midfielder Neil Lennon prior to the 1998 World Cup. The under-fire Geordie must have felt that the nation was against him in a similar fashion to 1996, when his long-running goal drought for his country saw him pilloried as a predictable, archetypal English forward whose assets saw him flourish domestically, but whose international credentials had yet to be displayed.

Indeed, if he had heard that a poll carried out by football website, *voiceoffootball.com*, suggested that 72 per cent of England fans did not want him in their team, he could easily have come to the conclusion that the entire country was against him.

The *Independent* offered him some comfort by noting: 'It is the sort of statistic that reminds you of those polls in the 1980s that suggested Margaret Thatcher was loathed by 80 per cent of the English. But they still voted for her. Shearer is a little like that, an English monolith. His time in the No. 9 shirt must be allowed to find its own fitting conclusion.'

The broadsheet also carried the inspirational words of Jack Hixon.

FAREWELL TO THE THREE LIONS

'He was top scorer in Euro '96 and he'll want to repeat that,' Hixon said of Shearer's impending international swansong. 'But that's just the usual ambition and the expectancy of the man himself. But Shearer is really at the height of his powers. When you think of the adversities he has faced in terms of physical injury and the criticism he had from the media when he wasn't putting it in the net with the regularity that he used to, his reaction has been magnificent.'

Thankfully for Shearer – if not for his legions of doubters – he was passed fit for England's opening game in Euro 2000 against Portugal. David Beckham enthused in the *Sun*: 'We could not have got a greater shot in the arm than the news that Alan is fit. Not only is he a great player, but he is also a leader. When you see players like him and Tony [Adams] in the tunnel, it's like watching two soldiers getting ready to go off to the front. Out on the pitch, there is no doubt defenders are intimidated by Alan. And not just by his reputation for goals, either. It's his sheer physical presence. He's a big fella, defenders worry about him – no one messes around with Alan Shearer.'

After racing into a two-goal lead against Portugal, courtesy of goals from Paul Scholes and Steve McManaman, the gifted Portuguese outclassed England with three strikes of their own, the best of which was a wondrous long-range effort from Luis Figo, which saw them prevail 3–2.

Few England players could emerge with credit from their sorry demise, which recalled the infamous collapse to West Germany in the 1970 World Cup when Sir Alf Ramsay's men led by two goals before Gerd Müller and co sent the Three Lions crashing out of the tournament.

The inevitable media backlash ensued, and Shearer was predictably a prime target for a poisonous press pack. The *Evening Standard*'s Michael Hart said: 'The England captain, playing in his last games before retiring from international football, demonstrated all the traditional virtues of the English game. No one could question his commitment, nor that of his team-mates, but as we have seen so often in the past, such qualities are no longer sufficient against the very best.' The *Scotsman* refused to gloat in the Sassenachs' sorrow, instead focusing on Shearer's often-overlooked caring-and-sharing qualities. 'Shearer provided a supportive shoulder for Michael Owen after the Portugal game. The young striker was more distressed than he would admit at being substituted at half-time, and Shearer understood. "We had a little game of golf and were able to have a chat about it," the captain said. "Contrary to what has been written, I get on very well with Michael and I enjoy playing alongside him. I said to him if he can lean on me in any way at all then he should. It's not nice being taken off, because you feel you haven't had a chance to influence the game, but the best reaction Michael can show is to go out and do the business on Saturday."'

For some, if Shearer were to be dropped it would not represent a terminal blow to England's chances of glory. His army of detractors cited the fact that, despite the absence of the injured Jimmy Greaves in the final throes of the 1966 World Cup, Geoff Hurst – who Kevin Keegan had invited to boost his players' morale prior to the Germany game – emerged to secure England's greatest triumph. Why, therefore, could the likes of Emile Heskey or Kevin Phillips not surface from the shadows and fire the Three Lions to success in Shearer's stead?

Yet again Shearer's formidable track record of thriving when under fire and on the receiving end of a press pummelling was about to be exhibited. As Kevin Keegan told the *Sun*: 'Alan Shearer has spent a lifetime proving people wrong and he has another opportunity against Germany. I still have every confidence in him – far more than most of you. Nothing that happened against Portugal makes me think otherwise. He is very focused and he wants to go out with a bang. Never underestimate him.' The *Sun*'s Steven Howard went on to say Shearer's demeanour included: 'A menacing look in his eyes that had terrified far more resilient opponents than the group of journalists who gathered round him.'

The heavily criticised forward responded bullishly to talk of his impending demise. He said: 'It has not crossed my mind that it could be my last game for England. And I don't see why it should be. As for all the criticism, I just don't respond. If I lead England to victory on Saturday, I won't have to answer to anyone. But this sort of thing comes with the job, with being England captain and with being me. And I still love every minute of it.'

Shearer and his team-mates were confident of victory against the Germans, who had drawn 1–1 with Romania in their opening game of the tournament, as they were regarded as a pale shadow of their ruthlessly efficient sides of old, despite being the tournament's defending champions.

But they were also confronted by a depressing weight of history as England had not beaten their old rivals since the 1966 triumph. The Three Lions had also been beaten on penalties by Germany in both the 1990 World Cup and the 1996 European Championships semi-finals, which would inevitably have left immense psychological scars.

A scintilla of comfort could, however, be drawn from Manchester United's thrilling defeat of German champions Bayern Munich in the previous year's Champions League final.

Prior to this momentous night, Bayern captain Lothar Matthäus had served a chilling reminder of Germany's stranglehold over England when he said: 'Your famous Gary Lineker once described football as a simple game and it is. Twenty-two men run around a field for 90 minutes and then the Germans win.'

The German coach who had overseen his country's 1996 defeat of England, Berti Vogts, was singing a similarly confident – or should that be arrogant – tune in 2000. He was quoted by the Press Association as saying: 'I couldn't believe my eyes at the way England played after going 2–0 up against Portugal. I couldn't understand why Kevin Keegan didn't decide to change the system. I thought Alan Shearer had a very poor game and perhaps he wasn't fit to play. I think a better combination for England would be Emile Heskey and Michael Owen or even Heskey and Kevin Phillips. However, I am German and want Germany to win, so I hope that Alan Shearer plays against us on Saturday.'

Vogts' overweening confidence was punctured by the man whose football career was redolent of a fabulous fable: England's saviour single-handedly saw off the challenge of Germany in Charleroi in a marvellous riposte to the barrage of criticism he had received in the build-up to the match.

Eight minutes into a tense, goalless encounter, David Beckham's whipped, looping, right-wing free-kick evaded the German defence and Shearer, the very epitome of bulldog English spirit, stooped to conquer his critics, decisively heading past Oliver Kahn in the German goal.

It was arguably his most important and enjoyable goal for England given the fact that had he not scored, his international career and the Three Lions' progress in Euro 2000 would have ended in miserable failure. His priceless strike also ended the unstinting thirty-four years of hurt that England and their fervent followers had endured since 1966. 'He's answered his critics again. The fans love him, but the critics don't. I just think he's the best at what he does and he's done it again tonight,' Keegan said of Shearer in the *Sunday Times*, before rounding on members of the media who had mercilessly mauled him. 'When you say a few people have been on at Alan, you are being very kind to your colleagues. He has answered his critics again. Just give him three or four days before you start on him again,' he said. 'You have knocked him. You have pummelled him. You have questioned his right to be in the side and to be captain. He has never, ever given anything other than 100 per cent. He got his goal tonight and tried to prove a lot of people wrong. When you look at some of the pieces the English journalists have written over the last year, you will know it is you people who are responsible for Alan retiring from international football. Not Alan. Not me. You people are.'

A relieved and delighted Shearer poured out his post-match thoughts to the *News of the World*. He said: 'I've never been more shattered after a game of football – but I have never been happier. I was completely drained at the end of the 90 minutes against Germany and it wasn't just physical effort. I was emotionally exhausted as well. It's been a tough few weeks for everyone connected with England – and me personally. We have been written off and branded as no-hopers in this tournament. But the stories which have been written can be ripped up. We're still in there. We've given ourselves a great chance of reaching the quarter-finals.'

Shearer added: 'To beat the Germans in a major competition for the first time since 1966 makes it even more satisfying. It is a memory to store away with my proudest football memories. Scoring the winning goal made it extra special for me. It's certainly up there with the best and most important goals of my international career.'

Shearer had picked up a booking in the blood-and-thunder encounter against the Germans after fouling striking Ulf Kirsten, but naturally Kevin Keegan did not want to entertain dropping his star man, despite the fear that he would miss the quarter-finals if he was yellow-carded against Romania. The Romanians, deprived of their talisman Gheorghe Hagi, who was ruled out after picking up two yellow cards in the tournament, represented a reasonable test of England's ambitions, although with only a point needed by the Three Lions to progress, a quarter-final berth looked an eminent possibility.

A far greater threat to England was the excessive triumphalism that had been whipped up in the wake of the German victory. There was, therefore, a horrible sense of inevitability that if England did not treat the Romanians with respect, their European dreams would wilt as a result of a surfeit of complacency.

It is debatable whether this contributed to England's downfall, an inexplicable and sorry surrender to the Romanians, who progressed to the quarter-finals with a 3–2 victory, or whether Shearer and co were simply not good enough. In any case, sadly, England's depressing self-destruction will be remembered more as one of the Three Lions' most disappointing losses rather than for it being Alan Shearer's last game.

It all started to go terribly wrong when defender Christian Chivu gave the Romanians a shock lead after 22 minutes and warning bells began to sound at the Stadio Communial stadium in Charleroi, Belgium. However, the tenor of the game apparently changed when Chivu hauled down Paul Ince in the penalty area and up stepped old warhorse Shearer to draw England level with his thirtieth goal for his country as the first half neared its close. In equalising, Shearer leapt alongside legends Nat Lofthouse and Tom Finney in the England goal charts. He also became the second highest goalscorer in European Championships' history with seven goals, two strikes behind the all-time record-holder, Michel Platini.

Michael Owen's goal early in the second-half seemed to have smoothed England's path to the quarter-finals, but the dogged Romanians levelled matters again through Dorinel Munteanu. Then, with only two minutes left to play, Phil Neville committed a foul that was tantamount to professional suicide. He needlessly lunged at Viorel Moldovan in the penalty area and Ioan Ganea ended England's Euro 2000 campaign and their legendary forward's international career with an expertly taken spot kick, sending the helpless Nigel Martyn the wrong way.

Tears streamed down the cheeks of Captain Fantastic as he sank dejectedly to his knees at the final whistle, distraught that his majestic

England career had foundered from one player's bungling ineptitude. He stumbled from the pitch wearing his tear-stained shirt, his head bowed, whirring with shattered dreams and 'what might have beens?'

Surely the football scriptwriters in the sky could have penned it differently? Surely England's hero could not suffer such an ignominious fate?

Yet football is a capricious and unsentimental beast, as Shearer knows only too well. There was to be no fairytale farewell, no repeat of the glorious goal that helped vanquish England's arch-rivals Germany and no possibility of a European Championship winners' medal to clutch proudly. Instead, as Shearer revealed in his *News of the World* column: 'I sat alone in the England dressing room, unable to move and unwilling to talk to anyone. I just wanted some time to myself. For half an hour I struggled to come to terms with the fact I would never again play for my country. And I felt completely empty. I don't think I have ever been as low after a football match as I was after our heartbreaking defeat by Romania. It was as bad – if not worse – than losing in two FA Cup finals with Newcastle.'

Shearer then made a stunning admission – he pleaded guilty to the sin of simulation, or in layman's language, he dived close to the penalty box in a desperate attempt to win a free-kick as the game against Romania entered its dying minutes. With breathtaking honesty, he confessed that he had resorted to such measures 'for his country'. The *Sun* suggested that Shearer's surprising confession was intended 'as an illustration of the extent of his patriotism, but it was also a glaring example of the depths to which the England football team has sunk.'

The *Daily Mail*'s Brian Scott had mixed feelings about both Shearer's unsavoury act and his openness in acknowledging it. 'Is this what England expects of its icons? Should John Bull be proud of a guy who is willing to sacrifice his integrity for the sake of gaining an unfair advantage over his rivals? Shearer, in fact, was just the latest in a long line of players at the European Championships to sign the Cheats' Charter, although there can't be many more like him who would acknowledge publicly having done so.' Scott added: 'Those who might wish to remember him for his great contribution to international football, underpinned as it was by thirty goals in sixty-three games, were left to ponder something unsavoury about him. Honest or dishonest? The jury is liable to return a split verdict on the question. The great pity is that he gave them cause in the first place to consider it.'

Shearer had arguably blotted his country's copybook with this minor indiscretion, but few fair-minded England fans will recall the incident and would certainly not be churlish enough to suggest that it obscures his more memorable moments for the Three Lions. One of Shearer's fiercest critics, *The Times*' Oliver Holt, asserted that it was high time that the Newcastle forward's lengthy service for his country had concluded: 'Those who have campaigned long and hard for Shearer's retention reaped the rewards last night. In an ineffective team, he was ineffectuality itself, the personification of a washed-up hero well past his England sell-by date. No one would wish this send-off upon him after such sterling service to his country, but he should never have been allowed to carry on playing for England until now. Only Keegan's hero worship of Shearer, which sometimes seemed to verge on deference, preserved his place in the side. At its most excusable, his persistence with the Newcastle United centre-forward was short-termism gone mad.'

It is interesting to juxtapose this savage appraisal of Shearer as an England has-been with the deluge of appeals for him to return to national service post-2000. If he were as impotent as Holt and other sceptics suggested in the first year of the new millennium, why were some high-profile names in the football firmament pressing for his inclusion in England's European Championship squad four years later?

FAREWELL TO THE THREE LIONS

In February 2004, the *News of the World* posed the question 'Should Alan Shearer Return For England in Euro 2004?' under which an emphatic 'Yes' was delivered by a clutch of leading lights in English football. For example, the then Portsmouth supremo, Harry Redknapp, said: 'Alan and Michael Owen are a great partnership and if I was picking the team for the European Championships he would definitely be in it.'

Birmingham boss Steve Bruce supported this view, declaring: 'Alan Shearer is the king of English centre-forwards in the current era as far as I am concerned. He has been at the top of his profession for almost a decade and, of course, it would be a massive boost for Sven if he was around for Euro 2004.'

Shearer himself had raised hopes that he could make a dramatic international comeback after stating, before England's Euro 2004 qualifier against Liechtenstein, that he was convinced he 'could still do a job for England'. He also confessed that he missed representing his country and felt that he could have done more for the cause. But Shearer remained resolute and adhered to his decision, insisting that it had been vindicated by his excellence for his club. In an interview with BBC Radio Newcastle, he said: 'I think my performances over the past four years have justified my decision to retire from international football. It is nice when you hear people say, "Come back and play for England", "Come back and play in Euro 2004." But as I said, the reasons that I gave have happened. I have been able to maintain a very high standard of football over the last four years and I'm not sure I would have been able to have done that if I had played for Newcastle and England, particularly with the injuries I had.'

So where does Alan Shearer rank among England's goalscorers of the past? Graeme Souness has asserted that he is the best of the lot and he was voted into one of the two striking berths, alongside Gary Lineker, in Channel 4 viewers' choice of a best-ever England XI in 2004.

ALAN SHEARER

It is invidious to give a definitive answer to this ubiquitous question however, as different eras throw up contrasting challenges and circumstances. For example, few, if any, England forwards have survived the depressing litany of injuries that Shearer suffered.

In 2005, he was placed fifth in the table of England's goalscorers in history, although his goals-per-game ratio was surpassed only by Nat Lofthouse, Gary Lineker and Geoff Hurst. It could be said that Alan Shearer possessed the same virtues that made each of these three men unique: he had the awesome aerial ability of Nat Lofthouse; the prolific goal-scoring prowess of Gary Lineker; and the gift of striking on the big occasion *à la* Geoff Hurst.

When considered in these terms, Alan Shearer can lay claim to being the greatest England striker of them all...

CHAPTER EIGHT

A Ruud Awakening

When Ruud Gullit launched a withering attack on Alan Shearer in June 2005, it was a revealing reminder of the pair's bitter power struggle almost six years earlier.

'Shearer has too much influence at Newcastle,' said Gullit in the Newcastle *Evening Chronicle*, in a scornful swipe at the former England No. 9, during which he scoffed at his decision to carry on playing.

But Gullit found out to his cost how great Shearer's influence at St James' Park was when he dropped the golden boy to the bench for the Tyne-Wear derby against Sunderland – and days later made a summary exit from the Newcastle manager's role.

Although Shearer has since denied influencing the Dutchman's departure from Newcastle, the denouement to Gullit's tempestuous Tyneside tenure has shades of the 1970s pop group Sparks' hit 'This Town Ain't Big Enough for the Both of Us'.

This town ain't big enough for the both of us
And it ain't me who's gonna leave...

ALAN SHEARER

In a similar vein to part of the song's chorus, Newcastle United could not accommodate this pair of formidable, yet wildly contrasting, characters. There could only be one winner when the two antagonistic forces collided: Alan Shearer, the Toon idol.

One could have foretold of the pair's rancorous relationship when the flamboyant Dutchman arrived at St James' Park two years earlier. Prior to Newcastle's clash with Chelsea in November 1996, Gullit, then the Chelsea manager, derided the £15 million Shearer had cost Newcastle earlier that summer. He told the *Daily Mirror*: 'Shearer's price is crazy and a waste of money in my opinion. I look abroad for players of the same or better quality – and I manage to sign them for a lot less.' He went on to say that he preferred Gianluca Vialli as a striker, claiming that Shearer had 'no tricks' and few facets to his game, other than the ability to score goals galore.

Typically, Shearer did not want to be drawn into a war of words, retorting: 'He's entitled to his opinion. It may not exactly coincide with mine, but it's certainly not a problem. People can say what they want, and I'll just get on with things like I normally do.' Imagine his dismay, then, when little more than two years later his chief critic was installed as Newcastle manager.

Most Newcastle fans relished the mouth-watering prospect of a return to high-octane entertainment, or to quote a Gullit buzzword, 'sexy', football, served up in the cavalier Kevin Keegan era. Fans sporting dreadlocked wigs and T-shirts bearing the slogan 'Clog on the Tyne' flocked to St James' Park to greet the Dutch master on his arrival there. Shearer, meanwhile, was now left contemplating his own future, as rumours circulated of his horror at the departure of Dalglish, his mentor.

He had forged a close relationship with Dalglish, with whom he had enjoyed unexpected Premiership success with unheralded Blackburn and the Scot was a coach who had unswerving faith in his abilities.

The arrival of the legendary Scot had also helped soothe Shearer's heartache at the departure of Kevin Keegan, his boyhood hero, who had brought him back to his native North-East in 1996. Now Newcastle's No. 9 was facing a near-impossible task – of impressing a boss who was not impressed with him.

The Gullit era could hardly have got off to a worse start as Liverpool walloped Newcastle 4–1 at St James' Park, with Michael Owen overshadowing his England strike partner Shearer with a blistering hat-trick. John Richardson, writing in the *Daily Mail*, believed a showdown between Gullit and Shearer was looming after Newcastle's dismal display and defeat. 'Shearer's body language during Sunday's 4–1 defeat against Liverpool, during which he was overshadowed by Michael Owen, suggested that he was not enamoured with the events of the past week. When your new boss has already described your £15 million fee as "a waste of money", as Gullit did before a Newcastle-Chelsea match in 1996, the outlook is, at best, unsettled.' Oliver Holt in *The Times* quipped of Gullit's desire to play sexy football: 'If he wants this lot to play sexy football, he might need a few boxes of Viagra.'

In the wake of this so-called 'Ruud awakening', sources close to Shearer revealed that he was prepared to bury the hatchet with Gullit and strive to win trophies for his hometown club.

And the dreadlocked Dutchman also attempted to defuse any suggestions of a simmering feud between the pair at his first official press conference as club manager. 'Alan Shearer is one of the best strikers around, of course he is. He is part of the future of this club,' insisted Gullit. 'But he is like the cannons of Navarone. Ammunition must be given to him by other people, he can't do it by himself.'

His last comment referred to the fact that his principal marksman had gone nine matches without a goal in the Premiership – a tally previously unheard of for Shearer. However, a 1–0 away defeat to Aston Villa in September extended this barren patch and Gullit admitted that Shearer was becoming frustrated by his lack of goals.

ALAN SHEARER

Redemption for the downcast striker was just around the corner, however, as he netted twice in Newcastle's home win over his first club, Southampton. Despite this double delight, Shearer still seemed to shun his new manager, according to Louise Taylor in the *Sunday Times*: 'At the end, the stony-faced striker appeared deliberately to cold shoulder Gullit as he walked past his new leader en route to the tunnel.'

Despite Gullit's insistence to the contrary, speculation remained rife that the Dutchman wanted to offload Shearer. Graham Hunter of the *Daily Mail* believed Chelsea would head 'a stampede' of clubs – including Arsenal, Manchester United and Aston Villa, if Shearer were to be put up for sale.

Serie A was another possible destination for the much-talked-about striker, claimed Hunter, with Parma, Juventus and Roma among his alleged admirers in Italy. The feverish transfer talk surrounding Shearer was beginning to cause severe anxiety among the St James' Park faithful, so much so that the Geordie hero issued a statement confirming his intent to remain at Newcastle. He said: 'If I comment on speculation every time it is written, I will be in the press all the time and I would rather concentrate on preparing for my football. However, because the fans have specifically asked, I can say that I have spoken with the chairman and the manager and they have told me that they see me as an important part of Newcastle's future.'

Gullit endorsed Shearer's sentiments and claimed that the striker had reiterated such thoughts in private discussions with him and Newcastle chairman Freddy Shepherd. Meanwhile, the man at the centre of the brouhaha continued to impress continental spies by scoring in Newcastle's 2–1 European Cup-Winners' Cup first-leg, first-round tie against Partizan Belgrade.

His rich vein of form continued when he scored twice in the 5–1 away thrashing against Coventry, taking his goal tally to five in three games. Faced with yet another barrage of 'do you want Alan to stay?' questions at the end of the match, Gullit answered in the affirmative and declared that Shearer's recent goal haul was irrefutable proof that he was happy at St James' Park.

A rejuvenated Shearer also declared that confidence at Newcastle was 'sky high'. He added two more in the 2–0 home win over Nottingham Forest to demonstrate that, even if he and Gullit would never be best buddies, they had at least established a working relationship together. But Shearer and Newcastle's European exploits were brought to an abrupt halt when Partizan Belgrade squeezed past them on away goals in the European Cup-Winners Cup after securing a 1–0 win.

As the season wore on, however, Gullit repeatedly implored his board to furnish him with funds for a raid on the transfer market, with a powerful striker to partner Shearer identified as a top priority.

Newspaper reports suggested that Aston Villa's lanky frontman Dion Dublin had been targeted by the Newcastle manager, but no move ever materialised. Meanwhile, Steve Watson and misfiring French striker Stéphane Guivarc'h both departed for pastures new, creating some cash for Gullit's desired indulgence. In mid-November, the *Journal* analysed Newcastle's strife under the headline 'Is Shearer good enough for Newcastle?' and invited comments from readers. One felt that Gullit should bite the bullet and allow Shearer to leave.

'However, unlike some pundits, I do not believe that there will be a queue of big clubs ready to pay mega-bucks for a twenty-eight-year-old who, in my opinion, isn't performing anywhere near the standard of bygone years. I would be amazed if anyone stumps up £15 million on the basis of what Shearer has produced at Newcastle United. Take away his penalties and it doesn't look very impressive at all. What makes Shearer or his agent think that there is a bigger club than Newcastle United waiting to "rescue" him? In my opinion, perhaps it is us who should be questioning whether Shearer is still good enough to be playing for Newcastle?'

In late November, Gullit finally added to his firepower by signing Everton's maverick Scotsman, Duncan Ferguson, for £7 million. Newcastle chief executive, Freddie Fletcher, was adamant that Ferguson had not been bought to replace Shearer. 'The board have signed Duncan Ferguson to partner him with Alan Shearer up front,' he said. 'The object of the exercise is to have two really class strikers playing up front for Newcastle United.' However, the potentially potent strike force could not be unleashed on opposing defences initially due to Shearer's hamstring injury.

Nevertheless, Ferguson proved his worth by netting twice in the 3–1 victory over Wimbledon at St James' Park. However, when Shearer and Ferguson both started alongside each other on Boxing Day, Newcastle crashed 3–0 at home to rampant Leeds United.

Gullit's frequent trips home to Amsterdam were a source of much controversy for Newcastle supporters at the time, with his girlfriend Estelle – the pair would go on to marry in 2000 – claiming that the majority of suitable houses were too big for the pair. He had mixed success in the transfer market, meanwhile, signing twenty-year-old French full-back Didier Domi from Paris St Germain, but missed out on his compatriot Ibrahim Ba from AC Milan after the midfielder failed a medical. Shearer ensured that Gullit had further cause for optimism when he scored the winner – his first goal in eleven starts – for Newcastle in their 2–1 defeat of Crystal Palace in the third round of the FA Cup.

However, days later, he learnt that he would have to wait at least six weeks before he could develop his partnership with Duncan Ferguson after the Scot underwent an operation on his troublesome groin. Shearer could comfort himself with the fact that he had been cited as a model of professionalism to England's ever-increasing foreign legion.

A RUUD AWAKENING

The Professional Footballers' Association chief Gordon Taylor declared that Shearer embodied the best of British virtues after his Newcastle team-mate, the Italian defender Alessandro Pistone, became embroiled in a dispute with Ruud Gullit and was duly banished to the reserves. The Newcastle *Evening Chronicle* quoted Taylor thus: 'Alessandro Pistone is refusing to train with Newcastle's reserves but professional sport these days is all about stress and pressure. You just have to cope with it. Alan Shearer was forced to battle back from an horrendous injury, but he still carries on without complaint.'

Despite Shearer's excellence, Newcastle were struggling to emulate the verve and buoyancy of previous years, prompting the *Mail on Sunday*'s David Walker to launch a stinging attack on the club. 'Newcastle United, the club that was once the epitome of drive and enterprise, is sinking slowly but inexorably into a quagmire of mediocrity near the foot of the Premiership. The days when Sir John Hall and Kevin Keegan made United the most vibrant team in English football are long gone. They may not have won any trophies in their heyday, but the thrilling football Keegan's team produced earned them acclaim from football followers around the country. In the past year, Newcastle have been engulfed by a sporting malaise that shows no sign of abating.'

Indeed, pervasive rumours of dressing-room dissension at St James' Park continued to abound, a prime example of which was when Gullit stripped Rob Lee of the Newcastle captaincy and gave the honour to Shearer. Shearer felt as though Lee had been treated badly by the controversial Dutchman, whose rifts with Newcastle players were dominating the headlines. The *Evening Chronicle* said in late January 1999: 'Alan Shearer has been labelled "selfish" by his new paymaster, Paul Dalglish, has been accused of telling tales to dad, and Rob Lee is allegedly well dischuffed, while keeping a dignified silence. Or so the grapevine goes. Certainly all is not well and United's team spirit is not the sort where the manager can demand his players to run through a wall and know he'll be left with a pile of demolished bricks.'

However, February started in a more positive fashion for both Newcastle and Shearer, who silenced his critics by scoring his first Premier League goal for over four months in the 2–1 win over Aston Villa at St James' Park. Gullit led the plaudits for Shearer after the match. He said: 'I'm very pleased with his performance. There has been a lot of press on his back and he's put that aside now. It's one weight less on his shoulders. He showed today that he is not only a very good player but a good captain. He battled hard.'

Shearer's revival continued when he plundered two goals in Newcastle's emphatic 4–1 victory over Coventry at home. However, his astonishing inability to score against his former side Southampton continued when Saints downed Newcastle 2–1 at The Dell. His lack of success in front of goal during that match meant that Shearer had only scored one goal in seven games for both Blackburn and Newcastle against the south-coast side.

Croatian midfielder Silvio Maric was recruited by Gullit to improve the service to Shearer at the end of February, while Metz striker Louis Saha had joined until the end of the season to supplement his goals. Saha made an immediate impact in the absence of Shearer, who had been struck down by flu, by firing Newcastle into the quarter-finals of the FA Cup after netting the only goal in United's 1–0 win at Blackburn Rovers in a fifth-round replay.

The strains of 'Que Saha, Saha' – a witty ditty devised to celebrate Saha's FA Cup feat – became a familiar sound at St James' Park and the ebullient Frenchman was also quick to sing the praises of his forward partner Shearer, describing it as an 'honour' to play with him. A season of unfulfilled ambitions and disquiet for Shearer and Newcastle was suddenly transformed into one of burgeoning hope and expectation.

A RUUD AWAKENING

A possibility of a repeat of the FA Cup final the year before was teed up when Newcastle were paired with either Tottenham or Barnsley in the semi-finals of the competition after a terrific 4–1 victory over Everton in the quarter-finals in March. Shearer, who scored Newcastle's fourth goal, was full of optimism for his side's tilt at the Twin Towers and was eager to gain revenge over Arsenal, proclaiming: 'If we're going to win the competition, then we are going to have to beat the best somewhere along the line – because the best are still in it. I suppose at a push we would take the draw we have got in the semi-finals, but it's still going to be tough. I have always said that when you get to the semi-finals it is anybody's game.'

Buoyed by his team's recent run of success, Gullit then reportedly made an audacious £8 million offer for Celtic's prolific marksman, Henrik Larsson. The *Sunday Mirror*'s Brian McNally said that Gullit faced competition from Manchester United but reckoned that the Dutchman was determined to land the Swedish star, offering the incentive of double the wages Celtic could offer. McNally added: 'The Dutchman has been a big fan of twenty-seven-year-old Larsson since his days in Holland with Feyenoord and sees him as the ideal foil to play off his £23 million strike force of Alan Shearer and Duncan Ferguson.'

While Larsson potentially represented the future for Newcastle, the club's present was being expertly looked after by their striker extraordinaire, Alan Shearer, who bagged a brilliant brace in the FA Cup semi-final against Tottenham to earn his side a second successive final appearance. The first of his glorious double arrived in the 19th minute of extra-time from the penalty spot, after Sol Campbell was controversially adjudged to have handled the ball in the box. He then walloped in a second ten minutes later from 25 yards, off the underside off the crossbar and past Ian Walker in the Tottenham goal to send the Toon Army into ecstasies at Old Trafford.

ALAN SHEARER

Temporarily, at least, Shearer's rift with his manager seemed to have healed. The *Daily Mail's* Martin Lipton and Ivan Speck commented: 'Ruud Gullit and Alan Shearer will walk hand-in-hand down Wembley Way next month after Newcastle clinched a dramatic return to the FA Cup final. Shearer's two goals in extra-time were enough to beat Tottenham at Old Trafford yesterday and foster harmony between the England skipper and his Dutch manager where, six months ago, only mutual distrust existed.' An overjoyed Shearer told the pair: 'I thought last year was the best experience I've ever had, but this time it's even better. We're giving the fans another day out. We want to give them something to shout about this time.' Gullit was effusive in his praise for his two-goal hero, saying: 'Shearer is Shearer, he can score goals whenever he wants.'

Footballing fortunes have a habit of swiftly, and often unexpectedly, changing and this was certainly the case when Shearer and Newcastle enjoyed the proverbial 'bad day at the office' when they then collapsed 3–1 at home to Everton. Shearer enjoyed a day of mixed emotions, despatching a penalty against the relegation-threatened Merseysiders to reach his 150th goal in the Premier League but also missing his first Premiership spot-kick for Newcastle.

Forward reinforcements were still being targeted by Gullit to eliminate such irritating inconsistency, with Real Mallorca's striker Dani said to be a target for the Dutchman. May witnessed the welcome return to action of Shearer's strike partner, Duncan Ferguson.

The towering frontman was restored to Newcastle's first team for the Magpies' derby clash with Middlesbrough and was optimistic that his partnership with Shearer would reap rich dividends. 'It's great to be back. Alan and I have only played a couple of games together, but I think I can help him and he can help me,' said Ferguson.

The Scot would not immediately find his feet, however, while the dependable right foot of Shearer delivered a perfectly aimed penalty past 'Boro 'keeper Mark Schwarzer to earn Newcastle a draw in the Tyne-Tees derby. Nevertheless, there was talk that a post-FA Cup semi-final hangover was lingering at St James' Park, with the suggestion that Newcastle's players were unable to focus on anything but the wonders of Wembley. The Newcastle *Journal* said that measures were in place to clamp down on any such wandering thoughts. 'Ruud Gullit, stumbling over a question about the FA Cup final, peeled off a £10 note from a thickish wad and handed it to Newcastle's press officer, Graham Courtney. "Every time we mention the F-word we have to pay a fine," he smiled. "The only time we will talk about it is in the week of the match."' The *Journal* reporter Tim Rich added that Alan Shearer had stressed that he and his team-mates were not overly distracted by the forthcoming final. 'Newcastle are at least making an attempt to focus on their remaining Premiership fixtures, however irrelevant they may seem before Wembley. "Let's get one thing out of the way to start with: the players here are not going through the motions," were the first words of Alan Shearer's programme notes, and the way the England captain plays you know he meant it.'

However, there was no doubt that Newcastle's form had dipped alarmingly since beating Spurs in the semi-final – they had failed to win a Premiership fixture since 3 April against Derby – and were held to a 1–1 draw by Blackburn at St James' Park in their final league match of the season. Both Shearer – who would finish the 1998/99 campaign with 20 goals in all competitions – and Ferguson were left out of this match, though, so that they could be primed and ready for a crack at Premiership champions Manchester United in the forthcoming FA Cup final.

The Mighty Reds were bidding to complete the second leg of a majestic treble – they would face Bayern Munich in the Champions League final just four days after their trip to Wembley. Newcastle's Greek defender Nikos Dabizas predicted that his side's hopes of derailing United's triple trophy quest lay firmly at the feet of Alan Shearer, who was tasked with the responsibility of scoring the Magpies' first Wembley goal since 1955 and Jackie Milburn's effort after only 45 seconds of his side's 3–1 triumph over Manchester City. He told the *People*: 'As long as Alan is playing and we give him the right type of service to enable him to score we have a good chance. But we must help him. We know he can't do things as an individual, he needs crosses and service. That's up to us and if we don't get it right from the midfield we will pay.'

Newcastle dismally failed to carry out Dabizas' wishes and, with Shearer isolated up front, Alex Ferguson's men steamrollered their way to the second leg of an eventual historic Treble through goals from Teddy Sheringham and Paul Scholes. All in all it was a day to forget for Shearer and co and further doubt was cast about the Newcastle figurehead's uncertain future by a scathing media. The *Independent*'s Glenn Moore wrote: 'Shearer, again starved of service and no longer capable of making chances for himself, looked a disillusioned figure. How he must regret twice turning Manchester United down. There will not be a third chance. Shearer is no longer desired by the major clubs and this presents a problem for him and Gullit. The Dutchman may prefer a more technical player, but cannot sell Shearer for a cut-price fee without alienating the Newcastle support. Shearer, meanwhile, is running out of options to expand a medal collection which contains just one winners' bauble [the 1995 Premiership].'

The other half of Newcastle's forward pairing, Duncan Ferguson, was the subject of similar speculation, suggesting that he was disenchanted with life in the North-East and pining for his former club, Everton.

Later in May, however, Shearer could console him with the fact that he was one of six football luminaries to enter the FA Hall of Fame for his contribution to the Premier League since its inauguration in 1992. He was cast in wax alongside Manchester United's Eric Cantona and Peter Schmeichel, Arsenal's Dennis Bergkamp, Chelsea's Gianfranco Zola and former Newcastle favourite, Les Ferdinand of Tottenham. The super sextet, selected by a panel of experts headed by Sir Geoff Hurst following a nationwide poll, were showcased at an attraction in London which featured interactive displays and footage of classic matches.

With his place in Premier League history cemented, Shearer then sought to put an end to the persistent rumours surrounding his Newcastle future. He signed a contract extension, which would keep him at the club until 2004, when he would end his playing days and seek to enter football management.

Shearer – whose new deal reputedly achieved parity with Duncan Ferguson's £40,000-a-week salary, said he was confident that Newcastle – galvanised by summer signings Kieron Dyer, Alain Goma, Marcelino Elena and Franck Dumas – could improve their Premiership form and gain success in cup competitions. Ruud Gullit said he was thrilled at Shearer's long-term commitment to the Magpies: 'We're all delighted to see him extend his contract. Hopefully everything will go as well as we hope next year and we're looking for a lot of gold from Alan.'

After an injury-hit pre-season, Shearer was ready to roll for Newcastle's opening game of the season and his 100th in the black-and-white stripes, at home to Aston Villa. The Newcastle and England captain endured a torrid start, however, after being controversially shown the red card for the first time in his career for two bookable offences, both for unsporting behaviour. The *Guardian*'s David Lacey reckoned that Shearer was the victim of a serious injustice in a match which Newcastle lost 1–0. He said: 'Shearer's dismissal by Uriah Rennie for two bookable offences on Saturday against Aston Villa has made him as big a victim of injustice as Alfred Dreyfus. Others may be more sceptical. The first red card of Shearer's career followed an earlier booking for catching Villa's Colin Calderwood in the face with a flying elbow when the pair challenged for a high ball, an offence for which another referee might have sent him off. The second offence hardly seemed to be a foul at all, since all Shearer did was put himself between Calderwood and a dropping ball. All right, there was a hint of Shearer backing into the defender but, if every forward who did that was cautioned, Geoff Hurst would never had a career, let alone a knighthood. Bumping and boring has always been part of Shearer's game.'

Shearer asked Rennie to review the decision, but to no avail. 'I challenge anyone to watch on television the incident which got me sent off from any angle and at any speed and if, after total scrutiny, there is the slightest foul then I will accept the decision without further comment,' Shearer said. 'If, however, it is proven beyond all doubt that no foul was committed, then I would hope that something could be done.'

Ruud Gullit was raging at the treatment of his striker and was duly charged by the FA for gross misconduct. 'I've never seen a referee being such an influence as I've seen today, never ever in my whole career,' he had said of Rennie's performance. His and Shearer's moods worsened 48 hours later when Tottenham consigned Newcastle to their second defeat of the season by romping to a 3–1 victory at White Hart Lane.

Despite his frustrating and goalless start to the new campaign, bookmakers Ladbrokes suggested he was still worth a punt after making him 12–1 to be the Premier League's leading goalscorer for the fourth time in his career. The odds were also shortening on Ruud Gullit's Newcastle reign being curtailed in the 1999–2000 season after Newcastle's woeful start to the league season.

The controversial Dutchman sought solace in rekindling his playing career after he registered himself as a player before Newcastle's trip to Southampton – a fortnight before his thirty-seventh birthday. No such comeback materialised, however, but another Newcastle defeat did as, despite the Magpies holding a 1–0 half-time lead, thanks to a penalty from Shearer, they succumbed to a 4–2 drubbing. Three straight defeats left Newcastle propping up the rest of the Premier League in twentieth place and Gullit's position as architect of their fortunes in peril.

The under-pressure Gullit told Sky Sports he was contemplating his future after becoming increasingly dismayed by his expensive side's ailing fortunes: 'I have to think about what I saw today and what I have seen in the last couple of weeks. The thing is this team has great potential and sometimes they are very good and sometimes they are very bad and I cannot understand what is happening. It's very difficult for me, the fans and the television crowd to understand it.'

The Dutchman's resolve was also being sternly tested by a constant media intrusion into his private life and jibes about his girlfriend Estelle's alleged inability to settle in Newcastle. 'When the going gets tough, the tough get going,' sang American crooner Billy Ocean in the mid-1980s and Shearer wholeheartedly embraced his defiant message as Newcastle prepared to get their season back on track with victory over arch-rivals, Sunderland. He was in bullish mood ahead of the two North-East giants' derby confrontation, which had assumed even greater significance in the wake of Newcastle's losing streak. 'It's a big, big game for everyone,' said Shearer in the *Daily Mail*. 'I have a family who are Geordies and if we win it will make their day when they go into work. We must try and get it. As a team, we are in this together.'

The Tyne talisman had to field the inevitable questions about his frosty relationship with his manager. He replied: 'The relationship with the manager is strictly professional. As captain of this football club, all I want to do is to play for Newcastle and give 110 per cent. We all have to get it right. It's not his fault that we are in this situation, it's everyone's fault. This is a big football club, it has big names in it and when things aren't going well it's going to cause a stir.'

Such a response hardly quashed the media murmurings of the pair's strained relations, but irrefutable evidence of their fraught rapport arrived when Gullit stunned Newcastle fans by naming their hero on the bench for the Sunderland match. To compound matters, he stripped Shearer of the club captaincy and handed it to Welsh midfielder Gary Speed. It was fair to assert that Shearer had not been firing on all cylinders in Newcastle's opening four matches – scoring only once. Yet for a proud Geordie like Shearer, a game against Sunderland was seminal in the season and Gullit's decision to prevent him from playing in it was pure torture and the ultimate humiliation for the twenty-nine-year-old.

Former Southampton manager and Shearer's first England Under-21 coach, Lawrie McMenemy, explained to the *Independent* why Gullit's decision was tantamount to professional suicide. He said: 'I knew it was over for Gullit the day he dropped Shearer from the derby with Sunderland. Nowhere, not Glasgow or Milan, does more feeling go into a derby match, and the sight of Shearer on the bench watching a kid from the reserves play the biggest league game of the year, told me that Ruud had no idea about the people he was dealing with. Alan Shearer, at times like that, is Newcastle.'

Teeming rain matched the all-pervasive gloom shrouding St James' Park on the night of the match as Newcastle fans heard the horrifying and barely credible news that their idol would be absent from action, replaced up front by former Darlington player Paul Robinson. Paul Hayward of the *Daily Telegraph* said: 'When the Newcastle United team was read to the crowd at St James' Park on Wednesday night, and Alan Shearer wasn't in it, a fork of lightning flashed across the sky and the rain grew Biblical and stayed that way for the full 90 minutes.

A RUUD AWAKENING

Phewee! As Ruud Gullit discovered this week, you take care when you mess with Shearer. You never know who you might upset.'

Even when the Geordie legions hollered 'Shearer, Shearer' during half-time, their impassioned pleas to their manager to introduce the Newcastle icon into his favourite arena fell on deaf ears. He was eventually brought in at the expense of Robinson on 74 minutes, but was unable to reverse Sunderland's 2–1 advantage.

Cries of 'Gullit out' rang out at the final whistle and police feared that Newcastle fans' anger and frustration at both the result and the Dutchman's perceived dodgy selection policy could spill onto the streets. 'Last night, extra police were drafted onto the streets of Newcastle in anticipation of a possible backlash by fans. But a Northumbria police spokesman said all was relatively quiet an hour after the game ended,' reported the Newcastle *Journal*.

Gullit made matters worse when he stood by his Shearer snub. 'When we brought Alan Shearer on in the second half we lost. What is the conclusion to that?' he said. His decision to replace a legend with Paul Robinson was described as 'totally unbelievable' by BBC pundit Alan Hansen after the match. Rob Hughes of the *International Herald Tribune* predicted that Gullit could not match Shearer in any Tyneside tussle for supremacy. 'For however long, or however short his stay, Gullit has to cope with Shearer, whose contract is long and whose future, no one doubts, is to become manager and messiah. Shearer, you see, is something Gullit could never be: he is a Geordie, a native of this place where soccer is inseparable from the cultural identity,' he said.

There was little surprise on Tyneside when, days later, Gullit tendered his resignation citing the unbearable press intrusion into his private life, his league record reading an indifferent eleven wins, thirteen draws and eighteen defeats. Yet he had also clearly chosen to leave to avoid repercussions from his actions *vis-à-vis* Shearer. Player power, which might have engineered a dressing-room revolt had Gullit remained at St James' Park, swung into action and made the Dutchman's position untenable. Duncan Ferguson confessed that he and Shearer had both made their displeasure at being dropped for the Sunderland match patently obvious the day after. He told the Newcastle club magazine *Scene at St James*: 'It was obvious he was trying to make a point about Alan. But if you make a decision like that, to leave out Alan Shearer against your biggest rivals from down the road, then you've got to win the game if you want to keep your job. He didn't win, but then he had the cheek to tell the media that Newcastle were winning before he sent on Alan and me – the inference being that if he hadn't made those substitutions, Newcastle might well have won. I wasn't having that and I stormed into the manager's office the next morning to let him know that he was bang out of order. The door was still just about on its hinges when I came out – and Alan Shearer was next man in. I think Ruud got the message. He resigned the next day.'

It is self-evident, from this frank testimony and that of other Newcastle stars of that era, that Gullit had, in football speak, 'lost the dressing room' through his treatment of Shearer and other high-profile stars, which was perceived as arrogance and aloofness. Midfielder Kieron Dyer, for instance, told the *People* in November 1999: 'Ruud had a weird style. There were times when he would not come into the dressing room – even after those [bad] results. He would not say anything at all and he'd just let us get changed. That was very strange. I've never come across anything like it.' And Dyer added of Gullit's surprise omission of Shearer for the derby match: 'Everyone in the club was in shock when we found out the team. We all knew from the day before because in training we'd been doing set pieces and Alan was on the opposite team. We just thought the manager must have got the teams mixed up – but that wasn't the case. We tried not to concentrate on it, but it was still an astonishing decision. It wasn't easy to concentrate on the game with all that going on and we lost.' Even Newcastle chairman Freddy Shepherd remonstrated with the dogmatic Dutchman when he dropped Shearer, according to *The Journal* in 2001. Reporting Shepherd's comments during a radio interview with Newcastle legend Bobby Moncur, the newspaper said:

'He [Gullit] said "I'm going to leave him [Shearer] out," and I said, "You can't do it. Believe me, you don't leave Alan Shearer off the bench in a Sunderland derby. If you don't want to play him, that's up to you, but you don't leave him out of the squad. You've got to put him on the bench," and he did put him on the bench. But saying that, I think Ruud had left the game before. I think he would have loved to have gone out on a high by beating Sunderland, but I still think even if we had beaten Sunderland he would have left.

'I think he would have said, "I've beaten Sunderland, I've lost the players, I've got them on the bench, I've gone." I think that's what would have happened.'

Shearer's close friend and former team-mate, Rob Lee, has suggested that Gullit's fatal error was to try to usurp Shearer, a Newcastle idol, as the darling of the St James' Park faithful. Even people unconnected with Newcastle United sensed that all was not well between Shearer and Gullit; diners at the pair's favourite restaurant, the Italian eatery Uno's, have alleged that the estranged duo were often seen scowling at one another while eating at different tables.

To his credit, Shearer has been fairly restrained when discussing his views on Gullit and the controversial Dutchman's spell on Tyneside. He has been quite open about the fact that his astonishing demotion to the bench for the Sunderland match was 'the lowest point of my career', but has often resisted the temptation to seek vicious verbal retribution on his former manager in the press. He has, however, admitted in several interviews that the pair never 'saw eye-to-eye' and that he was disgusted by Gullit's treatment of senior players like Rob Lee. He also found Gullit's aloofness, compared to the harmonious relationships he enjoyed with Kevin Keegan and Kenny Dalglish, difficult to accept. Shearer even went a step further prior to Newcastle's FA Cup semi-final with Chelsea in 2000, when he disclosed that had Gullit remained manager 'a week longer' than he had, he would have been 'a yard behind' his friend, Rob Lee, in the queue to exit St James' Park.

Gullit, in stark contrast, has verbally attacked Shearer on a number of occasions since the undistinguished climax to his Newcastle career, clearly blaming his bête noire for playing a pivotal part in his demise. In March 2004, for example, in an interview with the *News of the World* he branded Shearer 'a rotten apple' and 'the most over-rated player I have ever seen'. Gullit added: 'I knew a player like him would score a lot of goals. But also that he was not going to win trophies for you. He thinks about himself all the time. It's always about his goals, and not about the team. I knew he was that kind of player all along, so I knew that we had to change if we were to succeed. I needed to change the way that Alan Shearer played, but he didn't want to change. In fact, he made it plain he didn't want to play for me... The problem was that he had so much power. It became a battle – and in the end, a battle I could never win.'

Yes, Ruud, Newcastle was never big enough for the both of you...

CHAPTER NINE

Saved by a White-haired Knight-to-be

He may not have been a knight in name in September 1999, but when ex-England boss Bobby Robson replaced Ruud Gullit as Newcastle manager, he might as well have been riding a white charger and wearing a gleaming suit of armour as far as Alan Shearer was concerned.

During a cataclysmic period in his career, the disaffected Shearer's appetite for goals, playing and maybe even life itself had been eroded throughout the Dutchman's wretched reign on Tyneside. He had suffered the shame of being sent off for the first time in professional football and the devastation of being left to languish on the bench for the un-missable match against Sunderland at St James' Park.

Age and injuries had wearied him, as a glorious career seemed irreversibly fixed on a moribund downward spiral, with a move from Newcastle looking an eminent possibility.

Shearer was comforted somewhat when Ruud Gullit bit the proverbial bullet, but was then left in limbo while he, Martin O'Neill,

Glenn Hoddle and a host of other renowned managerial figures were all touted as possible successors to the Dutchman.

Yet into the breach stepped an affable, sixty-six-year-old Geordie, born fifteen miles away from Newcastle in Sacriston, who was desperate to revive the fortunes of his hometown club and lifelong passion.

Arise, Sir Bobby!

On returning to his North-East roots and taking charge at Newcastle, Bobby Robson immediately perceived that urgent remedial work was required to resurrect Tyneside's God, aka Alan Shearer, whose abject misery continued in the first game post-Gullit when Newcastle suffered a 5–1 thrashing at Manchester United. He recalls in his autobiography, *Farewell but not Goodbye*, that the once-deadly marksman looked a shadow of his former self when he first met him in September 1999: 'Alan had lost his movement. He had become a static player, standing with his back to goal. Alan was running across the face of the [penalty] box – 15 yards in one direction and 15 yards in the other. He was making lateral runs, waiting for the ball to come to his feet. He'd lost the spins and turns and the old dynamism. I could see it straight away.'

Robson goes on to say that he believed that Shearer was young enough to recapture the gifts that had made him great, encouraging him to increase his mobility and tug opposing defenders hither and thither as he had done in his pomp. In all other aspects of his character, Shearer was as exemplary a role model as ever, the former Newcastle boss acknowledges: 'I realised very quickly that he was an exceptional guy with a good character, nice to be with and good on the training ground every day. Punctuality, professionalism, attitude in the changing room, team meetings, on the bus, in restaurants – Alan scored ticks in all these boxes; you name it, he was top. I've never met a better guy. He was a fighter and brave, and would empty his physical locker for you, however hard the game.'

SAVED BY A WHITE-HAIRED KNIGHT-TO-BE

Shearer repaid the compliment when he recognised Robson's saviour-like qualities during a BBC Radio programme to commemorate his manager's seventieth birthday in February 2003: 'I was down in the dumps here when he [Robson] came to Newcastle. I would have had to leave, that's how bad it was,' he said. 'I was playing in a certain way that wasn't good for the team and wasn't good for myself. He came in and spotted that and analysed me. He had a chat with me and he changed me around. He saved my career in a way, because I wasn't playing well at the time.'

Robson's influence on Newcastle was immediate, despite a 1–0 loss away to Chelsea in his first game, as his infectious enthusiasm and father-figure friendliness revivified Shearer and his team-mates.

CSKA Sofia of Bulgaria were dispensed with in the UEFA Cup, 4–2 on aggregate, and then, in Robson's first match in charge of Newcastle at home, the Great Redeemer's remarkable transformation of his struggling side was crystallised in 90 minutes of pure bliss for the Toon Army and Alan Shearer. Newcastle hammered Sheffield Wednesday 8–0 in electrifying fashion, in a performance which unleashed a raging torrent of goals – including five in total from Shearer.

The fantastic five-star show, which included two penalties, was a Newcastle player's best individual tally since 1946, when Len Shackleton scored six times in a 13–0 demolition of Newport County. Such a stunning return to form for Shearer ranked alongside Shackleton's sorcery and ensured that, if it hadn't been already, his name was etched into Geordie folklore alongside stellar Newcastle strikers of the past, such as Hughie Gallacher and Jackie Milburn. His marvellous goal haul, the most he had ever achieved in one match, meant that he became only the second player in Premiership history to score five goals, emulating the feat of Manchester United's Andy Cole against Ipswich in 1995.

Shearer was understandably jubilant at having made such a

blistering return to the goal trail. He said: 'I've never scored four goals in a match before, never mind five. Bobby said to me at half time that if I got six he'd buy me a Mars bar. I'll have to get my own now. The gaffer has put a smile on everybody's face in training again. There is a mutual respect there between the two of us, which is very, very important. He is down-to-earth, he is genuine and he is honest.'

There was further delight for Shearer when he was reunited with his former Blackburn team-mate, Kevin Gallacher, bought by Robson to provide much-needed pace and unselfish running to Newcastle's forward line. Once again, it proved a masterstroke by the old master, as in his first match alongside Gallacher, a rejuvenated Shearer plundered two goals as Newcastle downed North-East rivals Middlesbrough at St James' Park 2–1 in early October.

Shearer's partnership with gangly forward Duncan Ferguson was even more propitious and a fearsome weapon in Newcastle's armoury on their day. Indeed, even though injury conspired to limit them to sixteen appearances together, they shared thirteen goals between them in the 1999–2000 season. Manchester United witnessed at first hand how devastating the pair could be in harness when Shearer scored twice and Ferguson lashed in a brilliant volley in Newcastle's superb 3–0 victory over the champions in February.

It was also in February that Shearer committed himself fully to Newcastle when he signalled his intent to retire from England duty at the end of the forthcoming European Championships. And his club performances continued to be of the highest order, including a double strike in the 2–2 draw with Leeds at St James' Park in April, prompting Elland Road boss David O'Leary to exclaim: 'I wouldn't mind Shearer in my side. For a lad who was written off six months ago, he's not bad. I think he's quality and, while he might not be what he was, there are not many better.'

Shearer signed off his and Newcastle's encouraging league campaign

– which saw the Geordies finish in eleventh place after being in dire relegation trouble when Bobby Robson joined in September 1999 – in fine style when he scored his thirtieth goal of the campaign and the 300th of his career in the 4–2 win over Arsenal at St James' Park. 'Same old Shearer – always scoring', sang the Toon Army, before belting out lusty verses of 'There's only one Bobby Robson'.

If two ditties ever defined resurgent Newcastle's season, these were them.

A sensational season on a personal level for Shearer was, naturally, interspersed with moments when he was targeted by the boo-boys. Yet leaping to his defence time and time again was the comforting figure of Bobby Robson, who was always quick to throw a sympathetic arm around Shearer's shoulders when his striker came under fire. A particular instance of this came in late November, when Watford fans subjected Shearer to vicious abuse during their side's 1–1 draw at Vicarage Road with Newcastle. Robson told the *Daily Mirror* that he was anxious to ensure that Shearer did not crack under the ferocious flak he was often subjected to. 'It is me in danger of losing my rag rather than Alan, who is always so calm, cool and collected', said Robson. 'But however professional you are, anybody might buckle under the sort of abuse which is being hurled in Alan's direction and that is something we need to guard against. I will be having a quiet word with Alan to push home the message about how much he is appreciated by everybody in Newcastle, including directors, fans and myself.'

There was encouragement in Europe for Shearer as well, as Newcastle progressed to the third round of the UEFA Cup, before narrowly succumbing to classy Italian side Roma 1–0 on aggregate. They also exited the League Cup at the third-round stage, losing 2–0 to First Division outfit Birmingham, a game in which Shearer missed a 3rd-minute penalty. But the FA Cup again proved fertile territory for Newcastle, who had been beaten finalists in both 1998 and 1999.

ALAN SHEARER

With holders Manchester United opting to head to Brazil to participate in the World Club Championship, a repeat of this achievement looked promising for Newcastle. Indeed, the Magpies spectacularly hurtled along the road to Wembley at breakneck speed, as Shearer scored twice in a 6–1 romp over Tottenham in the third-round replay, before Sheffield United received similarly ruthless treatment when Newcastle brushed the Blades aside 4–1 in the fourth round.

In the fifth round, Shearer returned to his old stomping ground, Ewood Park, as Newcastle were paired with Blackburn. Prior to the game, Rovers boss Tony Parkes had urged his side's fans not to barrack Shearer, for fear of reprisal from the irresistible force that had propelled Blackburn to championship glory in 1995. Yet Parkes' pleas were not heeded and a geed-up Shearer responded with a two-goal fusillade that demonstrated emphatically to Rovers' fans the gross stupidity of their actions. 'An exuberant Shearer went down on one knee and pointed extravagantly at the Blackburn supporters in a way that would not have not been out of place in a 1970s discotheque. As an incitement to fury you could not imagine him being more provocative, but if supporters will berate, they can hardly complain when they get something back in response,' was Guy Hodgson of the *Independent*'s description of Shearer's reaction to his opening goal.

Shearer admitted that he was disappointed to have been on the receiving end of such a hostile reception from the Rovers support, given that he had been instrumental in their club's recent success, although he acknowledged that the treatment he received mirrored that of any away ground he visited. Shearer and co then celebrated Bobby Robson's sixty-seventh birthday in style by overcoming plucky Tranmere Rovers, 3–2 at Prenton Park in the sixth round to earn a semi-final showdown with Chelsea at Wembley. He and his team-mates were eager to erase past disappointments at Wembley, where no

Alan's faithful fans watch their hero in action at St James' Park.

In 2001, he received Honorary Freedom of the City when he was awarded the Freeman of Newcastle award.

Above: Alan's goal-scoring ability has never faltered. He was presented with another award for scoring 100 goals for both Blackburn Rovers and Newcastle United.

Below: A proud father leads his daughters, Holly and Chloe, onto the hallowed St James's Park turf.

Awarded an OBE for his services to football, he proudly collects the award at Buckingham Palace with his wife Lainya and daughters Holly and Chloe.

Above: Having sensationally left Shearer out of the tense Tyne-Wear derby between Newcastle and rival side Sunderland, it wasn't long before Ruud Gullit parted company with Newcastle United.

Below: Kenny Dalglish managed Alan at both Blackburn Rovers and Newcastle United.

Above: Sir Bobby Robson is another manager whose decision to leave the Newcastle captain on the bench seemed to spell the end of his career on Tyneside.

Below: Graeme Souness (*centre*), during his difficult reign at St James' Park. Just days after Shearer announced he was staying for another season, Souness had to conduct a press conference with his players, Kieron Dyer and Lee Bowyer *(left and right respectively)*, after the pair fought on the pitch during a match.

Above: When Craig Bellamy publicly spoke out against manager Graeme Souness, he also fell out with Shearer. The pair are pictured in training together before Bellamy's sharp exit from St James' Park.

Below: Having started his footballing days at Wallsend Boys Club, Alan often returns to lend a helping hand.

Above: Film stardom is always an option following his appearance in the football flick, *Goal!*.

Below left: Royal of the Rovers... Michael Owen and Alan Shearer flank Newcastle's latest signing – Camilla, Dutchess of Cornwall at St James' Park!

Below right: Alan receives his honorary degree in Civil Law from Northumbria University.

North-East league team had triumphed since Sunderland's shock success over Leeds in 1973.

Despite his club's continued FA Cup woes, the competition had been productive for Shearer, netting sixteen goals in only twenty ties for Newcastle. There was to be no seventeenth strike, however, as Newcastle's Wembley hoodoo persisted after two Gus Poyet goals to one from Robert Lee in reply enabled Chelsea to book their place in the final along with Aston Villa.

The 2000–01 season seemed pregnant with exciting potential for Shearer. He had bowed out of the international arena with England in the European Championships and, unencumbered by this extra burden, he was expected to be even more lethal than ever for Newcastle. Bobby Robson suggested as much to the *Daily Mirror*: 'He's thirty years of age, he's done his duty and playing centre-forward is the hardest position of all. He needs a break, which he didn't get last year. He didn't miss a single match for Newcastle or England, and I only took him off once when we were losing a cup-tie with ten men. It's time to let the young ones have a go now, like [Andy] Cole, [Robbie] Fowler and [Kevin] Phillips, and it's great for us that he's rid himself of that tension and pressure which goes with being England captain. Being selfish, we will benefit from him concentrating on Newcastle.'

Bobby Robson had purchased £7 million forward Carl Cort to supplement the formidable attacking talents of Shearer and to replace Duncan Ferguson, who had made a £3.75 million move back to his spiritual home, Everton. Argentinian midfielder Christian Bassedas and striker Daniel Cordone had also pledged their futures to Newcastle, while the likes of defenders Steve Howey, Lionel Perez, Alessandro Pistone and midfielder Silvio Maric headed for pastures new.

Bobby Robson had vowed to buy the best of British talent available where possible, although his self-confessed disinclination of cut-price foreign players seemingly did not extend to South America, from where Chilean midfielder Clarence Acuna was another addition in October.

Battle-scarred Shearer, however, would have to contend with another frustrating season punctuated by injury, a fate that would bedevil a number of other Newcastle stars throughout the campaign. He had developed tendinitis in his knee as England prepared for the European Championships and what started as an irritating niggle would develop into a career-threatening complaint. Nevertheless, Newcastle approached the new season with renewed zeal, following Bobby Robson's constructive first season in charge as consolidation of a Premiership place had been achieved.

When Kevin Keegan resigned as England manager in September, Robson was reportedly refused the chance by Newcastle chairman Freddy Shepherd to once again manage his country. Newcastle would also be playing in a re-developed, state-of-the-art St James' Park, which now ranked among the best football arenas in Europe with a new capacity of 52,173, catering for the overwhelming demand among Geordies to see live football. Shearer and his team-mates were also offered a lucrative carrot to improve on their efforts of the 1999–2000 season and achieve prestigious and money-spinning Champions League football.

The *Sunday Mirror* reported: 'The Geordies are willing to fork out a staggering £6 million in bonuses and incentives in a bid to return United to a competition they last graced in the 1997–98 season. That cash bonanza would be shared among manager Bobby Robson, his coaching staff and a twenty-two-man first-team squad. The Champions League windfall would mean that their top earner – England captain Alan Shearer – can expect a £250,000 bonus on top of his £2 million-a-year salary if Newcastle finish in the top two.'

Yet it looked as though all the cash hand-outs in the world would prove fruitless for Newcastle when confronted with the might of

Manchester United, who convincingly beat them 2–0 at Old Trafford on the opening day of the season.

However, a string of wins propelled the Magpies to the top of the Premiership tree in early September, a perch procured by a 2–0 victory at Coventry, which included another marvellous milestone for Alan Shearer. His penalty for Newcastle's opening goal was his 200th Premier League strike in only 275 games.

Bobby Robson led the tributes to his history-making striker after the match. 'That's twenty goals a year for ten years,' said Robson in the *Independent*. 'It's a phenomenal effort and he hasn't finished yet. And don't forget he missed two years because of injuries.'

For Shearer, the milestone represented a double delight as it came hot on the heels of the birth of his third child, Will, who weighed 8lb 6oz. The *Sun* quoted the delighted father, who admitted he had burst into tears when he realised the bundle of joy was a little boy, as saying: 'Mother and baby are doing well and life doesn't get any better than this. I am on a real high and if I can go out and score a goal for Will at Coventry, that would be marvellous.' He added: 'We picked Will because it is a good, strong Geordie name. Now we have a boy and two girls – Chloe, seven, and Hollie, five – and there are no more planned.'

The Press Association revealed that one opportunistic punter stood to benefit from Shearer's new arrival. 'A football fan stands to win £125,000 if Alan Shearer's newborn son ever plays for England. Builder Keith Loft, forty-two, has bet £500 at odds of 250–1 that the former England captain's son will follow in his father's footsteps. Mr Loft, of York, will collect his winnings if Shearer junior wins a senior international cap. William Hill spokesman Graham Sharpe said: "This is the biggest bet I can recall being placed on a child growing up to achieve sporting glory."'

The exotically named Lomano Lua-Lua, a Zaire-born striker, was the next player to join Bobby Robson's revolution when he signed from Second Division Colchester. His signing meant that Robson now had two more attacking threats at his disposal – including Carl Cort – as foils for Shearer and Kevin Gallacher.

Newcastle's Premiership campaign continued promisingly as autumn descended, with a 3–1 win at Middlesbrough, including a goal from Shearer. Meanwhile, Bobby Robson was already looking over his shoulder at his likely successor – his treasured forward. He remarked in the *Sun*: 'I think Alan has got sufficient qualities in him to be a very promising manager – and in due course a very good one. He has a way with people – this leadership quality, which makes people respect him. They look at him and listen to what he says. They get on with him and like him – he's a good guy to be with.'

But Shearer's unstinting brilliance in the Premiership meant that managerial ambitions would be thrust on the backburner for a few years yet. He scored the 100th goal for Newcastle under Bobby Robson's tenure while grabbing a brace for his team in a 2–1 victory over Ipswich Town at St James' Park in November. However, there would be an agonising repeat of Shearer's most depressing low in football when Sunderland scored their second successive 2–1 victory at St James' Park.

Shearer may have started up front this time, unlike the 1999 nightmare game which he witnessed from the substitutes' bench, but he endured more misery when he uncharacteristically missed a penalty, thwarted by a wonderful save from Sunderland goalkeeper Thomas Sorensen. Losing to Sunderland and being unable to convert with his normal expertise was a shattering double blow to Shearer, as observed by the *Journal*'s Simon Rushworth: 'Had Alan Shearer missed his own wedding, one feels he would have forgiven himself over time. Missing a penalty against Sunderland is another matter altogether and watching United's proud Geordie captain disappear down the St James's Park tunnel, it was as if a dark cloud had enveloped this normally pugnacious personality. Even in defeat Shearer inevitably comes out fighting, but his mournful expression on the full-time whistle, minutes after Thomas Sorensen had beaten away a regulation spot-kick, betrayed the true magnitude of just what "that miss" really meant.' The *Independent*'s Tim Rich revealed that Sunderland had proved a 'bogey' team for Shearer throughout his professional career: 'For all his Geordie upbringing, which on New Year's Day 1985 saw him walk several miles to see Peter Beardsley put a hat-trick past the old enemy, it is a fixture that has provided Alan Shearer with painful memories. Of his 266 career goals, only one has come against Sunderland and, with nine minutes remaining of a contest awash with drama, if not great football, he failed to convert the penalty that would have given Newcastle a draw.'

There was more pain to ensue for Shearer, despite Newcastle's 2–1 win over Liverpool at St James' Park, as he aggravated a back injury. Then, at the start of December, he suffered a recurrence of the tendinitis that had plagued him during Euro 2000, which led to Bobby Robson describing his stricken star as 'a flogged horse' and suggesting that Shearer would miss at least a month of action.

Shearer watched on helplessly as Newcastle were ripped apart by rampant Arsenal, who crushed the Geordie side – also deprived of Carl Cort due to hamstring trouble and Kevin Gallacher who had injured his calf – 5–0 at Highbury. He was also stung by Neil Lennon's residual bitterness at Shearer's fierce challenge on him in 1998, which whipped up a storm of controversy, given that it appeared that the Newcastle man had kicked the Leicester midfielder in the face. Lennon told the *News of the World*: 'I will never forget what he did to me. It was certainly the worst challenge I have ever had made on me by a fellow professional footballer. What really rankled with me then, and still does, is the fact that not once did he contact me privately to say sorry.'

Thanks to a steroid injection, Shearer braved the pain barrier and returned for Newcastle's 2–1 home win over Bradford City in mid-

December. He also expressed his support for under-pressure boss Robson, whose managerial magnificence had steered Newcastle to safety the season before but was now under severe examination following a series of indifferent results. Shearer told the *Daily Express*: 'There is no doubt he is the man for the job, the right man to lead us. And no one should ever doubt or underestimate what Bobby has done for this club. He has proven his worth many times over. And to turn things around the way he did last season was a near miracle. We are currently seventh in the league and, taking into account all the injuries we have had this season, it would be a fantastic achievement if we could finish one place better off in sixth and get that place in Europe. It would be great for a club of the size and stature of Newcastle.'

Yet while Robson had rescued both Shearer and Newcastle from oblivion in 1999, usurping Manchester United and becoming Premiership champions was a task on an altogether more daunting scale – especially given that the Tyneside club was £19 million in debt and scrabbling around for loan signings. Newcastle midfielder Gary Speed had his doubts about whether Shearer would ever be rewarded for his greatness with a trophy for Newcastle. 'It would be such a shame if the greatest striker of his generation didn't manage to win the Premiership with the club he loves,' said Speed in the *Mirror*. 'If anyone deserves to win a championship medal with Newcastle United then it's Alan Shearer, but at the moment we're not realistically challenging the likes of Manchester United and Arsenal. I know that Alan won the Premiership when he was at Blackburn, but to win it with Newcastle would mean so much more to him.'

His injured knee was a more pressing concern for Shearer, however, as his worst fears that he needed an operation were finally confirmed in late December. Once he had survived this latest phase of surgery, he pencilled in a March comeback after resuming training in early

January. However, it then emerged that he would require further medical work, this time to remove his tonsils!

In Shearer's stead, Kieron Dyer and nineteen-year-old Shola Ameobi formed a fresh and fervent makeshift attacking force, which led Newcastle to a 2–1 win over Leeds United and a 1–1 draw with Manchester United at St James' Park. These two encouraging results enabled Newcastle to finish the year 2000 in sixth place and well situated to mount a challenge for a Champions League place.

But for Shearer and friends there would be no visit to Cardiff's impressive Millennium Stadium in the first year of the venue's replacement of the demolished Wembley for the FA Cup final. Aston Villa shattered Newcastle's FA Cup dreams with a 1–0 victory at Villa Park in a third-round replay. In the Worthington Cup, meanwhile, Birmingham City bundled Newcastle out of the competition for the second successive season at the fourth-round stage.

Their anguish was assuaged slightly when Shearer broke the heartening news to Bobby Robson that he was on course to return from injury one month ahead of schedule, at the end of February. However, according to the *Sunday Express*' John Richardson, the biggest name in world football was coveting Shearer's predatory talents: 'Newcastle United skipper Alan Shearer has been sounded out about a sensational move to Real Madrid. Having retired from international football and now at the age of thirty, it seemed that his predatory talents were no longer the envy of top European teams. But *Express* Sport can reveal that Real Madrid have been in contact with Shearer's representatives over the possibility of him leaving Tyneside. It is understood that the European Cup holders are poised with an offer of around £10 million once the uncertainty of the transfer market is resolved.'

Meanwhile, Newcastle's ongoing ability to cope without him was a source of much amazement and admiration for Shearer in early

February. 'The lads have done very well. To have been seventh with everything that has gone on is a fantastic achievement,' he said in the *Daily Star*. 'Considering what's happened – injuries, suspensions, even a player going missing – it has been a remarkably good season. Whatever problems we've come up against, we've beaten them and kept our hopes of European qualification alive. Without the injuries, I think we would have been in the top six.'

Shearer, the self-styled courageous comeback king, returned to lead Newcastle's forward line as predicted on 24 February against Manchester City at St James' Park, but his return coincided with a disappointing 1–0 defeat. He was then incensed by referee David Elleray's performance during Newcastle's 1–1 draw at Everton in early March. Shearer felt Elleray, a former schoolmaster, had made a grave error of judgement when he awarded Everton a penalty, from which David Unsworth equalised the Newcastle forward's earlier goal. He attempted to remonstrate with Elleray at the end of the match, but was infuriated further when, after hammering on his door, the official chose to avoid any discussion with him. The *Mirror*'s David Maddock detailed the sequence of events: 'In measured tones he [Elleray] requested that Shearer return to the referee's room in half an hour, when the forward had calmed down sufficiently. Then, Elleray did what all smart school kids do when faced with an opponent bigger and more frightening than them ... he legged it! Rule No. 1: the "Scarper". Simple, but effective... The sight of Shearer dutifully returning half an hour later to hammer on the referee's door – only for it to swing slowly open and reveal an empty room – will live far longer in the memory than this insipid match. Asking where the hell Elleray was, Shearer's face was a picture as it slowly dawned on him that the ref had showered and changed in five minutes flat and then left ... and he'd fallen for it. Doh!'

Uncontrollable rage was superseded by unfettered joy when Alan

SAVED BY A WHITE-HAIRED KNIGHT-TO-BE

Shearer received the most prestigious award his city could bestow on him – he was made a Freeman of Newcastle on 9 March. He joined a galaxy of luminaries, such as Nelson Mandela, Sir Bob Geldof and Newcastle legend Jackie Milburn, in achieving the accolade.

For Shearer, who received an illuminated scroll along with fellow Freemen collecting the award including Olympic triple jump champion Jonathan Edwards, seeing his name alongside Milburn's made his 'heart burst with pride'. He told the *Evening Chronicle*: 'To see my name alongside that of Wor Jackie makes it extra special. He is a huge part of Newcastle history, not just Newcastle United history. Therefore to be bracketed with him is my final accolade.'

Shearer and his team-mates, all of whom had been given a day off training to witness the memorable event, attended a gala ceremony at Newcastle's Civic Centre, where the ex-England striker's name was carved on the banqueting hall wall. He added: 'You can't compare anything I've won with this. It's unique for me. I've been excited about it and my family is very proud. It's great that my wife and my parents were there to see it.' Shearer was similarly recognised in 2004 by the area which worships him when the Freedom of the Borough of North Tyneside was bestowed upon him.

He could then justifiably have a claim to another more dubious honour, that of Britain's unluckiest sportsman, when his troublesome knee injury flared up in training. Surely no footballer has been as inured to the cruelly capricious nature of football, which can transform a player's fortunes from ecstasy to agony at any given moment. Beware the ides of March, indeed, Shearer might have bewailed.

Shearer was said to have been 'destroyed' by his latest setback and immediately flew out to America to see top knee specialist Dr Richard Steadman in a bid to put an end to his never-ending niggles amid fears that not only was his season over, but also that his career could be at a ruinous end.

ALAN SHEARER

Legendary Liverpool manager Bill Shankly once opined that 'Football is not a matter of life or death, it's more important than that', yet the great man's words may have appeared as crass when viewed in the context of Newcastle's VIP for the home match with Middlesbrough in mid-March.

American teenager Mark Kintgen's horrific ordeal also thrust Shearer's injury traumas sharply into perspective. A survivor of the Denver massacre, which saw two teenagers go on the rampage at their school, Columbine High, killing their teacher and twelve fellow students, Kintgen had been invited to watch his beloved Newcastle. Kintgen, nineteen, had, according to the *Evening Chronicle*, 'became hooked on Newcastle after watching their match against Liverpool on American TV five years ago'. After watching Newcastle train and receiving a signed shirt from Shearer and his team-mates, he said: 'I think I just liked the shirts. At training this week I spent about ten minutes talking with Alan Shearer, who's really nice, and said "hello" to Kieron Dyer, who's among my favourite players'.

Shearer and Newcastle greeted yet more traumatised transatlantic visitors a month later. A report in the *Evening Chronicle* said: 'Soccer's unluckiest fans finally met their Newcastle United idols this afternoon. Dedicated Jimmy Whithead and his mates have travelled 21,000 miles from the US to follow the Toon – but have so far never seen a game. For each time they arrived on Tyneside, they discovered the match had been postponed. But the group of six, from the Central Park Rangers footie team in New York, finally met Bobby Robson and shook the hand of their hero, Alan Shearer, today'.

By now, shin splints had forced Kieron Dyer onto the sidelines with Shearer and Newcastle's form began to falter, as they slipped to thirteenth place by the end of March. Shearer, meanwhile, was declared one of the symbols of Newcastle, according to a major survey undertaken to establish perceptions of the North-East. The *Journal* reported that the North-East Regional Perception Study sought the views of businesses in the south of England, the USA, Europe and Japan following fears that Newcastle was still saddled with a cloth cap and whippet image. Reporter Nick Woods revealed: 'Of famous people and landmarks, respondents knew of the Angel of the North, the Tyne Bridge, Alan Shearer, Hadrian's Wall, Gazza and Jimmy Nail.' 'It's a Bittersweet Symphony that's life,' sang The Verve in 1997, and this certainly encapsulated Alan Shearer's vacillating existence of black-and-white extremes.

While he awaited a further operation on his injured knee, he received a financial sweetener in the form of a massive loyalty bonus for his commitment to Newcastle. According to the *Sun*: 'Alan Shearer has netted a cool £1 million – just for staying at Newcastle for five years. The huge loyalty bonus kicked in yesterday, giving him a May Day payday to add to his £17 million fortune. It is the icing on the cake of a whopper deal sealed when he joined the Geordies in July 1996 – in a then world-record £15 million transfer from Blackburn. His contract states: "If you are still at the club on 1 May 2001 and not involved in a dispute you will receive a £1 million bonus. You will get this in your pay packet for that month."'

After Shearer underwent do-or-die surgery in America, there were inevitable messages of support and encouragement emanating from St James' Park and sensationalised doom-mongering in the tabloid press about horrific end-of-career scenarios for the wounded hero. Team-mate Shola Ameobi said he was desperate for Shearer to survive his latest injury battle as he felt ill-equipped to assume his mantle just yet. Ameobi articulated his thoughts in the *Journal*: 'I still have a lot to learn from Alan. There's no doubt in my mind that he will continue to defy the critics and make a full recovery from this week's operation. People have tried to write him off before, but he's always bounced back and this time will be no different. As far as I'm concerned, the sooner he comes back the better because he has a quality which the young strikers at the club lack – experience.'

The *People*'s Martin Hardy claimed that Shearer's operation only carried a 60 per cent success rate. But Shearer insisted to the *Sun* that he was not contemplating the 40 per cent chance of failure. He said: 'I know a few doom-mongers have been trying to suggest that this is the end of Alan Shearer's career. Well, they are very wrong. When I come back – not if – there won't be any problem.'

Meanwhile, in mid-May, visitors to the St James' Park Metro station were given the chance to walk in the famous footsteps of Shearer and Bobby Robson. The pair were involved in a Hollywood-style event which saw them set their footprints in concrete at the station which, slowly but surely, was becoming a dedicated shrine to Newcastle United.

Newcastle eventually finished the season in eleventh place in the Premiership, a respectable position given the horrendous catalogue of players' injuries that Bobby Robson had to contend with throughout a troubled campaign. Their endeavours in the league may not have been enough to qualify for the UEFA Cup, but hopes of participating in the competition were kept alive, firstly when they were put forward as the Football Association's representatives for UEFA's Fair Play System. Newcastle subsequently missed out in this draw, in which they had been entered due to their high level of discipline during the 2000–01 campaign, but in June they were handed another European lifeline when they entered the UEFA Cup pre-season qualification tournament, the much-maligned Intertoto Cup, after Spanish club Malaga pulled out.

European football was craved on Tyneside, although Shearer was not particularly enamoured with the Intertoto Cup and neither for that matter were the Newcastle players, who had to cut short their holidays with very little notice in June. Shearer had told the *Daily Star* before Newcastle were confirmed as entrants in the Intertoto: 'I must be honest and say I don't think it's a good move to be in a tournament that starts in mid-July. The last thing you want is to be playing early doors and getting injured.'

Victories over Lokeren of Belgium and German representatives TSV 1860 Munich set up a final showdown with French side Troyes, who scored four goals at St James' Park to earn a 4–4 draw with Newcastle and progress to the UEFA Cup on away goals. Meanwhile, at the start of June, Shearer was named the joint fourth highest-paid player in the Premiership, according to the *Sunday Times*. He, Aston Villa's David Ginola and Chelsea's Marcel Desailly all picked up £40,000 a week, according to the broadsheet, £12,000 behind the league's highest earner, Manchester United's Roy Keane.

Shearer certainly splashed out the cash on a pre-season summer break in his favourite holiday destination of Barbados, where he and his family enjoyed the luxury surroundings with Rob Lee and his wife and children. The *People* claimed that his hedonistic activities during the holiday were putting his career in jeopardy: 'Shearer, wearing a heavy brace after an operation by the world's No. 1 knee expert Richard Steadman in Colorado, took to the waves on a Yamaha Waverunner, a jet-bike that's ridden like a motorcycle and is more powerful than a jet-ski. While it was believed that he was taking it easy with Toon team-mate Robert Lee at the exclusive £1,500-a-night Sandy Lane complex in the Caribbean, Shearer was risking further damage to his busted knee. And last night an expert revealed the potential dangers of riding a machine that can reach speeds of up to 40mph. Solent coastguard chief, Bob Terry, said Shearer could be risking his own life and those of everyone in the water nearby.'

The press coverage of Shearer went from the ridiculous to the sublime in mid-June, however, when it was confirmed that he was to receive an OBE in the Queen's Birthday Honours' List. On hearing of the exalted award, Shearer said: 'In the past year I have captained England, watched my first son being born, received the freedom of the City of Newcastle and have now been awarded this honour by the Queen. I realise that I am a very fortunate man.'

The fated and fêted star admitted to the *Evening Chronicle* that his off-the-field accolades and achievements had mitigated his distress at missing large chunks of the season through injury. 'To be truthful, what's happened outside of football has kept me going. It has given me the lift I required. Away from my job everything has been so wonderful. The contradiction is enormous – a footballer who temporarily can't play and a person receiving so many accolades because he's a footballer.'

The day Shearer picked up his honour at Buckingham Palace – Tuesday, 17 July 2001 – represented one of the summits in his amazing rags-to-riches tale that frequently defied belief. The Press Association reported Shearer's delighted reaction as follows: 'This is the stuff that dreams are made of – to bring your family to the Palace – it's just fantastic,' he said, proudly holding his OBE. 'I'm just so pleased that my family's here – the two girls [Chloe and Hollie] have been really excited for a long time.' Daughters Chloe, eight, and Hollie, six, were at the Palace investiture with the soccer star's wife, Lainya. 'Our little boy, Will, is only ten months old, so he's back in Newcastle with my mum and dad,' said Shearer.

His 'annus mirabilis' outside of football, which saw him festooned with awards, continued in late August when he was honoured by the Variety Club of Great Britain at Newcastle's Civic Centre. His former England managers Terry Venables and Graham Taylor both travelled to witness the event, as did former striking sidekick Les Ferdinand. Shearer's footballing fortunes also acquired a rosier hue when, in early August, he was given the go-ahead to resume full training after visiting Dr Richard Steadman in Paris. An appearance in the Newcastle side for the second leg of the Intertoto Cup final against Troyes was also mooted, although the match against Sunderland in late August was regarded as being a more realistic aim.

When he pulled on a black-and-white jersey again, he would be joined by the speedy but temperamental striker-cum-winger, Welshman Craig Bellamy, whom Bobby Robson had acquired from Coventry City as a replacement for Kevin Gallacher who, along with Daniel Cordone, was released on a free transfer. Robson had also strengthened the supply line to his No. 1 target man with a mercurial left-wing talent that he hailed a heady mixture of 'John Barnes and Ryan Giggs'. Frenchman Laurent Robert was purchased for £10 million from Paris St Germain and, while his willingness to fulfil his defensive responsibilities always left a lot to be desired, his crossing capabilities and potent dead-ball accuracy with his exquisite left boot were indisputable.

The new acquisitions, coupled with the rehabilitation of Shearer, gave Newcastle supporters reason for cautious optimism that Bobby Robson's reconstruction work would at least lay the foundations for European qualification in the season ahead. A 1–1 draw at Chelsea ushered in the new season, although this was merely the prelude to the main event – the North-East derby between Newcastle and Sunderland, arguably the biggest game of the season for Geordie fans, and imbued with extra excitement as it would witness the renaissance of one Alan Shearer.

John Lennon once said that The Beatles were bigger than Jesus and for football-mad chaplain at St Andrew's Church in Newcastle, the Reverend Glyn Evans, Alan Shearer was on a comparable level to the saviour of the world. Rev. Evans planned to hold a service for Newcastle fans prior to the game with Sunderland in the forthcoming season and would encourage them to sing two revised hymns: Instead of 'Shine, Jesus Shine', 'Score, Shearer Score', while 'To God Be the

Glory' would be replaced by 'To Bob Be the Glory' in praise of manager Bobby Robson. Naturally, some Christian leaders found this bizarre blend of Christianity and football distasteful.

Meanwhile, the reborn Shearer had warmed up for the showpiece occasion by scoring twice in a behind-closed-doors match with Hartlepool and duly stepped back onto the hallowed St James' Park turf to thunderous applause from the Toon Army after 74 minutes, when he replaced Shola Ameobi. The miraculous comeback would not be embellished with a goal, though, as Newcastle drew 1–1, thanks to a Craig Bellamy strike. Bellamy told the *Evening Chronicle* that he was more than happy that his contribution was overshadowed by Shearer's reappearance. 'Kieron [Dyer] said to me before the game "you watch when Alan comes on", and then every time he warms up you hear a massive cheer,' said Bellamy. 'And when he came on it was unbelievable – he is Newcastle. To play with him is a massive thing for me. I've been learning the game for so many years, watching players like Alan, so to be on the same park as him is a great bonus.'

Shearer's first start in a Newcastle jersey in more than six months was even more spectacular, as he scored twice in a 4–1 rout of Middlesbrough at the Riverside, precipitating incessant choruses of 'Same old Shearer, always scoring' among the Toon Army legions. With Nolberto Solano and Laurent Robert likened to 'a beautifully balanced, two-winged bird' by Bobby Robson, the Magpies were adding flair and exceptional service to feed Shearer's scoring frenzy.

High-flying Newcastle faced the ultimate test of their soaring progress when Manchester United visited St James' Park in September eager to swoop to conquer. Shearer urged Bobby Robson not to follow Sir Alex Ferguson, who had vowed that the 2001–02 season would be his last at the helm of Manchester United, into retirement. He told the *Mirror*: 'I hope Bobby stays on much longer than the next two seasons. We want him around for a long time yet. We need his experience, because you cannot buy his knowledge on the training ground or what he has achieved in the game. All the players, myself included, learn so much from Bobby on the training ground and we need him to stay.'

Sir Alex Ferguson then, in an extraordinary move, given the pair's past history, toasted Shearer's remarkable resilience and wonderful willpower in surviving his latest horrific injury. 'The amazing thing is that he has had several bad injuries, one at Blackburn when he did his cruciate ligaments then two at Newcastle, first when he broke his ankle and then this year, when he needed an operation on his knee,' said Fergie in the *Express*. 'There were even rumours that he was going to retire some time ago, but he has battled on. It is not easy to overcome long-term injuries. It does have an effect on you. You have to have a certain will about you to overcome them and, in fairness to him, he has shown that will. I suppose he could have retired, but he has always striven to get himself fit again and get back into the game.'

Ferguson's nemesis, who had twice snubbed his advances during his career, remained the bane of the Scot's life when he scored Newcastle's winner with only seven minutes remaining of a classic encounter with United at St James' Park – the adrenaline-pumping Premiership at its best – which ended in a thrilling 4–3 victory for the home side. Shearer also contributed to the downfall of Reds' captain, Roy Keane, in added-on time, when he prevented the irritable Irishman from taking a throw-in. Keane threw the ball at Shearer before lashing out at the Newcastle forward with a punch that did not connect, forcing referee Steve Bennett to brandish a needless red card.

Shearer was bristling with optimism that Newcastle, if they could repeat such exhilarating endeavours throughout the season and rid themselves of persistent injuries, possessed the pedigree to secure European qualification. 'If we can keep everyone fit, if we can get Carl Cort and Kieron Dyer back from long-term injuries, then we'll have a chance of qualifying for Europe, I really believe that,' he said. 'But it's all ifs and buts, it's up in the air at the moment because they are two quality players. We need them fit and a full squad to choose from. I still believe that there are better-equipped sides than us to qualify for the Champions League places. We're not thinking of that, we're on a progression and we're not there yet.'

What was more certain was that Newcastle once again bore all the hallmarks of Kevin Keegan's swaggering and beguiling attack-at-all-costs era, which promised goals galore at either end and verve and entertainment in thick supply. The Geordie Entertainers, led by a terrific trio of offensive weapons – Shearer, Robert and Bellamy – would ensure that the Tyneside faithful would enjoy as satisfying a season as 1996, when championship glory was so nearly their's.

The Tyneside trinity indulged themselves in the 2001–02 season, inspiring Newcastle to some resounding wins both home and away. The name of all three graced the scoresheet in October when Bolton were destroyed 4–0 at the Reebok Stadium. Then league leaders Aston Villa were vanquished with similar disdainful ease in November, when Shearer commemorated his 400th Premiership appearance with a sublime volley in Newcastle's 3–0 home win – his first goal at St James' Park in more than a year. Brian McNally described Shearer's fabulous contribution, which allowed Newcastle to power into third place in the Premiership, thus: 'Shearer stole in unnoticed to cushion a right-foot shot beyond Schmeichel and into the far corner of the net. It was a wonderful volley and one that brought back memories of the veteran hitman's glory days for Newcastle and England. Newcastle produced their best performance since that 4–3 win over Manchester United and looked a smooth, cohesive unit throughout. The blistering pace of Bellamy and Shearer's intelligent positional play wreaked havoc all afternoon.'

Yet, as in Keegan's unforgettable epoch, a less-than-convincing rearguard always made Newcastle look susceptible on their travels, as

SAVED BY A WHITE-HAIRED KNIGHT-TO-BE

West Ham's comfortable 3–0 victory at Upton Park at the end of September bore testimony. The League Cup – which seemed to change name almost as frequently as Shearer hit the back of the net and, in 2001–02, was in its guise as the Worthington Cup – had been something of a non-event for Newcastle in recent seasons. But they reached the quarter-finals of the competition, thanks to Shearer's two goals in a 4–1 thrashing of Ipswich Town, before the Magpies succumbed to Chelsea.

In turn, Shearer celebrated his 100th goal for Newcastle, putting him ninth on the club's all-time-scorers' list – headed by Jackie Milburn, who scored 200 times. It was a tremendous accomplishment by Shearer and a fitting reward for his perseverance and patience during the gloomy days of his injury turmoil. 'It's absolutely fantastic to reach this milestone – there's only a few players who've done it', said Shearer in the *Evening Chronicle*. 'Considering the injuries I've had, not only at Newcastle but also at Blackburn as well, I'm delighted with the record. Jackie Milburn scored over 200, so I can scratch that. I don't think I'll catch him, though hopefully there's a few more. I'm feeling good and sharp and there's no pain in my knee. I'm looking forward to every game. I was just pleased to do it here in front of the Newcastle fans – I did it at St James' Park for the Geordie public.' He went on to cite his favourite Newcastle goal as his first strike for the club – a stunning, long-range free-kick against Wimbledon on 21 August 1996.

Newcastle's attempts to secure the FA Cup also foundered at the quarter-final stage, when Arsenal outgunned the Geordies 3–0 in a replay at Highbury. In late November, Shearer was sent off at Charlton in Newcastle's 1–1 draw for only the second time in his career.

Shearer bitterly contested the decision by referee Andy D'Urso, who reached for his pocket after believing that the Newcastle hero had raised his arm to Charlton player Jonathan Fortune, who collapsed to the ground. D'Urso decided to rescind the red card after reviewing video evidence of the incident.

ALAN SHEARER

Newcastle's inability to win in London had now stretched to a perplexing winless run of twenty-eight games following their victory over Crystal Palace in 1997. The *Evening Chronicle* turned to desperate measures in a bid to bust this jinx, enlisting an exorcist, shipping two stuffed magpies to London and even calling on Newcastle fans to place their hands on an Alan Shearer picture to will their team to a long-awaited win in the capital – all to no avail.

Yet salvation was only a game away when Newcastle emphatically ended their London drought and stormed to the top of the Premiership with a 3–1 victory at Arsenal. Shearer netted a penalty, his first ever goal at Highbury, prompting Newcastle to be installed as 11–1 joint favourites with Chelsea to win the league.

More often than not, Shearer's innate ability to put the ball into the back of the net repeatedly put him in contention for major goal-scoring honours. This was certainly the case in mid-December, as he and Thierry Henry were made 14–1 joint favourites to score the Premiership's 10,000th goal. Shearer already had the satisfaction of scoring the league's 4,000th goal, when he netted for Blackburn against West Ham on 2 December 1995. But his ex-Newcastle team-mate, Les Ferdinand, pipped him to the latest milestone, hitting the jackpot in Tottenham's 4–0 demolition of Fulham. Two breathtaking victories in the vein of Kevin Keegan's thrill-a-minute tenure – a 4–3 win at Leeds and a 3–0 mauling of Middlesbrough at St James' Park – ensured Newcastle continued their table-topping exploits. However, Shearer and his fellow players ended 2001 in second place behind Arsenal, after Chelsea denied them a sixth-successive Premiership win with a 2–1 win at Stamford Bridge.

In any case, European qualification – the goal of the club prior to the start of the season – looked perfectly achievable and a coveted Champions League berth was also looking an increasingly realistic prospect. As 2002 began, Newcastle captain and marathon man Shearer clocked up his 500th league and cup game in football and his 200th appearance for the Tyneside outfit in the clash with Manchester United at Old Trafford. Bobby Robson asserted that his glorious goalscorer was now well and truly one of English football's greatest-ever strikers, a man capable of making yet more history in years to come. He enthused in the *Journal*: 'He has been, and still is, one of the Premiership's elite players and England's premier striker after Lineker. He is a fantastic player, with a great character, and he has the leadership qualities to match it, that's why he stands out. He is one of the game's greats, with more than 300 goals and a strike record of more than one every two games. You have to give credit for that; that's a marvellous career. He's also been a battering ram all his career and missed two full seasons of football through injury. To have survived and to have been so successful speaks volumes for the player's ability and attitude.'

Sadly for evergreen Shearer, his goal was not enough to prevent Manchester United from asserting their dominance over one of their nearest challengers with a clinical 3–1 win. Newcastle were still in the running for English football's Holy Grail, however, for the first time in seventy-five years. The *Express* decided to interview a veteran fan who recalled Hughie Gallacher and co's 1920s brilliance in view of Newcastle's latest championship charge. Ninety-nine-year-old George Harrison said: 'I am a big fan of Bobby Robson and he has done a fine job since coming to Newcastle. And the team plays some lovely football. I prefer the football of today to the old days. It is a lot quicker and there is so much more movement. I also like Alan Shearer a lot – and he has got very good elbows.'

Craig Bellamy's knee injury in February was a shattering blow to Newcastle's quest for success, although prodigious young midfielder Jermaine Jenas augmented Newcastle's clutch of impressive youngsters when he joined the Magpies from Nottingham Forest. Yet while Newcastle's championship aspirations faded in the spring,

ALAN SHEARER

Shearer – a man synonymous with superb statistics – eyed another landmark: his 200th Premiership goal. He duly became the first player to reach this target by scoring Newcastle's third goal in their 3–0 thrashing of Charlton on 20 April. The *Sunday Express*' Niall Hickman put into words Shearer's latest special moment, which rendered many observers speechless and prompted Newcastle players to form a guard of honour to salute him at the end of the match. 'Lua-Lua missed a great opportunity to extend the lead before Shearer had a one-on-one with Kiely six minutes from time. St James' Park held its collective breath again, but the Addicks 'keeper bravely dived at his feet to smother the shot. Those fans who left early fearing Shearer had missed his chance made a shocking error of judgment, as Speed slotted through a terrific pass two minutes from time. Shearer, making his 400th top-flight start, netted his 200th Premiership goal and his twenty-third of an increasingly influential season. Another chapter had been written in the history of a sheet-metal worker's son from Tyneside and, on a day when records were falling all around, maybe the most succinct is the fact that Shearer's strike meant 100 goals for the season for Newcastle.'

Shearer said of his 200-goal mark, which resulted in him being awarded a Barclaycard Merit Award: 'Maybe Robbie Fowler or Michael Owen will have a chance to catch it. But I will still be going for a year or two yet and, hopefully, I can add to the tally.'

Lomana Lua-Lua joined Shearer in the record books as his goal in Newcastle's triumph was the 5,000th his side had scored at St James' Park. The former gymnast performed an astonishing display of about seven or eight somersaults in celebration of his magic moment on a day when Geordies everywhere jumped for joy. Newcastle's victory meant that one point from their final three league games would allow the reinvigorated Shearer to parade his scoring skills alongside the likes of Raul and Del Piero in the Champions League.

SAVED BY A WHITE-HAIRED KNIGHT-TO-BE

At the end of April, the irrepressible maestro struck two equalisers in his club's 2–2 draw at Blackburn to clinch Newcastle's place in European club football's premier trophy in which he had habitually struggled to translate his awesome domestic displays, with only one goal to his name in the competition. An ecstatic Shearer told the *Mirror*: 'It has been an incredible transformation. We were going to the Nationwide League two years ago and now we're in the Champions League. I think the fans deserve it, but so do the players and the manager for turning that round. I wish I could play Blackburn every week! I got a couple here last time and it was a happy hunting ground in the past, but I don't suppose any two goals have meant more than these.'

Shearer's sensational season had sparked repeated calls for his inclusion in England's World Cup squad, but he was insistent that he would be enjoying a summer sojourn rather than a pressure-filled month in Japan and South Korea. West Ham manager Glenn Roeder was one of a multitude of football pundits, players and bosses who believed Shearer was making a mistake. Talking to the *Evening Standard*, he said: 'Alan looks as good as ever to me, if not better. He personifies all that is good about an English footballer. He is strong, both physically and mentally. He is an old-fashioned type of centre-forward, but one who still has no peers in the modern game. I am sure he would be going to Japan if he still wanted to be involved with England but, knowing the sort of person he is, I would think there is absolutely no chance of him changing his mind.'

The endless stream of accolades kept coming for Shearer in May as he was crowned North-East Footballer of the Year and claimed the region's Goal of the Season trophy for his strike against Aston Villa in October, although his twenty-three league goals was one less than Arsenal's Thierry Henry, who scooped the Premiership's Golden Boot award. Yet it later emerged that Shearer felt that Premiership officials had robbed him of Henry's prize. The *Mirror*'s Simon Bird reported in December 2002: 'Last season Shearer finished on twenty-three league goals, one behind Henry. But he is still fuming that the committee robbed him of a perfectly good goal in the 4–3 win over Manchester United at St James' Park, which deflected in off Wes Brown. And the controversy deepened when Henry was allowed one of his goals that was not even on target when he shot. The Newcastle skipper said: "I do feel I should have had it last season, but the dubious goals committee, or whatever they are called, cost me the title. They took that goal off me even though it was going in anyway, and they gave Henry one against Leicester that was off target and deflected in, and they still gave it to him."'

Shearer's final league goal of the season was scored in Newcastle's 3–1 loss at Southampton, for whom former team-mate Matt Le Tissier played his final match. In any case, even though no trophies had been won, Newcastle's fourth place in the Premiership had earned them another crack at the Champions League. The season had been arguably one of Shearer's most satisfying in his career, given both his club's resurgence, the wealth of goals – he scored twenty-seven in all competitions – and the numerous personal attainments he accumulated.

Indeed, it was clear that Newcastle's fortunes were inextricably linked with their talisman, as they seemed to prosper when he did and, as had been the case in the Ruud Gullit era, toiled in perfect symmetry with his slump. Newcastle had re-emerged as a Premiership heavyweight, fuelled by the youthful exuberance of the likes of Dyer and Bellamy, and driven by an ardent desire to entertain and attack. Shearer, meanwhile, had reassumed the mantle of the Premiership's goal king and now had the opportunity to wow a wider audience via Newcastle's meetings with Europe's élite through the Champions League.

In June 2002, the architect of the Newcastle revolution received recognition for his immense contribution to football when he was knighted. In just three years, Sir Bobby Robson had taken a dispirited side from relegation candidates into the promised land of the Champions League, as well as reviving a once-lethal striker who was suffering a seemingly terminal decline. Shearer paid tribute to the newly crowned knight in the *Evening Chronicle*: 'I'm delighted for him and he deserves it. He's been a credit to the game for so many years now. We've all been hoping he would get it, but now he's finally been rewarded, I don't think there's much chance of us calling Bobby "Sir" now. He will still always be "Gaffer" to us, and he wouldn't want it any other way.'

Shearer, meanwhile, enjoyed a restful and relaxing pre-season break, admitting that he had not missed international exertions with England in the World Cup. A refreshed Shearer spelt trouble for Premiership defences, he told the *Daily Star*: 'This has been my first close-season clear of football since I was a kid at Southampton. I've had a relaxing time with my family and friends, with plenty of sunshine and plenty of golf. The only time I missed the England thing was when I came back for training and found that Kieron Dyer had been given an extra ten days off. But seriously, I'm rested and feeling great. I can't wait for the new season to start.' As the *Mirror*'s Michael Scully noted: 'Fitter. Stronger. Happier. More productive. Radiohead surely couldn't have had Alan Shearer in mind when they came up with those lyrics. But they sit well alongside the Newcastle United skipper's name now.'

Newcastle prepared for the forthcoming campaign by purchasing creative attacking midfielder and the 2002 European Young Player of the Year, Hugo Viana, from Sporting Lisbon and highly rated young defender Titus Bramble from Ipswich. However, a casualty list that included Craig Bellamy, who had undergone knee surgery for tendinitis, and Laurent Robert, who had cracked a bone his back, hampered the Tyneside club's build-up. Yet even without the walking wounded, Newcastle defeated Zeljeznicar of Bosnia 5–0 over two legs in the preliminary round of the Champions League to be paired with Juventus, PSV Eindhoven and Dynamo Kiev in the group stage. Newcastle's initial Champions League form followed a similarly woeful pattern to their initial league progress as they fell to three straight defeats – 2–0 away to Dynamo Kiev, in which Craig Bellamy was sent off and banned for three matches for head-butting Tiberiu Ghioane, 1–0 at home to Feyenoord and 2–0 away to Juventus. They found goals at a premium, while their defensive frailties were brutally exposed by the European aristocrats.

No one, not even a scriptwriter working on a film of Alan Shearer's career or the most optimistic member of the Toon Army, could have envisioned such an Houdini-esque reversal of fortunes, however. Three straight victories would propel Newcastle into the second group stage of the Champions League – a scenario that was barely credible following such a disastrous beginning. A 1–0 win over Juventus at St James' Park in October laid the foundations for the startling comeback, although elimination from the European arena still looked the likeliest outcome. Then, thanks to Shearer's unerring accuracy from the penalty spot, coupled with his steely nerve, Newcastle snatched a 2–1 victory over Dynamo Kiev. *The Times*' George Caulkin wrote:

At thirty-two, Shearer knows that he has few chances left. He had described this match as his most important in Europe and, although this was not the blunderbuss performance that had punished Juventus the week before, his pride and perspiration were at the heart of another famous victory. With a second-half penalty against Dynamo Kiev, which he won and converted, Shearer inched his club closer to an extraordinary achievement. By the final whistle, Shearer was baying at the ball-boys, urging them to play for time. In the

SAVED BY A WHITE-HAIRED KNIGHT-TO-BE

heart-thumping circumstances it was understandable, because reaching the second group stage could be worth as much as £10 million to the club and far more in terms of prestige. If that remains an unlikely achievement, it is no longer beyond the realms of possibility.

It was now a case of win or bust for Newcastle as they entered the intimidating cauldron that is Feyenoord's De Kuip stadium in early November. Step forward the inspired Craig Bellamy, returning from six months out with a knee injury, to send the travelling Toon Army into raptures when he scored a last-gasp winner in a pulsating 3–2 victory. In staging such an extraordinary escape act against all expectations and logic, Newcastle became the first-ever side to recover from three consecutive losses in the Champions League and progress to the second phase.

The amazing, heart-stopping triumph represented one of Shearer's most satisfying nights in a football career punctuated by soirées soaked in splendour. Speaking in the *Sun*, he said: 'It was just a great occasion for all of us – the players, the manager, the fans, everyone. It doesn't get any better in terms of the sheer excitement at the way everything happened. What an achievement after losing our first three games – only an idiot would have backed us to qualify after that! We left ourselves with a mountain to climb, but we got there in the end. What we've done ranks right up there with anything I've achieved in the game.'

The Champions League is a constant conveyor belt of quality sides and formidable challenges, which both Barcelona and Inter Milan – two of Newcastle's opponents in the second group stage – perfectly encapsulated. Add the omnipresent German representative, 2002 Champions League finalists Bayer Leverkusen, into the equation and Newcastle knew that they would have to exceed their jaw-dropping heroics of the first phase. They could not have anticipated a more calamitous beginning, however, as Inter Milan ran riot at St James' Park to record a resounding 4–1 victory after Craig Bellamy's propensity for petulance resulted in him being shown the red card after only five minutes. Bellamy had aimed a kick at Marco Materazzi, yet Shearer was involved in his own fracas, which, while not picked up by the referee on the night, was condemned by video evidence after the match. UEFA alleged that he had elbowed Fabio Cannavaro and meted out a harsh penalty – a two-match European ban.

Shearer vehemently protested his innocence and insisted that he, too, had been subjected to illegal treatment from the Italians throughout a stormy encounter. He later admitted that the television images did portray a punishable act, although he was adamant that it had not been deliberate.

If the task Newcastle performed in negotiating the first phase of the competition was on a par with an unenviable uphill struggle, they would now have to perform the football equivalent of scaling Mount Everest if they were to survive in Europe beyond the second group stage. Denuded of the services of Bellamy and Shearer for the trip to Barcelona meant that a backs-to-the-wall, larcenous triumph would be required in the Nou Camp if Newcastle, who were peering over the precipice at Champions League oblivion, were to stave off the slick Spaniards.

As it turned out, Newcastle were unable to withstand the classy Catalans, who made it an unhappy return to his former club for Sir Bobby Robson by prevailing 3–1. When the Champions League resumed in February 2003, Newcastle hinted that they might be on the verge of staging another European 'get-out-of-jail' act when they comprehensively overcame Bayer Leverkusen 3–1 in Germany. And, in the return game at St James' Park a week later when Newcastle replicated this scoreline, the Germans felt the full force of Alan

SAVED BY A WHITE-HAIRED KNIGHT-TO-BE

Shearer's pent-up frustration at being prevented from spearheading his side's Champions League bid when he plundered a superb hat-trick – his first in Europe and the fifteenth of his professional career. He was also at his inspirational best when he twice put plucky Newcastle ahead at the San Siro, only for indomitable Inter Milan to deny the Geordies a memorable victory with two equalisers. Then Barcelona ended Newcastle's exhilarating European voyage when they attained a clinical 2–0 win at St James' Park in March.

Shearer and Newcastle may have been eliminated, but they had left an indelible imprint on the Champions League after some rousing, seat-of-your-pants performances that were full of dash and daring, vim and vigour, and courage and resolve. He admitted he was buoyed by his young side's rapid improvement when faced with, what had been on paper, more accomplished outfits. He told the *Observer*: 'You could see some of our young players growing up at the San Siro (against Inter Milan). It's called accelerated learning. Playing at the highest level quickens your development. If I played golf with Seve Ballesteros every day I'm sure I would improve more quickly than if I played against my missus.

Shearer, too, had demonstrated that, even at the venerable age of thirty-two, he could still mix it with continental class acts such as Kluivert and Vieri and, at his imperious best, he was as good a match-winner as any in Europe. Sadly, Newcastle's domestic cup displays looked horribly inadequate when juxtaposed with their exciting European endeavours. Wolves upset the odds to send Shearer and his under-performing team-mates tumbling out of the FA Cup in the third round, edging an enthralling game 3–2, while they exited the Worthington Cup at the same stage when Everton beat them at St James' Park.

In the Premiership, meanwhile, Newcastle recaptured the swash-buckling form of the previous season in the Premiership opener, when they overwhelmed West Ham 4–0 at St James' Park, with the ubiquitous Shearer unsurprisingly adding his name to the scoresheet. Shearer had never before scored in Newcastle's opening match of the season and the awe-inspiring way in which he rectified this was demonstrable evidence of his unparalleled forward powers as he lay down the gauntlet to other Premiership strikers, according to the *Northern Echo*'s Steven Baker: 'An unerring swing of the right boot sent the ball fizzing into the back of the West Ham United net and Shearer raced away, arm aloft, to take the acclaim of his adoring public. Two minutes later, Shearer was being booked for what could politely be termed a "striker's tackle" on Trevor Sinclair. That vignette summed up the tireless Newcastle captain's evening, as he laid down a challenge to the pretenders to his crown as the greatest striker in Premiership history. Thierry Henry, Ruud van Nistelrooy, Michael Owen et al might lay claim to the title of English football's most deadly marksman, but as he began his sixteenth season as a professional yesterday, Shearer underlined the threat he will pose to the game's stingiest defences as he defies his advancing years.'

However, by September, Newcastle had slumped to just one place off the bottom of the Premiership after a rash of defensive errors saw them ship goals on a consistent basis. Bobby Robson sought to address this defensive fragility by swooping for Leeds' accomplished young England defender, Jonathan Woodgate, during the January transfer window for £9 million.

Shearer would prosper even when Newcastle struggled, however, chalking up another notable record during the season, scoring his 300th league goal, aptly enough at his old club, Blackburn, in Newcastle's 5–2 defeat in mid-October. Blackburn manager Graeme Souness was effusive in his praise of this striker par excellence. He told BBC Sport: 'I'd like to say how wonderful it is that Alan has scored his 300th goal and where else but here? We should remember what he gave to this club. He's the greatest English centre-forward that I've ever seen. There is not a single bigger reason than him for Blackburn winning the Premiership. I knew he would score today, I thought we might have to score twice to win the game, but maybe not three. Nobody should score 300 goals at this level, it's ridiculous.'

At the end of November, another fantastic feat was added to Shearer's burgeoning collection of individual milestones when he thumped in a scorching free-kick to score his 100th league goal for Newcastle in the 5–3 loss at Manchester United. Yet his side's shoddy defending once again took the gloss off this immense achievement, which saw him emulate the feats of Tom McDonald in 1931, with whom he shared sixth place in Newcastle's top-ten league goalscorers' chart, led by Jackie Milburn with 177 goals. Not only was Shearer acclaimed as a great goalscorer, but his aptitude for scoring great goals was another facet of his superlative capabilities. A sweetly struck, venomous 25-yard volley in Newcastle's 2–1 win over Everton in early December was his best goal for the club, according to manager Sir Bobby Robson. In an interview with the *Northern Echo*, he said: 'I don't think Alan has hit a better shot in the past and I don't think he'll ever hit a better one than that. It was absolutely perfect – a thunderous shot. He scored a very good free-kick at Manchester United last week and I liked his volley against Aston Villa last season. But you won't see anything better than that because it was a perfect strike. It was a blur as it went past the goalkeeper.'

The wonder goal cemented Newcastle chairman Freddy Shepherd's belief that Shearer could now be called the greatest player in the club's history in the same week that Sky commentator Martin Tyler labelled him the best-ever Premiership striker. 'Alan Shearer has been everything we hoped he would be and more,' Shepherd remarked to the *Evening Chronicle*. 'His goals record speaks for itself but, you name it, he's got it. His all-round character and skill are amazing. And he has been a captain fantastic for us. Certainly, when the chips are down, you can rely on Shearer to roll his sleeves up and we could not ask any more from him.'

Shearer admitted that his enduring brilliance had prompted him to consider playing on beyond the end of his contract, which was due to expire in June 2004. 'At the moment I don't think it will be a problem to play like this for another eighteen months, and I might do another year after then,' he admitted to the *Northern Echo*. 'I'll judge it nearer the time. I decide how I feel at the beginning of every season. If I feel I have another season in me, I'll give it a go. The advice everyone gives you is to play for as long as you can. Everyone can't be wrong, so you'd be a mug not to listen to them. I'll play for as long as I possibly can.'

Indeed, Shearer was widely expected to sign a two-year extension to his current deal in the summer of 2003. The *Sunday Mirror*'s Brian McNally suggested: 'In-form Shearer, whose current contract ends in June 2004, is expected to sign a two-year extension worth around £6 million this summer. The Newcastle captain earns around £50,000 a week at present and the new deal would give him an extra £10,000 a week. Newcastle have moved quickly to ensure Shearer finishes his playing career at St James' Park as he enjoys arguably his best Premiership season since his £15 million move from Blackburn in July 1996.'

Newcastle mounted another serious assault on the Premiership in the early part of 2003, reaching fourth spot by the turn of the year. Their incredible forward was intent on scoring the goals that underpinned their challenge and, along the way, was keen to savour more slices of history. In Newcastle's 2-1 victory over Manchester City at the end of January, he emulated Tottenham defender Ledley King's efforts three years previously by scoring the Premiership's quickest-ever goal. Displaying customary opportunism, he charged down City goalkeeper Carlo Nash's nervy clearance to slot home after only 10.5 seconds. It was the fastest-ever goal in official competition for Newcastle, although Malcolm Macdonald had scored after only four seconds in a pre-season game with St Johnstone in 1973, and Jackie Milburn was said to have netted at a similar juncture to Shearer in 1947, although official time-keeping procedures were not in place in those days.

Shearer's frequent acquaintance with the record books continued on 15 March when his goal in Newcastle's 2-0 win at Charlton allowed him to jump ahead of Hughie Gallacher and become his club's third highest goalscorer with 144 goals. Proof, if it were needed that, even at the age of thirty-two, Shearer's enduring sniping skills were beyond compare.

Newcastle still could not match majestic Manchester United, however, as any notions that the Toon Army had of Premiership success were brutally quashed by Sir Alex Ferguson's side at the end of April, when they roared to a 6-2 win over Newcastle at St James' Park. 'Newcastle hit a wall of China proportions ... a dirty, big great one. The torture of Titus Bramble is too painful to recall; the contribution of Olivier Bernard too difficult to remember. Every note struck by Alan Shearer suggested an old swinger who has crooned once too often, and Hugo Viana's disdain of the tackle should have him renamed Hugo the First,' was the *People*'s Andy Dunn's colourful and damning synopsis of Newcastle's sorry showing.

One abject performance could not detract from ten years of terrific displays, however, and days later Shearer was named the Premier League Player of the Decade. 'Given the number of top-quality players who have graced our league since its inception, it really fills me with immense pride to have been given this award,' he said of his latest honour, which followed a poll of supporters worldwide on the Premier League website.

Shearer would miss the denouement of the season, however, when he chipped a bone in his ankle during Newcastle's win at Sunderland in late April. Thankfully, there was every indication that, following a summer's rest and recuperation, he would be available for selection at the start of the following season and that there would be no repeat of the protracted injury anguish that had befallen him in the past. Seventeen league goals and a total of twenty-five in all competitions represented another excellent haul for him in 2002–03, while Newcastle once again secured a place in the Champions League by finishing third in the Premiership.

So, could Newcastle now make the next quantum leap in 2003–04 and finally deliver the silverware that Alan Shearer's enormous talent and desire demanded?

Sir Bobby Robson had presided over an era that, in terms of impact on the European scene, unremitting verve and vibrancy, outstripped anything that Kevin Keegan had achieved on Tyneside. On their day, Newcastle could compete with any side in the Premiership, although inconsistency and defensive lapses continued to undermine their challenge.

Up front, the partnership between Bellamy and Shearer – who was the subject of interest from Liverpool in the summer of 2003 – promised to reap yet more rich dividends. But this would be a season when Sir Bobby Robson believed that the elder of the pair was no longer able to be a consistent performer; as it transpired, it was a belief that would set the wheels in motion for his eventual demise.

Newcastle's midfield, meanwhile, ranked with the best in the Premiership and was strengthened further when aggressive attacking midfielder Lee Bowyer, snapped up on a free transfer from West Ham, became Sir Bobby Robson's only summer recruit. While his temperament was often questionable, Bowyer had impressed at Leeds as a goal-scoring midfielder of some renown and was hungry to reignite his career at Newcastle. He had also impressed in the Champions League for the Elland Road side in 2001 and was hoping to sample more of the same for his new club who, in August, were faced with a tricky tie in their quest to qualify for the lucrative group stages of the competition.

Serbian champions Partizan Belgrade, managed by former German midfield legend Lothar Matthaus, stood before Bowyer, Shearer et al and a £15 million bonanza. A 1–0 win in Belgrade, coming one day after Shearer's thirty-third birthday, looked to have assured a smooth passage towards such rich rewards. The scene was set for a comfortable victory at St James' Park in the return in Sir Bobby Robson's 200th match in charge of Newcastle. Instead, what ensued was one of his most distressing nights in football. Partizan Belgrade withstood the Newcastle onslaught and took the game to extra-time and then to every Englishman's most dreaded nightmare – penalty kicks.

Normally Alan Shearer's response to this match-deciding lottery is an emphatic thump of the boot, which usually results in the ball burying itself in the roof of the opposing goalkeeper's net. This time, however, his attempt was reminiscent of fellow Geordie Chris Waddle's ballooned blast in the 1990 World Cup semi-final against West Germany as he skied his effort yards over the bar. Kieron Dyer, Jonathan Woodgate and Aaron Hughes were also unsuccessful in the ultimate test of nerve and Newcastle succumbed 4–3 on penalties to leave Shearer and every tormented Tyneside fan reeling.

Every cloud has a silver lining, as they say, and amid the all-prevailing doom and gloom that had descended on Tyneside, Shearer could console himself with the fact that Newcastle had been afforded the safety net of the UEFA Cup, which, in any case, offered a more realistic chance of success than the Champions League. NAC Breda of Holland and Switzerland's FC Basle were the first victims of Newcastle's bid to make amends for the Partizan Belgrade defeat. Next up, in February 2004, were Norwegian minnows Valerenga and, although Newcastle again progressed with minimum fuss, the game would be no laughing matter for Lee Bowyer – who was deemed ineligible from European competition for six matches given that he had mistakenly not been registered – and Shearer. The *Daily Star* reported: 'Norwegian comedians upset Alan Shearer with a saucy interview. They rang ahead of Newcastle's UEFA Cup tie at Valerenga to quiz him on whether he "shakes" or "milks" his willy after taking a pee. Shearer was then asked: "What music do you listen to when you are cleaning the blood of a homeless man out of the boot of your car?" The Newcastle legend kept his cool, answering "no comment" and "pass". But he clearly wasn't amused.'

Shearer was then, much to his chagrin, informed by Robson that he would not be in Newcastle's starting line-up for the first-leg tie. For a man who lives, sleeps and breathes football, being deprived of playing when he is injury-free is a massive, gut-wrenching disappointment. He equivocated his despair in the *Mirror*: 'I have only played once in the last ten days. I do not feel any different to last season. I am very disappointed and surprised. I was told this afternoon. I was kicking every ball. I was disappointed to be left out. Angry. Did we underestimate them? No, it was a tough game.'

Robson later justified his controversial decision in his auto-biography, writing: 'Alan played more games than any Premiership striker I could think of. He was the only one who didn't take breaks and his main rivals in the Premiership were much younger than he was. I told him that. I tried to make him understand that, for a man of his age, trying to play in every single match was self-defeating. His competitive nature was admirable, on the one hand, but also an obstacle when I wanted him to step back from the firing line.'

Robson's reasoning is perfectly logical when applied to any other player reaching the twilight of his career, but Alan Shearer is a special case. Leave him out at your peril, as Ruud Gullit had discovered and as Robson, too, would find out later that year.

After a 1–1 draw in Norway, Newcastle progressed to the last sixteen of the UEFA Cup when Shearer and Shola Ameobi's two goals paved the way for a comfortable 3–1 win over Valerenga at St James' Park. Newcastle then crushed Real Mallorca 7–1 on aggregate, with Shearer scoring three times over the two legs before netting in his side's 2–1 win over PSV Eindhoven at home to complete a 3–2 aggregate victory and secure a place in the UEFA Cup semi-finals. Shearer knew that both glorious success and heart-breaking failure were only two games away as he spoke to the *Guardian*'s Michael Walker prior to Newcastle's clash with Marseille, his biggest challenge yet in a black-and-white shirt.

He was now standing on the brink of leading Newcastle to their first piece of silverware since 1969 and Bobby Moncur's men's fabulous Fairs Cup triumph. 'What's in front of us is huge,' said a stern Alan Shearer before his side flew out to Marseille. 'We now have a great chance to win a trophy – we've always said that's what we're in this competition for and that hasn't changed – and a chance to make this season a truly great one. But we're aware, too, that it could be bitterly, bitterly disappointing and a huge letdown. There can't be any middle ground now, there can't be anything in between – it's either great or nothing. We've had FA Cup finals, semi-finals and other big games in the past few years and they were all important at the time. But the next ten days could be the most important of my time at Newcastle, because they're here and they're now. It's crunch time.'

A 0–0 draw at St James' Park meant that away goals could be vital in France, yet such theories were rendered academic when Didier Drogba and co secured a 2–0 victory.

Once again Shearer had emerged with immense credit from his pivotal part in Newcastle's memorable UEFA Cup run, which yielded six goals for the Tyne hero. He scored twenty-two in the league, meanwhile, including his 100th goal at St James' Park in Newcastle's 4–0 rout of Tottenham in December. But Newcastle were denied another opportunity of pitting their wits against Europe's best when a fifth-placed finish meant that they missed out on Champions League qualification and all the associated razzmatazz.

The FA Cup was once again barren territory for Newcastle in their perpetual hunt for honours. 'I would swap everything for a medal in this competition, I really would,' announced Shearer before the start of the third round. 'I have obviously only won one thing in a team game and it's a team game we are in. But I have won a lot of individual awards and I really would swap the lot of them for an FA Cup medal. There's no doubt about that.'

His love affair with the world's greatest domestic cup competition continued after Newcastle cruised past Southampton in the third round, registering a convincing 3–0 victory at his first professional club. Liverpool put paid to any ambitions he had for another FA Cup final when they prevailed 2–1 over Newcastle in the fourth round, however. Bobby Robson's decision to leave his talisman out of Newcastle's third-round Carling Cup-tie with West Brom at St James' Park raised both a few eyebrows and disgruntled chants from the Toon Army and no doubt contributed to a 2–1 extra-time defeat.

It was the beginning of the end for Robson and Shearer's propitious union that, until now, had appeared capable of sweeping upwardly mobile Newcastle to the top. For Robson, his days were effectively numbered when Freddy Shepherd confirmed before the start of the 2004–05 season that this would be the septuagenarian manager's last campaign in charge of Newcastle. This inevitably created uncertainty about the future within the minds of Newcastle players, including Shearer, who was again pursued by a raft of clubs, including Blackburn Rovers and Celtic. He was rocked further when his fellow Magpies' mainstay Gary Speed departed for Bolton and injury-hit defender

SAVED BY A WHITE-HAIRED KNIGHT-TO-BE

Jonathan Woodgate signed for Real Madrid, although his sadness was tempered when Stephen Carr, James Milner and Dutch forward Patrick Kluivert bolstered Newcastle's ranks. For Shearer, Kluivert's arrival and Newcastle's ultimately unsuccessful bid to prize England's Euro 2004 hero Wayne Rooney from Everton was further evidence that his manager no longer had faith in his ability to withstand 90 minutes. Robson reveals in his autobiography: 'The day I replaced Alan in a pre-season friendly against Celtic, he expressed real displeasure. He was not abusive or even impolite. He was just unhappy. As he left the field, he remarked, "So, you don't want me to play 90 minutes any more, do you not?" "Alan, sit down," I replied, "there are other players in the team." If he's going to be a manager and a player comes off and says what he said to me that day, how will he respond?'

Robson certainly had every right to make such a move, although as we have seen, Shearer's standing at Newcastle makes a mockery of the old adage that 'no player is bigger than a club'. It is also alleged that the powers-that-be at Newcastle apparently believed that Shearer was eminently more valuable to the club than Robson given the vast disparity in their respective wage packets when Sir Bobby arrived at St James' Park. It has been reported that Robson was offered a £400,000-a-year deal, in comparison to Shearer's £3 million contract.

Alan Shearer *is* Newcastle and challenging his omnipotence was to be Robson's fatal flaw. Like Ruud Gullit before him, leaving Shearer on the bench for the trip to Aston Villa in late August, no matter whether it was deemed as a justified gambit in view of his poor form and Newcastle's winless start to the season, saw him out of a job. In the wake of Newcastle's 4–2 defeat in Birmingham, Robson was tersely told by his chairman Freddy Shepherd that he was being 'relieved of his position' due to the poor run of results. It is open to debate as to whether Shepherd had acted in response to Shearer's demotion to the bench, but there is every chance that he, as a passionate Newcastle

ALAN SHEARER

United supporter, was unappreciative of the treatment of the St James' Park saint. Shearer also refused to condemn Robson, publicly exonerating his manager in his programme notes for Newcastle's next home game with Blackburn in September. He wrote: 'We haven't had the best of starts to the season, with no win in four games and, after the Aston Villa defeat two weeks ago, it sadly came to an end for Bobby Robson, but I want to stress that it had nothing to do with Bobby leaving me out of the starting XI at Villa Park. The manager came to see me at the team hotel on the Friday evening before the game. We had a good professional discussion about it and I can promise you there was certainly no argument and certainly no bust-up. I merely asked him why, and he gave me his reasons.' While this statement resonated with echoes of 1999, it was clear that the Robson-Shearer split was far less acrimonious than the Gullit-Shearer divide had been.

A year after his departure from Newcastle, Robson still seemed rankled by the fact that he had succumbed to Shearer in the St James' Park power struggle. He confessed to the *Guardian*: 'I didn't know how tricky it would be, handling Shearer. I was a strong and experienced manager used to dealing with famous players like Romario and Ronaldo, Figo and Nadal. But Shearer occupies a special position in Newcastle. I think he's a good guy but I was a little disappointed by his reaction when I left him out. Still, at the same time I understood he wanted to play every game. I think he's changed his attitude but then he didn't appreciate the need to be rested.'

Sir Bobby had saved Shearer from the strikers' scrapheap and had encouraged him to recapture his fearsome force of old in a golden age for Newcastle. Trophies may not have been garnered, but individual records and goals flowed in plentiful supply, while legendary status on Tyneside was assured.

In view of all this, Alan Shearer will be eternally grateful to his old knight in shining armour...

CHAPTER TEN

Injury Torment and 'Bouncebackability'

Injuries are the worst nightmare of any professional footballer. Ordinary men, many with no experience of a life outside the confines of a grass pitch, often describe being deprived of playing the game they love as being akin to 'a living hell'. Alan Shearer would certainly subscribe to that simile.

While his astounding career will be remembered as a goal-ridden one, it will also be defined by his catalogue of catastrophic and critical injuries. Shearer became wearily reconciled to a succession of football obituaries, often heralded with a stark headline such as 'Shear disaster!', materialising with monotonous regularity in the tabloids every time his body failed him. His powers of recovery, not once but several times, are a true testament to the man's greatness and his unflinching tenacity. Shearer's admirable response to his successes and setbacks is redolent of the maxims promoted in Rudyard Kipling's poem 'If':

> If you can meet with Triumph and Disaster
> And treat those two impostors just the same

ALAN SHEARER

In both 'triumph' and 'disaster', the extraordinary Geordie's impeccable professionalism, dignity and self-belief have remained unstinting throughout his career. Injury invariably intervenes like the cruel hand of fate when a footballer's fortunes are at their optimum. This was certainly the case for Shearer when, by December 1992, he had amassed twenty-two goals for Blackburn in a swashbuckling season – more than justifying the £3.3 million Rovers had paid out for him that summer. His coruscating club form had cemented his place in England's forward line.

Then, on Boxing Day, during Blackburn's 3–1 home win over Leeds, a seemingly innocuous challenge from defender Chris Fairclough caused what, at the time, appeared to be little more than a 'knock' to his right knee.

Indeed, Shearer played an instrumental part in Blackburn's victory, scoring twice, before departing the Ewood Park turf not long before the end of the match. For the Rovers player, there did not seem be any danger of a protracted period on the sidelines as he declared himself fit for his side's Coca Cola Cup quarter-final away to Cambridge in early January. However, once again his right knee forced him to limp off after a tackle from Cambridge captain, Danny O'Shea. Initial diagnosis, or mis-diagnosis as it proved, was that Shearer had damaged cartilage in his right knee, necessitating an operation. However, swelling and traces of blood on the knee following the operation hinted at a more serious injury than had originally been predicted. 'Even with my limited knowledge of medical matters, I knew there was something seriously wrong,' he later admitted in his autobiography.

His worst fears were confirmed when, in February 1993, a visit to orthopaedic surgeon Professor David Dandy in Cambridge dropped a bombshell by revealing to Shearer that he had snapped his cruciate knee ligament and that he would be out of action for between six months to a year. For Shearer, the shock was so great that he suffered a serious nosebleed on hearing the news.

Thirty years previously, the career of another lethal centre-forward from the North-East, Brian Clough, was wretchedly curtailed by a similar injury. And, ironically, another legend from the same part of the world, Paul Gascoigne, nearly suffered the same sorry fate after infamously injuring himself during the 1991 FA Cup final, although his knee was said to be more severely damaged than his fellow Geordie's.

Shearer duly underwent an operation on his knee and Professor Dandy ruled him out for the rest of the season, but offered his patient a modicum of encouragement when he expressed the hope that he could return at the start of the 1993–94 campaign. The injured striker's misery was compounded further when a series of blood clots and an infection developed on his knee, making it a long and painfully drawn out two-month saga for the young Shearer. Once the reconstruction work on his right knee had been completed, Shearer knuckled down to an intensive period of rehabilitation, both at Blackburn and the Lilleshall Rehabilitation Centre in Shropshire.

Football, for a fanatic like Shearer, was uppermost in his thoughts throughout, as he admitted in the *Daily Mail* in August 1993: 'Once I was out of the hospital, I went to every Blackburn match, home and away, and I had to go and watch the lads train every morning. I couldn't have stayed at home and moped – what would have been the point? The encouragement from the supporters at the club was absolutely unbelievable.'

As the months limped on interminably, Shearer's frustrations intensified as he was prevented from playing a part in Blackburn's title charge, while doubts about his ability to recapture his previous skills began to develop insidiously. He articulated his injury torment in an interview with the *Observer* on 26 December 1993: 'It was the lowest point in my life. It shattered me. It's human nature to fear the worst and I got depressed during the long rehabilitation when, after weeks of hard work, day in, day out, the knee didn't seem to be getting any better. Then I heard people saying I'd never be the same and that my career was finished. That just spurred me on.'

But he needn't have worried – he completed a remarkable comeback when he appeared for Blackburn during a pre-season trip to Ireland. Thirty-four goals in forty-two games for Blackburn in the 1993–94 season provided incontrovertible evidence that injury had not blunted his cutting edge. 'I expected to be back, but whether I thought the goals would come as regularly is another matter,' he said to the *Mail on Sunday* on Boxing Day 1993. Mike Pettigrew, Shearer's physiotherapist during his recovery period, embellished the belief that he possessed an astonishing ability to recover quickly. He told the *Sunday Mirror* in 1996: 'Some players take up to two years to recover, Alan did it inside eight months. From the day surgery was decided upon, he said: "It won't beat me. I'll be as good as ever." That's his nature, challenging and dedicated.'

Injuries would return malevolently to interrupt Shearer's net-bulging activities, however. Three groin operations in a ten-month period between 1996 and 1997 followed for the ill-fated star. He suffered from a complaint known as 'Gilmour's Groin', named after the Harley Street specialist who repaired the damage, due in large part to the pressure exerted on his groin by his enormous thighs. The left-hand side of his groin was operated on at the end of the 1995–96 season, forcing him to miss Blackburn's final two games of the season and he then faced a desperate race to be fit for England's Euro '96 campaign. At the time, Shearer was enduring a long-lasting goal drought in his country's colours and missing the European extravaganza on home soil would have meant further heartache for the stricken striker. Round-the-clock physiotherapy from England physiotherapist Alan Smith restored him to full fitness, however, and his spectacular Euro '96 heroics need no elaboration.

Yet his groin was to prove troublesome once again later that year when he was forced to take another trip to the Princess Grace Hospital in London for surgery after injuring himself during Newcastle's 5–0 thrashing of Manchester United on 20 October. This time it was the right side of his groin that was affected, an area he had aggravated during Euro '96. Yet, in true Shearer style, he once again demonstrated phenomenal restorative powers to return for Newcastle's match against Chelsea only one month after his 24 October operation. His injury would, according to medical experts, have sidelined lesser men for six to eight weeks. Nick Duxbury of the *Independent* quipped Shearer had duly earned a reputation as 'the world's fastest healer' on 22 November 1996.

He could also have had a convincing case for being named the world's most unfortunate footballer, after he required a third groin operation in less than a year in February 1997. Yet again the rumour mill went into overdrive and some tabloids churned out incorrect and unfair predictions that Shearer would miss the rest of the season.

In actual fact, he was only unavailable for selection for five weeks – although during this period he was absent for Newcastle's two-legged UEFA Cup quarter-final, which they lost against French side Monaco. Shearer's response to his latest setback? A philosophical shrug of the shoulders and an incredible acceptance and perspective of the potential for bouts of luck to blight a footballer's career. 'Well, that's football for you,' he said phlegmatically in an interview with the *Independent*'s Ian Stafford during his latest spell away from playing on 10 March 1997. 'You can make plans, but the game has a habit of making decisions for you. You never know what's around the corner. Right now I'm injured again, and it's a particularly bad time to be injured. But it's a small hiccup compared to everything else that's gone right for me.'

ALAN SHEARER

This 'annus horribilis' of 1997 would plummet to new depths of despair for Shearer in July. During Newcastle's pre-season game against Chelsea in the Umbro Tournament at Goodison Park on 26 July, he ruptured his ankle and fibula. 'It had appeared to be the least dangerous ball that Shearer had gone for all afternoon against Chelsea when, in the 90th minute, he stretched for a pass from David Batty and seemed to catch the studs of his right boot in the wet turf. Shearer immediately collapsed in obvious pain and departed Goodison for a local hospital soon after,' said the *Observer*'s Alan Hubbard and Michael Walker of the disastrous incident, which incredibly saw Shearer have his dislocated right ankle put back into place without anaesthetic.

Shearer's manager, Kenny Dalglish, predicted that his injury-ravaged star would be out for 'a wee while, months rather than weeks' after it was initially thought he had only broken his right ankle. However, at that stage, Dalglish was not aware of the true, horrific extent of the injury and X-rays confirmed that a broken fibula could wreck Shearer's season.

Nevertheless, he had to confront the shattering reality that not only would he miss Newcastle's push for honours, but he was also in danger of missing the 1998 World Cup if England qualified. His club was thrown into turmoil, on and off the field, in the wake of the calamitous turn of events. Not only had they lost the services of a prolific striker, but their PLC's shares also dropped alarmingly when full details of Shearer's injury emerged. The *Extel Examiner* reported on 29 July 1997: 'At 9am shares in Newcastle United were down 2 pence at 114.5, having closed down 7 pence yesterday. The company floated at 135 pence a share in April.'

John Gorman, the England assistant manager in 1997, was quoted in the *Daily Record* as saying, after he had called Shearer in hospital: 'Alan is a crucial player and what has happened is devastating news for us. Alan was his typical, positive, usual self. He told me that he knows he's just got to get on with it. That's the sort of guy he is.' Shearer was also defiant about the long lay-off ahead and adamant he would return before the season's end. 'I'll be back for Newcastle for their bid to win something and I'll be raring to go for England next summer, when I intend to finish top of the goal charts at the World Cup finals, just as I did in Euro '96,' he insisted in *The Times* on August 1997.

However, Shearer's plucky public pronouncements masked his own private hell which lasted a traumatic 172 days. It was, he claims, 'the longest and toughest period of my professional life' when his renowned mental fortitude would receive perhaps its stiffest examination yet. There were unspeakably awful moments, such as when his plaster cast was cut off to reveal 'a mangled mess'. Then the committed family man was prevented from taking his ailing wife Lainya a cup of tea of tea as he hobbled around in despair on crutches.

On the same night as England's stoic defensive performance nullified the Italians in Rome to earn World Cup qualification, the plucky striker took his first step along the long and arduous road to recovery during a holiday in Barbados. He put his weight down on his injured ankle, walked for the first time since the injury without crutches and suffered no ill-effects, all of which reinforced his determined public declarations that he would return within six months. Newcastle fans were given false hopes of an even more miraculous and early comeback when he walked around the perimeter of PSV Eindhoven's ground with physiotherapist Derek Wright prior to the Magpies' Champions League clash on 22 October.

As Christmas approached, there was further cheer for England and Newcastle fans when Shearer appeared smiling and relaxed during the World Cup draw in Marseille. He told Martin Lipton of the *Evening Chronicle* on 4 December that the forthcoming year's World Cup was proving a huge driving force during his injury ordeal. 'All the time I've been injured the World Cup has been the big carrot waiting for me when I get fit,' he said. 'There's no doubt that playing in the World Cup can be a huge inspiration for you as a player. It's the world's biggest tournament; everybody will be watching, and that's bound to give you a kick, give you something extra and get the adrenaline pumping through you.' On 3 December, the *Daily Mail*'s Nigel Clarke said that Shearer had pencilled in a February return to action. He said: 'Shearer's amazing ability to put mind over matter has, once again, helped him conquer a career-threatening injury and, in two months' time, he hopes to emerge from the gloom that has enveloped him since his awful accident in August.'

But Clarke suspected that, beneath the smiling façade and superficial optimism, Shearer was having a harrowing time. 'So good is Shearer at hiding himself behind it that few, if any, know his real feelings or whether he bleeds in private like most do when confronted with setbacks. Nobody has ever seen him weep, either in despair or delight. Strong-minded, resolute and stubborn, he applies himself in private with the same dedication he brings to his public as perhaps England's most famous player.' Shearer confirmed Clarke's suspicions in his autobiography. He described the unbearable mental and physical anguish he was experiencing as being like a marathon runner hitting the wall and confessed that he reached rock bottom in December.

The low lasted for just under a week, though it must have felt a lot longer than that. Various engagements, such as the visit to the World Cup draw on behalf of his sponsors Umbro, helping co-ordinate the FA Cup draw and starting the Great North Run kept him busy and upbeat, however. Then there were the Christmas festivities to enjoy with Lainya and his children.

Slowly but surely, Shearer was emerging from the deep, dark pits of depression and starting to value both his life and career again. The intensive training regime he was undertaking, including a workout with the Newcastle squad at their Durham training ground in the morning, and then a strenuous personal session in the gym in the afternoon, was beginning to pay welcome dividends.

His increasingly rapid recovery amazed everyone. He had spectacularly defied medical predictions that his career was in serious jeopardy or, in the best-case scenario, would be resurrected by March at the earliest. This extraordinary force of nature actually returned to action in mid-January.

Not for the first time, Alan Shearer defied the odds and completed another astonishing comeback in mid-January. And he was determined that there would be a positive lasting legacy from his injury nightmare. He agreed for the plaster cast he had worn to be auctioned off at Newcastle Civic Hall on 30 January to raise funds for St Oswald's Hospital. The bizarre piece of football memorabilia was bought for £1,500 by a Norwegian lady, Wenche Romslo, who duly showcased it on her husband Dag's Color Viking ferry that ran from Tyneside to Norway.

Fast forward to 2000 and a horrible sense of déjà-vu struck, both in terms of the harsh timing of his injury and the sickening ramifications it would bring for Shearer. Just as had been the case before the European championships in 1996, his participation in Euro 2000 in Holland and Belgium appeared to be in serious doubt after he injured his knee during England's warm-up game with Malta. Pain-killing injections for tendinitis allowed him to complete his planned swansong from the international scene, but it was only a temporary reprieve. The niggle persisted and it was decided that, for the umpteenth time, he would go under the knife. Newcastle manager Bobby Robson bemoaned both his and his striker's bad luck. Speaking to the *Sun*, he said: 'Losing Alan is my biggest disappointment in fifteen months here. He's had cruciates, ankle, back and tendinitis, but he has soldiered on. He is a brave warrior and we're going to miss him.'

An operation on Shearer's injured knee was duly carried out on 23 December after a third steroid injection – the first of which had been administered during Euro 2000 – had failed to do the job. He was sidelined for nine weeks, making his comeback in Newcastle's 1–0 win over Manchester City on 24 February. But just over a week later during a practice match, he jarred his knee yet again.

It must have seemed to Shearer that the footballing gods were conspiring against him. Few footballers have been blighted with such bad luck as Alan Shearer, yet even fewer exponents of the beautiful game possess the incredible strength of character to survive such a physically and mentally exacting toll. He could have predicted the football world's reaction and written the newspaper headlines himself. Indeed, inevitably, talk of the end of his career was again rife in the media when he jetted out to see top knee specialist Dr Richard Steadman at his clinic in Colorado.

Steadman was credited with saving the career of Brazilian superstar Ronaldo and had also treated, among other leading sportsmen and women, former Liverpool players Jamie Redknapp and Patrik Berger, as well as Australian golf legend, Greg Norman. With such impeccable credentials, the omens for Shearer's rehabilitation looked bright. Shearer was later to reflect in the *Evening Chronicle* on 23 June 2001, that with the help of Newcastle surgeon Rob Gregory, he had determinedly tracked down Steadman: 'I decided immediately enough was enough and that I had to track down the greatest knee specialist in the world regardless of cost or where he was. If he was in Outer Mongolia I would have gone. This was my career.' The *Mirror* reported on 21 March 2001: 'Fears are growing for Alan Shearer's career – as he jetted out to America in a desperate bid to cure his long-term knee problem. Surgery has so far failed to cure the condition and Shearer will see the world's top knee specialist, Dr Richard Steadman, for treatment and therapy after he admitted being left "destroyed" by the breakdown in his recovery from an operation in December. A St James' Park source said last night: "There is a feeling that if anybody can help him it's Dr Steadman."' Shearer's consultation with Dr Steadman revealed an urgent need for another make-or-break knee operation, which the injury-plagued striker vowed would be his last. Inevitably, there was talk of his powers being greatly diminished through months of physically and mentally damaging injuries.'

However, he was comforted by the heart-warming encouragement of fellow professionals and close friends and associates that he could emerge both a more accomplished player and a stronger person. Former England striker Mark Hateley empathised with Shearer's predicament, as he too had lost a large chunk of his career to injury. Hateley was sidelined for eighteen months when he had carbon-fibre knee ligaments inserted while playing for Monaco. He told Richard Williams of the *Independent* in March 1999: 'In my view Alan isn't even in his prime yet. At twenty-nine, thirty, thirty-one and thirty-two, I was at my strongest and having my best years. Whatever Alan may have lost, he's also become stronger.' And Dave Merrington, his former youth coach at Southampton, and the man who brought him to the attention of the football world, Jack Hixon, sprang to the defence of the wounded hero. 'Mentally, it won't bother him at all,' Merrington said. 'He's never let an injury get in the way of his single-mindedness. As time goes by, of course, injuries like that can have a certain effect, but if you're a good enough player, and you're mentally as strong as Alan is, you adjust.' Hixon added: 'I believe that Alan's moral fibre is great enough to have enabled him to overcome an injury that would have prejudiced the future of any ordinary player. It's been a battle to get his edge back, but his moral edge has never deteriorated.'

ALAN SHEARER

Newcastle United fans' website, *Toonerama*, revealed in 2005 that further surgery was in the pipeline for Shearer to extend his career. The amusing spoof report claimed that Austrian professor Heinz Kritzfield was prepared to undertake an operation which would see Newcastle striker Shola Ameobi's head transplanted onto Shearer's shoulders! The website goes on to say: 'United have officially denied the story, however an informed insider has suggested that the club are looking into the professor's claims that "it would be a perfect case of an old head on young shoulders". But despite the fact that Shearer is the son of a sheet-metal worker from Gosforth who would do everything he could to bring success to the club, a close friend has suggested that he may turn down the opportunity. "Alan is a family man," he said and "although he loves the club he has to think of his wife and children. If he has to be round Shola's house all the time, who would creosote the fence?"'

When Shearer signalled his intention to retire at the end of the 2005/06 season, he cited the fact that his debilitated knees were in terminal decline and could no longer withstand the relentless rigours of English football. Given his ailment-ridden career to date and his veteran status by virtue of his thirty-five years, it would have been a considerable surprise had he escaped further torment in the treatment room and remained injury-free throughout his valedictory football campaign. Shearer being Shearer, he could not bow out of the game, which had foisted on him both glory and pain, without his anatomy yet again slightly overshadowing his feats on the football pitch.

Firstly, Shearer travelled to Germany in November 2005 to undergo surgery on his injured hernia, but the worst was yet to come; the denouement of his career would be couched in conflicting terms – describing both yet another glorious goal and the depressing failure of his battle-scarred body once again.

At least Shearer was allowed to experience the joy and jubilation of ending his magnificent career with a goal in Newcastle's emphatic 4–1 win over fierce local rivals Sunderland in April 2006. But the final throes of Shearer's football odyssey simply had to countenance a sorry ending to quell any excessive euphoria and to satisfy the criteria for a tragic legend's tale. After 71 minutes, he fell awkwardly on his left knee after a heavy challenge from Julio Arca and, despite receiving treatment from Newcastle physiotherapist Derek Wright, Shearer could not shrug off the nagging injury and reluctantly decided to depart what had been his equivalent of the workplace for almost 20 years.

Regrettably, rather than leave the game he adored in scenes of triumphant celebration, Shearer endured a rather more unsavoury exit as scornful Sunderland supporters rose as one to roar abuse. It seemed a wholly inappropriate ending for one of English football's greatest ambassadors.

However, while Shearer's career had often assumed comic-book proportions, Roy Race he is not. He was already fearing the end, when he admitted afterwards: 'That's it for me. I hope it's not. I will have a scan in the morning but if it is medial ligaments, then I'm done.'

Shearer did not need to be a soothsayer to predict that his demise had been determined. Nor did Newcastle manager Glenn Roeder and chairman Freddy Shepherd, who were both pessimistic about their star's chances of recovering from his latest affliction. Yet Roeder was still upbeat despite the overwhelming sense of dejection he was feeling. He wanted to pay tribute to his man's stubborn refusal to let injury defeat him – a salutary lesson for footballers everywhere.

Roeder enthused: 'Alan Shearer was summed up in the two seconds before we could get him off the pitch. He was hobbling with what looks like potentially a bad ligament injury and a Sunderland player was carrying the ball forward and he turned around and tried to make a tackle where most players would have been lying on the floor curled up. That just sums up Alan and why he's had the career he's had and why he's the person he is. It's a shame they don't make more people like that.'

Eulogies about Shearer's sterling spirit during the darkest of days on the sidelines emanated from other sources, too. Sir Alex Ferguson, who had been left stunned and seething by Alan's decision to overlook Manchester United twice in favour of other clubs, decided it was time to let bygones be bygones and saluted the man who got away.

He said: 'There are no hard feelings that he turned Manchester United down. Football is football. I'm sorry he didn't join us but there you are. Alan is the professionals' professional. The great thing about Alan is that he's had some serious injuries. It takes a lot of determination and will to get back from serious injuries but he has done it a number of times. That's the hallmark of someone who has great courage. This injury has just come at a bad time for him.'

The *Daily Telegraph's* Henry Winter was equally lavish in his praise for Newcastle's favourite son, writing: 'Amid all the understandable wailing from Wallsend to Washington over Monday's injury, it was fitting that what appears Shearer's final act in a Newcastle strip should be an attempted tackle on a Sunderland player despite being on one leg. Competing to the last.

'This is a warrior who never surrendered for Southampton, Blackburn or Newcastle, and never, ever for his country.'

Several days later, and Shearer confirmed the prognosis he had envisaged – he had torn his left medial ligament and would therefore be forced to wear a knee brace for several weeks. In short, his distinguished career was over.

He confessed: 'Deep down I knew when I limped out of the Stadium of Light that it was probably the end and I think the fans knew it as well. They know I don't stay down unless I'm badly hurt. It's disappointing, but I've got no regrets. I've had a great career.'

INJURY TORMENT AND 'BOUNCEBACKABILITY'

So, that was that, a sad and wholly unsatisfactory farewell had seemingly been confirmed for one of English football's greatest servants.

However, Alan Shearer did not want to leave his admirers with the lasting memories of him as a 'crock'. Although he was unable to play a full part in his testimonial match for Newcastle against Celtic in May 2006, he kicked off proceedings resplendent in his black-and-white stripes, looking every inch the Geordie hero rather than a hobbling cripple.

He was determined that he would take his final bow out on the pitch, on which he had graced with distinction and dignity, and salute the adoring legions who had worshipped his every vicious volley, thunderous penalty and emphatic header.

He just had to have the last say and duly fired in a late penalty to allow Newcastle to edge a pulsating match, 3-2, epitomising the fact that in amazing Alan Shearer's life, triumph always overcomes disaster and pathos is constantly punctured by pride and passion.

Undoubtedly, injuries have, for many, overshadowed Shearer's career achievements and raised the nagging question 'what if?' about his potential for more personal prizes and capacity for club success, had his body been ailment-free. It is tempting to wonder how many goals he would have accumulated at international level had persistent health worries not heavily influenced his England retirement in 2000.

Yet it is perhaps churlish to ponder too long on what might have been, given that Shearer succeeded in inordinate ways in spite of his lachrymose legs. Frequently beset by bad luck, his immense mental resilience, which has been honed in adversity and is central to his being, has come to the fore time and time again. John Rawling ventured in the *Guardian* in March 2003 that Shearer might even have developed areas of his game following his crippling injuries. He said: 'Maybe the dodgy knee just made him smarter in using tricks, some admittedly fairer than others, to challenge for the ball and knock it to those around him. That loss of mobility, however marginal, may have improved his ability to read a match and hone his already impressive positional awareness. And it could be that, subconsciously, knowledge of his physical frailty made him a more lethal finisher, as if he knew it could all end at any moment.'

In 2004, the word 'bouncebackability' – the ability to bounce back after a period of failure – started to seep into dictionaries everywhere.

Alan Shearer is its embodiment.

CHAPTER ELEVEN

Painting a Different Picture

While his football achievements, bar a regrettable dearth of club trophies, are widely lauded, Alan Shearer's personality remains something of a sticking point. According to his critics, he is the archetypal bland and boring footballer; a colourless character with a monotonous voice and uninteresting life.

In short, he is caricatured as Creosote Man, a legacy of the well-spun yarn that he favoured creosoting his garden fence over wild carousing when his team, Blackburn, were confirmed as champions of England in 1995. Yet this enduring myth is actually ill founded; Shearer insists it was actually his father-in-law who was undertaking the fence-enhancement work, and that he only went out to supply him with drinks.

Nevertheless, even if this revelation debunks the notion of Shearer as a dreary DIY man, Wor Al is still regarded as a one-dimensional drab individual. In the view of his detractors, Shearer's former Blackburn team-mate Tim Flowers encapsulated his supposed anodyne personality perfectly when he jokingly dubbed Alan 'Mr Mogadon', after the sleep-inducing drug, and 'the Nigel Mansell of football'. His penchant for banal utterances was certainly the source of much frustration for journalists during his football career, as was his dislike of talking about himself; he was a firm believer that his endeavours on the field of play were eminently more voluble about him.

Jonathan Northcroft wrote in *Scotland on Sunday* in February 1997 that, while on the pitch Shearer was both 'vivid and concise', during interviews, 'probably nobody has managed to stay awake while conducting one, let alone reading someone else's. To paraphrase Woody Harrelson in *White Men Can't Jump*, "It's hard goddam work making something this pretty seem this dull"'.

Granted, he frequently trotted out trite and tired 'over the moon' and 'the lads done well' football clichés during his career, but to characterise Shearer as a footballer completely devoid of substance and personality would be doing him a great disservice. *The Times*' Simon Barnes reckoned, for instance, that Shearer had consciously decided to hone an overtly ordinary image and public façade and therefore represented 'a throwback' to a bygone age before the cult of celebrity footballers like David Beckham.

He wrote, 'Shearer is a fascinating and unusual man who had an extraordinary talent and he has chosen to come across as dull, uninteresting and utterly ordinary. He is football's plain-clothes man, the great undercover worker for high and rare talent. He has painted his masterpiece and the fact that he has chosen to do so in creosote makes him more, not less, unusual.'

Barnes's view is reinforced by Shearer's famous declaration on signing for Newcastle – 'I'm just a sheet-metal worker's son'. It is a mantra that he and others have often repeated. It is as if Shearer stresses his working-class-hero credentials to remind people that he is just a footballer and not an affected superstar. He does not care for fuss, false proclamations and delusions of grandeur. He prefers a no-frills, football-filled existence shorn of the trappings of fame and fortune craved by many of his contemporaries. OK, for many people, ordinary equals dull, but there is more to this much-maligned Mr Mundane than meets the eye.

Explore the Shearer psyche further and you soon discover the reasons for his wilful ordinariness. He may not be as articulate and erudite as the likes of former footballers Graeme Le Saux or Gavin Peacock, for instance, but his terse and uninspiring replies to journalists were due to an avowed suspicion of the media's machinations which can see the most innocuous of comments blown up by hungry hacks, who hanker after juicy quotes to flesh out their stories, into sensational soundbites.

He admitted his caginess towards reporters in his autobiography as follows: 'I get on well with a lot of journalists in the written press and from radio and television, and always try to be helpful and polite with them. But there are one or two lurking around the corner whose motives are suspect. They can take a quote completely out of context and draw you into a controversy of their own making.'

Alan Shearer never wanted to be distracted from his lifeblood and passion by the outside interferences and annoyances of tabloid tittle-tattle. His career was interrupted enough with a succession of horrendous injuries without being burdened further by the weight of public scrutiny into his private life. While other players may have been appreciably more interesting and newsworthy through their notorious nocturnal habits and their sexual preferences, Shearer remained a virtually unsullied, model professional. And for that, he deserves a great deal of respect.

In 1997, he told the *London Evening Standard*, 'My football is the main priority. Nothing will ever get in the way of that. I play football on the pitch and, if other things follow on from that, that's great. It all boils down to what happens on the park.'

ALAN SHEARER

While Shearer's guarded approach succeeding in warding off unwanted intrusion from malicious media men, it also prevented many of us from seeing a joker *par excellence*. Indeed, this apparent doyen of deadpan, diplomacy, discretion and dullness has a latent mischievous sense of humour that was regularly exposed to close friends and team-mates, making a mockery of his 'Captain Clean' and 'goody-two shoes' images. He has confessed that he was not averse to a few dressing-room pranks and his former team-mate and close friend Rob Lee has even compared him to a milder version of Paul Gascoigne, the so-called 'Clown Prince of Football', due to his inclination for wacky antics.

While at Newcastle, he regularly assumed the role of serial practical joker who revelled in deriving humour from cutting the toes out of his team-mates' socks, tying their football boots together and using comic tools such as shaving foam and toothpaste to generate guffaws galore. Shearer himself has gleefully recounted how he caused gales of laughter among his Newcastle team-mates when they dared him to mention an Abba song while doing post-match analysis for Sky television. Wearing his trademark deadpan facial expression, Shearer completed his mission as expertly as he had dispatched many a penalty kick on the field of play.

He said, 'It doesn't matter what the score is in football. The winner takes it all.' He then remembers struggling to stop himself from collapsing into a fit of the giggles.

Shearer even warmed up for the momentous declaration that he would be finishing his England career during Euro 2000 by spraying a Newcastle security guard with a fire extinguisher two days before his pressurised public announcement. However, while for other footballers – Gazza being a prime example – assuming the role of entertainer off-the-field becomes a perilous pastime, Shearer realised when it was time to be serious and that football and not comedy was his bread and butter.

PAINTING A DIFFERENT PICTURE

While in general his clowning around took place within the confines of the dressing room, his comic potential has occasionally been vaunted to a wider audience. For instance, fast-food chain McDonald's exploited Shearer's supposed pallid personality in one television advertisement which shows him wandering around Newcastle, reminiscing about his past and his affection for the place where he was born and bred. The advertisement concludes with Shearer going into McDonald's to order a burger. Then one member of staff turns to the other and says, 'He's really boring, isn't he?'

He has also generated mirth unwittingly when, in 2006, a clip showing him singing lustily along to 'Elevation' by Irish rockers U2 while driving his car, apparently near his home in Pontelant, Northumberland, aroused feverish discussion on the Internet. The 30-second clip was captured on a mobile phone by one of his two daughters, Chloe and Hollie, and then apparently posted on the chat website Bebo by the pair under the joint Internet alias Clo Hoe.

It was heralded with the Internet slang 'lmao' or 'laughing my arse off' and it certainly produced this reaction among the Bebo fraternity. One person wrote, 'What a guy', while another enthused, 'Tell ure [sic] dad he is a legend.' Newcastle United fan websites were deluged with similar messages of support and praise for their idol's singing prowess.

However, the 35-year-old's management company SFX initially considered the footage no laughing matter and contemplated legal action to have it removed from cyberspace. But perhaps they believed that, rather than cast their client in a negative light, it was helping to change the public perception of him as humourless and boring.

An SFX spokesman said, 'We have looked into it on Alan's behalf and realise that the footage is completely innocent and is simply capturing Alan spending time with his family. As a result we will be taking no further action.'

As the spokesman said, what resonated most with the public from this risible piece of film, apart from his debatable singing ability, was the fact that Shearer was portrayed as an ordinary family man. Indeed, he dotes on his wife, Lainya, and children, Chloe, Hollie and Will. He has always greatly appreciated the reassuring, vitally important anchor of family in his life to keep him grounded and untroubled by the pressures of professional football. The love and support of his nearest and dearest are the only things that matter more to Shearer than football. Even when he was abroad due to football commitments, he would always make a special effort to call his family every night. He lives only five minutes away from his parents' home and enjoys heading down to the local pub on a Sunday with his father, Alan. It is a homing instinct that may be considered unadventurous – he snubbed the likes of Barcelona and Inter Milan during his career, for example – but it is nonetheless heart-warming, charming and reassuringly normal, recalling the homely habits of old–fashioned footballers of yore.

Close friends and associates are also crucial to Shearer's *modus vivendi*. He keeps in regular contact with many of the friends he grew up with on the Gosforth council estate, proving that he has never forgotten, and will never forget, his roots.

His business adviser Tony Stephens and 'guardian angel' Jack Hixon, the scout who discovered him, are two people with whom Shearer has forged fervent friendships, he acknowledges in his autobiography. Members of the football fraternity have also lauded his kindness and loyalty. The current Crystal Palace coach Peter Taylor has told how he received a call from Shearer when Alan decided to end his international career. Taylor, who established a close rapport with Shearer while working with England as one of manager Glenn Hoddle's assistants during the 1998 World Cup, confessed he found this particularly touching given that, at the time, he was manager of lowly Division Two side Gillingham. The former Republic of Ireland forward

PAINTING A DIFFERENT PICTURE

Niall Quinn has also enthused about Shearer's encouragement and inspiration over the telephone. When Quinn was in the depths of despair after suffering a career-threatening injury like Shearer, he was heartened to hear from empathetic Alan who urged him never to give up on regaining his old form and fitness.

While he will never fully satisfy people that he is more than an apparently soporific soul, one cannot argue that Shearer is as thoughtful and helpful a footballer away from the game as you can find. Such is his ardent desire to help others that he will even have a centre named after him to support disabled children and adults – 'The Alan Shearer Centre – Free mind, Free body, Free choice' on the outskirts of Newcastle. The St Cuthbert's Care charity respite facility will feature a hydrotherapy suite, bubble pool and sensory rooms, cinema, Internet cafe and eight bedrooms. Not only did Shearer donate £250,000, swelling to £320,000 with Gift Aid tax relief, from his £1.64 million testimonial fund towards the initiative, but he also donned a hard hat and visited the construction site to view the scheme's progress. It may be de rigueur these days for footballers to lend their name and provide financial assistance for charities to enhance their public image, but would most players go one step further to champion their chosen cause? No, certainly not, but then Alan Shearer is different; he is the epitome of decency, dignity and class.

In an interview with the *Journal*'s chief reporter, Paul James, Shearer explained, 'From my point of view, it was important not just to say, "There's a cheque, get on with it". It was important for me to come and see the building and I'm looking forward to coming back when it's complete. I'm a very lucky man. It's great that I'm able to give something back, which was the reason I gave the money from my testimonial to local charities.'

The National Society for the Prevention of Cruelty to Children (NSPCC) was also a beneficiary of Shearer's testimonial fund, earning

£420,000 from its long-time ambassador. Countless other charities and worthwhile causes have benefited from his input and monetary support to confirm him as a thoroughly nice chap and Good Samaritan.

In total, the following charities and organisations profited from Alan Shearer's generosity: Nordoff Robbins Music Therapy, £608,000; NSPCC, £347,000; St Cuthbert's Care, £250,000; Newcastle General Hospital A & E, £95,000; Freeman Hospital, £95,000; Royal Victoria Infirmary children's services, £95,000; Wilms' Tumour (Institute of Cancer Research), £25,000; Little Hearts Matter, £25,000; Bobby Moore Fund for Cancer Research, £25,000; Samaritan's Purse, £25,000; Cramlington Juniors FC, £15,000; Wallsend Boys' Club, £15,000; Friedreich's Ataxia Research, £10,000; Gosforth High School, £10,000.

He has visited schools to pass on football tips, set up his own soccer academy and also provided encouragement and succour to sick children in hospitals, especially at Christmas. On one visit to the bedsides of stricken youngsters spending the festive period on the wards, he admitted that he had felt in bad spirits before he arrived given that he was injured at the time. But, on seeing the heart-warming smiles creep across the faces of the patients who were overjoyed to see him, he regained perspective about how fortunate he was. While many high-profile footballers drowned in wealth often lose sight of the things that truly matter in life, Shearer has remained grounded and generous to people and clubs that have helped him reach the privileged position he now enjoys.

At the 40th anniversary dinner of his former team Wallsend Boys' Club in 2005, he donated one of his signed shirts, helping to raise a total of £40,000 to preserve the future of the renowned football academy; and, in 2004, he was the guest speaker at a charity fundraising event, in aid of the Hartlepool and District Hospice, which was organised by Century FM radio DJ Paul 'Goffy' Gough, who had lost his sister, Angela O'Hara, to cancer.

PAINTING A DIFFERENT PICTURE

Suddenly, after stripping away the creosote from the popular pre-conceptions of Alan Shearer, you find a normal, everyday man who achieved greatness and had quite a few laughs along the way, while furnishing others with the fruits of his success. He is a dying breed and should be cherished, not chided for something he will never be. Young, up-and-coming footballers would do well to follow his impeccable example.

CHAPTER TWELVE

Unexpected Extra Time

Talk about a tale of the unexpected.

Alan Shearer's astonishing u-turn in April 2005 on his seemingly cast-iron decision to retire at the end of the 2004–05 season stunned the football world. 'I could have been knocked down by a feather duster,' declared a shocked John Gibson of the Newcastle *Evening Chronicle*, mirroring the sentiments of Magpies' fans everywhere when they heard the momentous news. 'I was staggered and had to check the news twice over. It is, of course, April Fool's Day.'

It is widely accepted that there are few certainties in the fickle world of football in the modern era and that players, often said to be manipulated by opportunistic agents, are frequently prone to changes of heart. Some cynics could have predicted Liverpool lynchpin Steven Gerrard's last-gasp decision to remain at Anfield in the summer of 2005 given that the same 'Should I stay or should I go?' saga had unfolded the year before. But few football fans could have envisaged Shearer's sensational announcement; it completely confounded perceived wisdom.

ALAN SHEARER

His extraordinary career has often been said to be one of comic-book proportions and this latest chapter was almost comparable to the twists and turns of Roy Race's seemingly never-ending Melchester Rovers stint as detailed in *Roy of the Rovers*.

The Geordie has not only become legendary for his phenomenal feats on the football field, but was renowned for his steadfast refusal to change his mind. When he declared in 2004 that he would play on for one more season, most people were convinced that it was a *fait accompli*.

He had already persistently resisted the constant clamour from England fans to reverse his decision to retire from international football at the age of twenty-nine in 2000. His steely single-mindedness has also shone through in many of his major moves. Spurning Sir Alex Ferguson and Manchester United not once, but twice, would be inconceivable for most footballers, but Alan Shearer has never been one to bow to public pressure, he has always plotted a career path that was in the best interests of him and him alone. Until April 2005, that is.

'The man who wasn't for turning had just turned 180 degrees until he was facing t'other way and that's what is surprising. Nay, amazing!' proclaimed John Gibson in the *Evening Chronicle* again. Shearer admitted to a disbelieving media on 2 April that he had been 'too hasty' in contemplating the curtailment of his playing days. Outside influences had, for once, made the Geordie idol stop and ponder. Spearheading the 'Shearer must stay' lobby were Newcastle manager Graeme Souness and chairman Freddy Shepherd. Shearer confessed: 'These two got into my head and made me think.'

Souness had publicly declared his admiration for Shearer prior to moving to Tyneside, hailing him as 'the finest centre-forward England has ever seen'. The tenacious Scot therefore made it his personal mission to coax and cajole, pester and badger his highly prized striker into staying the moment he had been installed in the Newcastle hot seat.

In September 2004, he said: 'If Alan Shearer scores twenty goals this season then I will be plaguing him not to retire. If you have a striker who can get that for you, you bite their hand off.'

The 2004–05 season was punctuated by such bullish utterances from Souness. For instance, he told the *Northern Echo* on 15 January 2005: 'Alan Shearer is important to this club. Not only on a Saturday afternoon before 3pm, but in every other walk of footballing life... He represents everything that is good and great about football, and everything that is good and great about this club. If he stays on, he will be an enormous help to me, even if he wasn't playing every week. It [a coaching role] would not be out of the question, because I want him around the place.'

His determination to do everything in his power to retain the playing services of Shearer also represented a clever act of self-preservation from Souness, who was acutely aware of the fates suffered by both Bobby Robson and Ruud Gullit when they left the Toon idol languishing on the bench.

A successful outcome of this passionate crusade would help endear the Liverpool legend to the Magpies' masses, many of whom had opposed his appointment after Sir Bobby Robson's sacking. It would also save Souness from having to replace the irreplaceable by buying a top-class centre-forward at the end of the season.

His options in the striking department began to look glaringly inadequate in view of the Tyneside torments suffered by two other Newcastle frontmen. Welshman Craig Bellamy had made no secret of his annoyance during the season about, in his opinion, being played out of position by Souness, who favoured a central striker pairing of Shearer and Dutchman Patrick Kluivert.

His public spat with the Scot reached boiling point when Souness accused Bellamy of feigning injury after he had asked him to play in midfield away against Arsenal in January 2005. Bellamy hit back, insisting that Souness was lying and was summarily jettisoned from St James' Park to Scotland and a loan spell with Celtic.

Meanwhile, Souness also had his doubts about the gifted, but irritatingly inconsistent and injury-plagued, Kluivert, who had been a high-profile purchase by Sir Bobby Robson from Barcelona in the summer of 2004. The Newcastle supremo shared the Toon Army's frustrations that the Dutchman was massively under-performing and questioned his motivation. It soon became apparent that – as was proved in the summer of 2005 – Souness and Newcastle had decided not to take up the option of another two years of seeing considerable talent wasted.

Months after his disappointing spell on Tyneside ended, the outspoken Kluivert astonishingly appeared to blame Shearer for his failure to make a significant impression at St James' Park. He told *Voetbal International*: 'There is only one man responsible for the fact that I did not become a big hit in Newcastle, his name is Alan Shearer. The man is God in the North. I think Shearer is a fantastic footballer, but Graeme Souness should have played Craig Bellamy and me together all the time. We formed the ideal partnership; Souness should have preferred both of us above Shearer.

'I know Bellamy felt the same but that did not make a difference. Every week it was Shearer and Kluivert or Shearer and Bellamy. Newcastle United Football Club is all about Alan Shearer, it is as simple as that. Nobody can beat him, nobody can touch him and nobody can do anything about it.'

While the old adage 'no player is bigger than the club' applies at most football institutions, its validity is less certain when considered in the context of Alan Shearer's considerable influence at Newcastle United. Not that this was necessarily a bad thing for Graeme Souness – quite the opposite, in fact.

UNEXPECTED EXTRA TIME

The troubled Scot always knew that he could rely on the former England captain for support during a turbulent first season in charge on Tyneside. Newcastle chairman Freddy Shepherd even went as far as describing the pair as 'soul-mates' and Shearer loyally stood shoulder to shoulder with Souness as the Magpies lurched from one crisis to another during the 2004–05 season.

Just days after announcing his decision to stay on, he joined his boss in condemning the moment of madness by Lee Bowyer and Kieron Dyer during the 3–0 home defeat to Aston Villa when the two midfielders brawled shamefully on the pitch.

Meanwhile, Freddy Shepherd was another member of the Newcastle hierarchy who was desperate for Shearer to remain. In 1998, Shepherd and fellow Newcastle director Douglas Hall were caught in a tabloid sting, which saw them making a series of derogatory comments about Newcastle including dubbing Shearer as 'Mary Poppins' – a sarcastic swipe at his goody-two-shoes image. Seven years later, the Newcastle chairman was anxious to ensure that Shearer did not, like the fictional child minder, pack up his bag and fly away.

He used his persuasive skills to good effect by promising Newcastle's prodigious son a player-coach role that would lead to eventual management of the club he loved. Shepherd revealed to the *Sun*: 'In an ideal world, I would always want a Geordie to be manager of this club and I have always seen Alan Shearer as playing some part in this football club when he finishes playing.'

Crucially, Shearer also shared Souness' and Shepherd's staunch conviction that he could play at the highest level for another season. He said: 'I am doing this because I think my performances have carried on at a level I am content with. Most importantly, the manager and the chairman believe that, too. I am confident that I can carry on at that level for another year.'

By Shearer's lofty standards, seven league goals and twenty-two in all competitions did not represent a vintage season. However, when considered in the context of his advancing age and Newcastle's lacklustre campaign, it can be viewed as a remarkable return. He also proved that he was still capable of excelling on the European stage, notching fourteen goals in eleven games in the UEFA Cup.

Shortly after announcing that he was prolonging his Newcastle career, a superb goal and a terrific all-round display in the 1–0 first-leg UEFA Cup quarter-final win against Sporting Lisbon illustrated that he was still a force to be reckoned with in Europe. Henry Winter, writing in the *Daily Telegraph*, summed up Shearer's performance thus: 'Shearer gave Sporting's centre-halves a real bruising welcome to the North-East, backing in, dropping off, running wide, confusing Beto and Anderson Polga with either his clever movement, or muscling them out of his way.'

His detractors couldn't even say that with the onset of age, the veteran striker had lost vital yards of pace as, even during his prime, Shearer was never blessed with searing acceleration off the mark. His bursts of pace tended to be sporadic and perfectly timed to allow him to steal into the box and perform his predatory tasks. What's more, despite the passage of time, his renowned muscularity and 'nuisance' factor also remained intact.

Another significant factor in Shearer's amazing about-turn was his optimism that, at long, long last, Newcastle were about to end their seemingly interminable trophy drought. The St James' Park side had not won a major trophy since the Fairs Cup – now known as the UEFA Cup – triumph in 1969.

In the spring of 2005, Newcastle were chasing glory on two fronts – the UEFA Cup and the FA Cup – although they were ultimately denied silverware in both competitions.

Just as George Best or Paul Gascoigne's careers are somewhat cruelly considered to be ones of wasted potential, some football pundits believe that Shearer's talents warranted more trophies for his time in football to be deemed an unqualified success. A solitary Premiership crown won with Blackburn was certainly scant reward for one of England's finest-ever forwards and the most prolific Premiership goalscorer in history.

A further season at St James' Park guaranteed him at least three more cracks at club success in the Premiership, FA Cup and Carling Cup. 'The last few months have been fantastic for everyone and the spirit in the camp is fantastic, too,' enthused Shearer. 'We can go on to bigger and better things here and I want to be part of what is happening. I believe this football club is moving in the right direction and I believe we can win things.'

He also succumbed to the overwhelming pleading of his adoring faithful who bombarded him with scores of e-mails and letters in a bid to persuade him to shelve his retirement plans. Shearer said: 'The response from the public has been incredible. I have thousands of e-mails and faxes at home and I've been through every one of them. That was the point when I thought, "Hang on, am I making the right decision?" The majority were telling me I was making the wrong decision.'

But perhaps the most telling and tangible show of faith from the Toon Army came when, during Newcastle's UEFA Cup game against Heerenveen, St James' Park rose as one and sang in unison: 'Give us one more season, Shearer.'

And the views of his nearest and dearest, particularly his wife Lainya, had to be taken into account when he contemplated extending his illustrious career. Shearer quipped: 'It was a tough decision, but the right one for everyone concerned – especially my wife, who I don't think was relishing the prospect of me being at home 24/7!'

But he denied that his decision was motivated by the fact that he was edging tantalisingly close to another Newcastle legend, Jackie Milburn's, club record of 200 goals.

ALAN SHEARER

Whatever the reasons, Shearer's decision was greeted with widespread delight on Tyneside. Graeme Souness said:

> I cannot tell you how delighted I am by the news. Everybody at this football club should be thrilled, and if all my future signings turn out to be as good as this one, I'll be extremely happy... I tried to get into his roots, into his head, telling him, 'This is your club, the club you love, and if you really love it you have got to stay here and help me for another year to be a success and help the club challenge the big boys and win things.' And he has made the right decision for all the right reasons.
>
> I don't believe it was such a big decision for him. He loves this club; he has a hell of a lot to offer Newcastle – not just goals but every aspect of this club.

'It is the news every fan wanted to hear, and also the news the board and the manager Graeme Souness wanted to hear,' Freddy Shepherd added. 'His new contract will read "player-coach" and we are looking forward to another year of Alan Shearer at Newcastle.'

Although some Newcastle fans expressed misgivings about Shearer's ability to excel in the Premiership at the age of nearly thirty-five, the vast majority was equally jubilant about their hero's unexpected change of heart. They began to drool over the prospect of Shearer being paired with his former England strike partner, Michael Owen, a supposed summer target for Souness after the former Liverpool star became disillusioned with the paucity of his first-team appearances for Real Madrid in Spain.

Surely, then, the script had been written, *à la* Roy Race, for Shearer to fire a revitalised Newcastle to much-sought-after success both at home and abroad? However, Shearer's football fortunes do not quite have the fantastical flavour of those of the Melchester Rovers' legend.

There was more of a gloomy fog on the Tyne than a bright new dawn for Newcastle following his early April announcement. Joy turned to abject despair in just a day as Newcastle plummeted into a vortex: first when Lee Bowyer and Kieron Dyer clashed disgracefully during the 3–0 home capitulation to Aston Villa on 2 April. Shearer and Newcastle's woes deepened further when they suffered a crushing 4–1 loss to Sporting Lisbon in the quarter-final of the UEFA Cup.

Despite suffering a succession of career-threatening injuries and two consecutive FA Cup final losses with Newcastle, Shearer lamented to the *Sun* on 18 June 2005, that: 'The defeat in Lisbon was the lowest point in the whole of my career – by an absolute mile. I have never felt worse, more pained, more empty than that night in Lisbon, believe me. And that includes the night I lay in a hospital bed with my ankle pointing in the wrong direction.'

Days after their exit from Europe, Newcastle's sole chance of domestic silverware was then thwarted by a rampant Manchester United. United's one-sided, 4–1 thumping of the hapless Geordies in the FA Cup semi-finals led Paul Hayward in the *Daily Telegraph* to implore Shearer to change his mind yet again.

Hayward said: 'Memo to Alan Shearer: you changed your mind once, so you can change it twice. In the hour of Newcastle's obliteration here yesterday, an internal voice must have been telling the local hero to walk away from the smouldering ruins of his hometown club's embarrassing campaign.'

Hayward twisted the knife further when he declared that Manchester United's romp hammered home a chastening reminder to Shearer of his refusal to move to Old Trafford and savour silverware galore earlier in his career. He said: 'On the evidence of an abysmally one-sided FA Cup semi-final, Shearer will smash Jackie Milburn's club record of 200 Newcastle goals with ease but leave the playing staff at St James' Park with little else to show for ten years of toil. This is the unspoken calamity of Manchester United's contemptuous 4–1 win.'

The deeply depressing double whammy of defeats had exacted a devastating psychological toll on Shearer as Newcastle's season lay in tatters. He reportedly implored Souness – although Shearer subsequently insisted it was a joint decision – to omit him from Newcastle's away trip to Fulham in early May, claiming that he was 'physically and psychologically drained'.

Some members of the media seized on this plea as proof that Shearer was not fit to continue his playing days. The *Northern Echo*'s Scott Wilson believed his requested omission raised the question of 'Should he be guaranteed a starting spot next season?'

The beleaguered striker was also, according to various media reports, allegedly the target of abuse from Newcastle's tempestuous Welsh striker, Craig Bellamy. The *Scottish Sunday Mail* reported on 24 April 2005 that Bellamy – still smarting from being shunted to Scotland following his bitter feud with Souness – had sent a series of taunting insults to Shearer via text messages after Newcastle's FA Cup defeat. 'They included insults: "Your legs are gone. You're too old. You're too slow." Another – which made him "turn purple with rage" – reportedly read: 'You couldn't even kiss my a**e,"' said reporters Brian McNally and Euan Stretch of the alleged contents of the text messages. The article claimed that, even earlier that year, Bellamy had left Shearer an abusive voicemail and sent insulting text messages to both Graeme Souness and Freddy Shepherd when reports suggested he was due to be sold to Birmingham for £6 million. It added that a spokesman for Bellamy had responded to the shocking allegations by insisting: 'The text messages were not sent by him. The mobile phone was lost while he was in Ireland and reported as such.'

Off-the-field turmoil was mirrored by Newcastle's continued on-the-pitch demise. What in April had looked like becoming a season of growing promise for Shearer and his team-mates was now rapidly turning into a calamitous campaign. Even Shearer's fantastic feat of playing his 500th league game in Newcastle's turgid goalless draw at home with Crystal Palace was couched in negativity, indicative of the despondency enveloping St James' Park.

The Newcastle *Journal*'s Luke Edwards said on 2 May 2005: 'It was the Newcastle captain's 500th career start but, such is the burden currently weighing so heavily on his shoulders, that he looked as though he had played the last 100 back-to-back. At thirty-four, Shearer should not be expected to lead the line on his own at the tail-end of his seventeenth year in the top flight. There is only so much a club's talisman can take and this was his tenth Premiership match without a goal, a barren patch which dates back to the 1–1 draw with Manchester City on 2 February.'

An exhausted Shearer was then left on the bench for Newcastle's trip to Everton in the next match, which ended in dismal failure once again, as the Magpies lost 2–0.

He now couldn't wait for the end of Newcastle's awful season; one that had spiralled depressingly downwards after he had sprung his spring shock.

Freddy Shepherd attempted to cheer up the sorrowful Shearer by again making public his desire to see the striker become Newcastle boss in the future. His declaration raised further speculation that the axe was about to fall on Souness' faltering reign, as Newcastle prepared to bring their season to a close by entertaining Chelsea at St James' Park.

Meanwhile, Newcastle were again linked with a sensational £20 million swoop for Michael Owen, all of which overshadowed the persistent rumours of Souness' uncertain future. And the Magpies, who scored when Shearer's thirty-third- minute flick-on was bundled into his own net by Chelsea midfielder Geremi, salvaged a measure of pride from the wreckage of a dreadful campaign when they held the Premiership champions to a 1–1 draw. It was a creditable performance in which to bring the curtain down on Newcastle's worst-ever Premiership season – they matched their lowest total of 44 points and ended up entrenched in mid-table mediocrity by finishing fourteenth.

Shearer would have been forgiven for thinking that the close season would prove a welcome reprieve from the controversy and criticism that had ravaged him and Newcastle at the tail-end of 2004–05, but his lengthy career has inured him to tabloid journalists' apparent glee at revelling in the misery of superstars whose reputations they help to cultivate.

Alan Shearer was akin to wounded flesh being picked at and devoured by crow-like hacks, hungry to sate their readers' craving for meaty tales during a post-season football famine. On 3 June 2005, the *Daily Star* featured an astonishing attack on the forlorn forward from his former boss – Ruud Gullit.

The pair had enjoyed a stormy relationship during the Dutchman's brief spell in charge of Newcastle between 1998 and 1999 and Gullit was seemingly still bitter about his acrimonious departure from St James' Park, one that had been precipitated by his decision to drop Shearer to the bench for the derby with Sunderland. He said: 'I definitely think Alan Shearer should have quit at the end of the season like he was going to do. It would be better if he'd stopped. Shearer has got too much influence at Newcastle. If he had stopped it would have helped the team move on.'

Shearer was then cheered by the news that he was to be awarded a testimonial as a fitting culmination of his playing career at the end of the 2005–06 season in Newcastle's 3–1 first-leg victory in Slovakia.

The additions to Newcastle's squad of midfielders Emre and Scott

Parker and defender Craig Moore were also encouraging, offset by the departures of big-name stars such as Patrick Kluivert to Valencia, Laurent Robert to Portsmouth and Craig Bellamy, who joined Shearer's former club, Blackburn Rovers. Despite this flurry of transfer activity at St James' Park, Newcastle's squad was still looking woefully inadequate for the challenges ahead, including a possible gateway into the UEFA Cup – via the Intertoto Cup.

Shearer scored twice in a 2–0 win over Slovakian side ZTS Dubnica at St James' Park to help Newcastle progress to the semi-finals of the competition 5–1 on aggregate in July 2005. And his brace brought him within only seven goals of Jackie Milburn's club record of 200 strikes. Indeed, he would have been even closer to a place in the history books had UEFA not deemed that a second goal initially attributed to him was an own goal.

The modest Magpie did not want to discuss any potential record-breaking achievements after the match, however, repeating the familiar mantra that 'the club is more important than the individual'. He admitted afterwoods: 'The record is not a motivation and this is the last time I will talk about it, because team-wise it's irrelevant. The team is far more important. If I get goals then great, but I don't want it to become a distraction.'

A stiffer test of Newcastle's European credentials now lay ahead, however, as the Tyneside club were paired with the classy Spaniards, Deportivo La Coruna, in the Intertoto Cup semi-finals. This seminal clash would highlight Newcastle's desperate shortage of attacking resources and provoked an urgent need for forward reinforcements.

Throughout the summer, Graeme Souness had been linked with a myriad of stellar strikers, including Alan Smith, Christian Vieri, Nicolas Anelka and Luis Boa Morte, but had singularly failed to make any acquisition for a variety of reasons. According to Shearer's former Blackburn and Newcastle team-mate, Kevin Gallacher, securing a worthy replacement for the retiring Shearer was a near-impossible task. Gallacher said in the Glasgow *Evening Times*:

> Getting somebody to take over from Alan Shearer at Newcastle United is like getting somebody to take over from Pelé with Brazil. It is next to impossible. Alan's great strength is, purely and simply, that he scores goals. As his team-mate you just know that, if you get a ball into the box and he is there, he is 99.9 per cent certain to put it in the back of the net. That quality is invaluable. Patrick Kluivert, who has proved himself to be a world-class player with Ajax, Barcelona and Holland over the years, failed to live up to Shearer's standards last season.

Indeed, Souness' luckless hunt for firepower in the transfer market highlighted the significance of Shearer's u-turn earlier that year, and the veteran was deployed as a lone striker in the first leg of the tie with La Coruna, who triumphed 2–1.

But Lee Bowyer's precious away goal gave the Geordies a glimmer of hope that European qualification was still within their grasp. Shearer's last crack at elusive continental glory was dashed in the return leg, however, as the Spaniards deservedly defeated Newcastle 2–1 at St James' Park. The crestfallen striker was characteristically determined to portray a brave public face after playing his final game in Europe. He said: 'Even though we are out, I thought there were plenty of positives. I thought we played some decent stuff at times. If I'd put one in early it may have given us a lifeline, but we missed a couple, their goalkeeper made some good saves and we hit the bar. They are a good side, but it was a mistake that cost us the second goal.'

As the start of the new Premiership season approached, Shearer was realistic about his personal goals for the forthcoming campaign. 'When I sat down with the chairman and the manager before I signed my contract, I was fully aware I wouldn't be playing every single game this year,' he admitted in the Newcastle *Journal*. 'That's physically impossible for me because of what has gone on in the past. To keep me fit and sharp and hopefully scoring goals, I understand I will not be able to play every game and I accept that.'

Meanwhile, there was also renewed speculation in the media about the possibility of Michael Owen joining Shearer to form a mouth-watering strike force. Graeme Souness made no secret of his craving to capture Owen and, with Manchester United and Liverpool both denying their interest in the Real Madrid star, he tabled an £11 million bid for the England man.

But Shearer refused to believe that Newcastle were in pole position to acquire the former Liverpool ace, telling the *Journal* on 8 August 2005: 'There will be a few after Owen's signature. I know one or two have denied they are in for him, but we all know what football is like. Some people are just not prepared to say they are in for him yet.' He added: 'Our manager would love him here, he would be a great asset. I had great times with him and England.'

One player who definitely would not wear the famous black-and-white stripes was the Italian defender Francesco Coco, who was poised for a season-long loan move from Inter Milan, but failed to impress Souness during a trial. And gifted England midfielder Jermaine Jenas also looked to be bound for the St James' Park exit door after admitting he wanted to leave the 'goldfish-bowl' environment at Newcastle. Jenas, who eventually moved to Tottenham not long after the start of the season, hit the headlines again when he was sent off during Newcastle's opening Premiership game of the 2005–06 campaign at Arsenal, which the Gunners won 2–0.

Shearer had shrugged off a calf injury to take his place as a lone striker but, shorn of striking support, was below his best. A dull 0–0 draw at home to West Ham again highlighted Newcastle's need for another striker and the Magpies responded with a £9 million bid for Deportivo La Coruna striker, Alberto Luque, which was eventually accepted by the Spaniards.

Luque joined after Newcastle fell to a disappointing 2–0 defeat at Bolton and duly made his debut alongside Shearer when the Magpies entertained Manchester United at St James' Park. But despite a promising display from the Spaniard – which included having a goal chalked off for offside – second-half goals from Wayne Rooney and Ruud van Nistelrooy handed the Manchester club a comfortable 2–0 victory. Newcastle's dire shortcomings in front of goal were clear for all to see, as they had now failed to score in their first four matches of the season.

However, the purchase the Toon Army craved was Michael Owen and Newcastle duly obliged, after the Spanish giants accepted a club record £17 million bid for the Real Madrid man. Owen said that he would have preferred a return to Liverpool, but declared that if no offer was forthcoming from Anfield, he would join Newcastle on a season-long loan.

Souness knew that the capture of the talented Spaniard Luque could not fill the gaping void Shearer's planned departure at the end of the season would leave and was desperate to secure the signature of Owen, a striker who possesses comparable goal-scoring capabilities to the Tyneside legend. Shearer wholeheartedly supported his manager's determined pursuit of the diminutive player. 'I am no different to anyone else at this football club, I would love him to come here,' he said. 'He would improve any team in the Premiership and we are no different.'

Meanwhile, Shearer was the subject of a flattering eulogy from a Swedish cultural studies student. Jenny Lindstrom penned her 14,000-word thesis on the exploits of her hero after spending four months in Newcastle exploring his symbiotic relationship with the city. 'The relationship between Alan Shearer and the city of Newcastle is so unique,' gushed Jenny in the *Evening Chronicle*. The student had received funding from the University of Linkoping in eastern Sweden to pursue her labour of love.

'You ask yourself as you walk the streets and hear people chant his name and wear his name in print on their backs if it is possible for one single person to be this worshipped, in this day and age. I want to describe how a modern day hero is created and how one person can become a superman and an icon for a whole city.'

Shearer was living up to such exalted praise by proving a key figure in Newcastle's persistent pursuit of his ex-England colleague, doing his utmost to sway Owen into joining the Tyneside club. He told BBC Radio Five Live: 'I've had several phone conversations with him and spent a fortune calling Madrid, but I don't have to tell him what passionate supporters we have. I know if he came here he would be loved. They love their goalscorers up here and he would be a hero,' he added.

His tireless efforts were rewarded when Owen sensationally elected to move to Newcastle for a club record £17 million on 31 August 2005 in favour of returning to Liverpool. Parallels between Shearer's momentous arrival on Tyneside nine years earlier were unavoidable and demonstrated that Newcastle went where other clubs feared to tread by continually and boldly pursuing the world's best players, including Wayne Rooney in 2004.

Newcastle's massive outlay, their unexpected triumph in capturing their man from under the noses of their rivals and the ecstatic response of their fans bore all the hallmarks of Shearer's joyous homecoming.

Following his initial reservations, Owen was persuaded to put pen to paper on a four-year contract. Shearer had been part of a four-man Newcastle delegation – including Graeme Souness, Newcastle first-team coach Dean Saunders and Freddy Shepherd – that met Owen in

Northumberland on the same day that the striker had held talks with Liverpool boss Rafa Benitez.

Graeme Souness and Freddy Shepherd had pulled off an incredible coup: one that perhaps outstripped their success earlier in the year of persuading Shearer to continue at Newcastle. Shepherd, who could barely conceal his delight, said of his amazing swoop: 'Bringing Michael here will rank alongside the signing of Alan Shearer as my proudest moment at Newcastle.'

Souness shared his chairman's jubilation, telling Newcastle's official website: 'In football, the hardest thing to get is someone who puts the ball in the back of the net and Michael is the best at doing that for England. I'd say it's the biggest transfer I've been involved in as a manager of any football club.'

Newcastle fans were understandably stunned by the club's astonishing signing. Ian Gilmour, of the Newcastle United Supporters' Association, admitted to BBC Sport: 'I am totally speechless. I cannot believe it, if I am honest with you. I thought Owen was going to Liverpool and I am very surprised that he has come to St James' Park.'

Owen was given a hero's welcome at St James' Park, reminiscent of Shearer's unforgettable arrival at Newcastle nine years earlier, when he was unveiled in hazy September sunshine to an adoring faithful numbering some 15,000 ecstatic fans. 'Owen can be as important for us and as big as Shearer,' said thirty-two-year-old factory worker Sam Rose, from Kenton in the *Evening Chronicle*. 'He will be a hero here. Just look at the reception he got today and he's not even played yet. His signing has lifted the whole club.'

Yet some sceptical pundits questioned his commitment to Newcastle given his admission that he would have joined Liverpool had the Reds been willing to meet Madrid's asking price for the player. But Owen has insisted that he would be completely focused on helping to revitalise Newcastle's flagging fortunes and declared that he was desperate to experience the raw passion of the Premiership again. And Freddy Shepherd dismissed suggestions that Owen's spell in the North-East would be a fleeting one. He said: 'I have heard a little rumour that Michael has a clause in his contract which states he can leave Newcastle United in one year's time. I can tell you now that he hasn't.'

However, one season would be the length of time that Owen would play with the retiring Shearer and the twenty-five-year-old stressed that his friend had played a crucial role in persuading him to move to Tyneside through a concerted charm offensive. Shearer underlined the adulation from Newcastle's passionate fans which would await Owen, should he move to St James' Park.

He even went as far as offering Owen his No. 9 shirt for the season; an 'unbelievable gesture' according to the former Madrid man and one that he rejected. Shearer told the *Sun*: 'I am as excited as I've been as a Newcastle fan in a long, long time. I didn't get much sleep on Monday evening, then I spent early Tuesday morning talking to Michael and his agent.'

Owen was delighted to be reunited with his former England forward partner, commenting: 'He's been a good friend for a long time. It's his last season here and it will be an honour to play with him. He shares a lot of the same interests as I do and he was one of a few reasons to join. Following Shearer is not easy. I can only guarantee I will give 100 per cent, score as many goals as I can, but help the team win as many games as possible.'

While Owen's Tyneside transfer dominated the headlines, popular Peruvian midfielder Nolberto Solano slipped back into St James' Park almost unnoticed when he re-joined Newcastle from West Ham. The *Northern Echo*'s Paul Fraser believed that Owen was the missing ingredient in Newcastle's line-up and one that hinted at goals galore. He said: 'It [Owen's arrival] now means Souness can abandon his three-pronged attack that has worked to the detriment of Shearer's ageing legs and concentrate on supplying his lethal front two with the necessary ammunition. With Albert Luque on the left, there remains the matter of who will be asked to play on the right flank with Nolberto Solano suddenly emerging as a possibility. But, regardless of whether that role is afforded to Solano, Kieron Dyer, Lee Bowyer or James Milner, Souness has surely found the correct formula for the thing most lacking from his side's play – goals.'

The *Express*' Mick Dennis was less impressed with the thought of Shearer and Owen forming their England alliance for their club and ventured a damning assessment of the elder of the pair. He said:

> It is said that Shearer and Owen were terrific pals when they played together for England, but if that is true, then their body language was extremely misleading and Shearer must have displayed a generosity of spirit off the field to the youngster which was not apparent on it. It is extremely unlikely that they will gel now in the Premiership because Shearer is so far past his sell-by-date. Look closely at him. Don't use Sky's player-cam coverage, because you will think the picture has frozen. Instead, try to study Shearer in the flesh, as I did when Newcastle surrendered at Bolton last month. His team were shocking and he was a big part of the problem because he was so turgidly immobile. Two or three times he plodded along the touch-line to confront a defender in a one-on-one and played for a ricochet off the opponent's shin.

Shearer, so often the top dog among Newcastle's forwards since 1996, insisted that he was happy to play second fiddle to his heir apparent during his final fling.

He had every faith in his new strike partner emerging at the top of the scoring charts and insisted that he would be perfectly satisfied at this outcome – even though he would be supplanted from his regular role as both Newcastle and the Premiership's leading scorer.

Owen's debut for Newcastle, at home to Fulham on 10 September 2005, was as feverishly anticipated as Kevin Keegan's or Shearer's had been at St James' Park. Yet it all ended up as a massive anti-climax as Newcastle laboured to a 1–1 draw, with Charles N'Zogbia upstaging the new boy with a goal from a late free-kick.

The overwhelming optimism that had gripped St James' Park was well and truly punctured and the unhappy rumours that had infected Newcastle prior to Owen's arrival resurfaced again like an unremitting bad smell. Graeme Souness was again said to be facing the axe, with Shearer supposedly poised to step into the manager's breach at St James' Park.

The Times' Matt Dickinson wrote: 'There have been mutterings that Alan Shearer could retire as soon as he breaks Jackie Milburn's record of 200 goals for Newcastle United, rather than wait until the end of the season. Shearer denies it and, on recent form, it might look presumptuous to assume that he will have the choice. Shearer needs six goals to equal Milburn's tally and unless they all come from the penalty spot, the former England forward must fear that he will still be chasing the record next May. He has not scored in his past seventeen Barclays Premiership matches which, even considering the inevitable fading of his powers at thirty-five, is remarkable for a man who can smite a ball with violent force, if given half the chance.'

Now only rivals Sunderland kept Newcastle away from the ignominy of the Premiership's basement and there was further turmoil to follow when it emerged that Albert Luque would be sidelined for up to two months after tearing his hamstring during the Fulham match. Enough was enough for Souness, who not only demanded an extra training session but had also held an impromptu crisis meeting with his players in a bid to seek solutions to their escalating crisis.

ALAN SHEARER

A trip to Blackburn heaped yet more pressure onto the Scot, given that he would be reacquainted with Craig Bellamy, the fiery Welshman with whom he had clashed repeatedly during their stormy few months together. For Shearer, meanwhile, not only was he returning to his old hunting ground but he was also desperately in need of scoring a goal to silence an ever-increasing army of doubters.

The genial Geordie enjoys nothing better than sticking up the proverbial two fingers at his unforgiving critics and defiantly did so again when he scored his first Premiership goal for twenty-five hours in Newcastle's unexpectedly easy 3–0 victory at Ewood Park. He broke the deadlock with a blistering free-kick, before Michael Owen scored his first Newcastle goal to make it 2–0 and Charles N'Zogbia capped a tremendous display on the left-wing with a third.

Shearer was now one step nearer to eclipsing Jackie Milburn's historic goal haul and even the Blackburn supporters rose in unison to acclaim the hero they had loved to hate since his departure from Ewood Park in 1996. 'It was Shearer's 195th goal in a black-and-white shirt, leaving him six short of breaking Jackie Milburn's club record and, in the context of the unrest at Newcastle, it must be as valuable as either of the strikes in FA Cup semi-finals or that goal at Heerenveen in February, which temporarily silenced chants of "Sack the board", said the *Guardian*'s Michael Walker. 'Thirteen minutes after scoring, Shearer was replaced. He has had a difficult relationship with Blackburn's supporters since he moved from Ewood to St James' Park in 1996. But Shearer was back here for Tony Parkes' testimonial in May and received a good reception. Yesterday, when he walked off, all four sides of the ground were on their feet.'

Relieved, Graeme Souness rubbished suggestions that Shearer's weary legs would not survive a gruelling Premiership campaign. He insisted 'I think you would be an absolute fool to lose faith in Alan given his track record. I work with him every day and I don't see any desire missing. Opportunities for strikers don't come along and then they all come along at once. I hope that this is the start of a run for Alan and it was good for Michael to get off the mark as well.'

Souness also supported his striker when Shearer became embroiled in controversy after being left bruised and battered during Newcastle's stormy 1-0 Carling Cup win at Grimsby in October. Shearer, who scored the winner, required three stitches in his lip – accusing pugnacious Grimsby defender Alan Whittle of causing the injury with a flying elbow. BBC Sport reported that Shearer was raging at the incident: 'It would have been easy for me to go out there and do him because that is what I wanted to do but I had to be sensible,' said the 35-year-old Shearer. 'He has done me, it was blatant. The referee was five yards away and did nothing.' Whittle expressed disappointment with Shearer and remains unapologetic. Both players were involved in a shoving match as they exchanged angry words at the final whistle at Blundell Park. 'He didn't want to shake my hand at the end and I haven't got a problem with that,' he told BBC Radio Humberside. 'But I'm disappointed with him. If you dish it out you've got to take it.' And Whittle has been backed by his club.

The League Two outfit released a statement which read: 'We feel that there was no deliberate intent on behalf of Justin to catch Alan with his arm. The referee was very close to the incident and no action was taken.'

Shearer's combative style aroused controversy again during the 2005/06 season when Arsenal manager Arsène Wenger hit out at the Newcastle man following his side's 1-0 defeat at St James' Park in mid-December. He was reported as saying: 'Shearer always plays the man first – we have to decide if we want football or judo. Every challenge in the air from Shearer was a foul first.'

On this occasion, Shearer's response was that 'he didn't care' about the Frenchman's comments, which were perhaps borne of bitterness at Arsenal's faltering Premiership challenge.

What Shearer did care about passionately, however, was stamping his name in the Newcastle history books yet again.

As 2006 began, he was tantalisingly just one goal away from equalling Jackie Milburn's 200-goal record for Newcastle. Success or failure in his quest for this landmark would have a significant bearing on how his planned final season in football would be assessed. Yet he would have to chase the record shorn of the support of his striking cohort Michael Owen, who broke the fifth metatarsal bone in his foot during Newcastle's 2-0 defeat away to Tottenham on December 31, and was expected to be sidelined for several months. Owen's prolonged absence was sure to reignite renewed appeals for Shearer to postpone his retirement once again. Prior to this, Graeme Souness had already expressed the belief that Newcastle's favourite son was capable of another season in his beloved black and white shirt, although Shearer was adamant that 2005's shock announcement would not be repeated.

Whatever happened in the final months of the 2005/06 season, given how Shearer's career had panned out in the past, his swansong was sure to be utterly eventful and undoubtedly memorable...

CHAPTER THIRTEEN

Breaking the Record

A lan Shearer's career at Newcastle United is considered by a some observers to be a story of wretched unfulfilment given his frustrating inability to win silverware with his hometown club. His critics quite justifiably point out that a lack of tangible rewards from his 10 years at his boyhood heroes is a depressing legacy from his controversial decision to spurn Manchester United on two separate occasions.

However, if you measure the success or failure of Shearer's time at St James' Park purely in terms of club achievements, then you are guilty of a serious injustice. A fusillade of goals for Newcastle, allowing him to accumulate milestones and records aplenty, resulted in him attaining hero worship and become a living legend on Tyneside. Winner's medals are the ultimate goal of every professional footballer, but even these cannot compete with the everlasting love from your own supporters. Becoming an idol for the club he supported as a boy will even see Shearer become immortalised in bronze after it was announced that a statue of him and Jackie Milburn would be created in 2007. Only the

ALAN SHEARER

very best footballers are accorded such an honour and very few of
them are, unlike Shearer, still living and breathing to this day.

However, while Shearer effortlessly racked up a multitude of
personal achievements in the black-and-white stripes, one attainment
remained elusive and unfulfilled until his final season: the record to
beat all records – the prestigious honour of Newcastle's greatest
goalscorer. Securing this honour during the 2005–06 campaign would
allow Shearer to justifiably lay claim to being Newcastle's greatest
centre-forward of them all, statistically at least, superior to the likes
of Hughie Gallacher, Malcolm Macdonald, Wyn Davies and the man
who was the original goalscorer supreme at St James', Jackie Milburn.

A burning desire to eclipse Milburn's 200 league goals had, it was
widely believed, underscored Shearer's conviction to reverse his
decision to call time on his career in 2005 and would partly make
amends for the lack of club success throughout his 10 years on
Tyneside. Shearer denied that securing another record to add to his
abundant collection of personal highlights had influenced his decision
to continue his playing days. But earning his most coveted piece of
history yet must have weighed heavily on his mind throughout the
2005–06 season and was also a central theme in the press whenever
his name was mentioned.

Frenzied 'will he, won't he?' conjecture dominated the thoughts and
discussions of the Newcastle legions and the *Observer*'s Spencer
Vignet even posed the light-hearted question of how Shearer would
celebrate breaking Milburn's record. He wrote, 'Would he bungee jump
off the Tyne Bridge in a Ruud Gullit wig, or perhaps streak through the
latest exhibition at the Baltic gallery singing Lindisfarne's 'Lady
Eleanor'? Anything but the trademark grin and raised right arm.'

The response to Vignet's query was simple; yet the questions of if,
when and how Shearer would supplant Milburn as Newcastle United's
most prolific forward could not be answered as easily. The predictable

unpredictability of football and Alan Shearer's fickle fortunes ensured this was the case. Nothing has ever been a cast-iron guarantee in Shearer's football career, with its twin passions, joy and pain. Yet failure to attain the record would have been plain cruel to a man whom fate had conspired against in the past through a litany of horrendous injuries. Everyone of a Newcastle persuasion was willing the retiring hero to stamp his name in the history books one more time.

Even Jackie Milburn's son, Jack, publicly voiced his support for Shearer's quest, even though he might have been praying inwardly for his father's record to remain intact. He told the *Northern Echo*, 'It looks as if he will pass 200 and I think it's great news. I'm sure my father will be sat on a cloud up there shouting "go on, Alan" every time he gets a goal.

'My father would be the first to say congratulations to Alan if he were still around, I'm sure of that. He is a Geordie lad and the whole of the city are excited by the prospect of him breaking the record. The whole city has just been excited by the "will he, won't he" retirement situation. That just shows how highly he is regarded around the place.'

Yet Mr Milburn Junior, whose father passed away in 1988, could not resist pointing out that Wor Jackie had in fact scored another 38 goals, which were not officially recorded, during the Second World War. However, despite this, he could not be churlish and resent the fact that Shearer was poised to dethrone his father as Newcastle's goal king.

He added, 'My father scored 238 goals if you consider the games played when there weren't any league games. Those games were played in front of 60,000 people so you can't say they weren't serious. I say it a little tongue-in-cheek though because Alan has done remarkably and he could well go on to get that total anyway.'

So, just who was Jackie Milburn and why is he a revered folk hero on Tyneside, rendering his record such an enviable target for a goal-hungry Alan Shearer? Young aficionados of football may be distinctly unimpressed by the feats of a footballer who plied his trade in the baggy-shorts, black-and-white television era of the 1940s and 1950s. However, his name and unforgettable achievements still resonate with every Newcastle fan, young and old to this day.

Milburn was the Wayne Rooney of his day, who was renowned for explosive shooting with either foot, often from seemingly impossible angles, as well as his stunning ball skill and phenomenal speed off the mark; the latter attribute was employed to good effect when Milburn was a professional sprinter. By apposite coincidence, the initials of his first three names, John Edward Thompson, spell the word 'JET'.

It is also worth pointing out that his fascinating story bears some uncanny similarities to the man who was on the verge of overtaking his goals haul. Milburn hailed from a working-class background; he was born in the North East mining town of Ashington in 1924. He left school at the age of 14, tried his hand at a variety of jobs, but his innate footballing ability meant that he soon came to the attention of Newcastle, who took him on trial. Milburn responded brilliantly by scoring six goals in one game and was duly signed as a first-team player for the statutory £10 registration fee.

His prodigious football skills captivated Newcastle fans, who immediately nicknamed him Wor Jackie (Our Jackie), as they cherished him as one of their own. However, rather like Shearer, Milburn was always a reluctant hero who was unassuming and private off the pitch. Like the man who would succeed him in the black-and-white shirt, he shunned the limelight and preferred to articulate himself on the football field and let others speak about him, which they would normally do with awe-struck amazement and a string of laudatory adjectives. However, unlike his successor in the number-nine shirt for Newcastle, Milburn did not pursue a clean-living lifestyle; he was a heavy smoker, whose pre-match routine involved eating a meat pie and having a cigarette.

BREAKING THE RECORD

Among his legions of admirers were his nephews, Sir Bobby and Jack Charlton, although Milburn was only an uncle in the hearts and minds of the pair as he was actually their mother Cissie's cousin. Sir Bobby admitted to the *Sunday Times* in 2005 that so powerful was Milburn's magnetic appeal that, if he was not playing, many Newcastle supporters were not as interested in watching their team play. When he did take to the field, every Newcastle supporter was transfixed on this personification of poetry in motion, whose beguiling elegance, sublime skill and awesome power were sights to behold.

Sir Bobby went on to express his delight that the Magpies' modern-day Milburn was set to overtake the past master's benchmark given that the name and achievements of Wor Jackie had been brought to the fore again.

He said, 'When Shearer does it, I'll have a little thought about Jackie and how marvellous he was. Shearer's a marvellous player and a born goalscorer but he's a different type – he never runs at people. When he beats the record, it won't knock any of the gloss off Jackie. He hasn't spent his whole career at the club and isn't so identified with Newcastle as Jackie.'

Charlton continued, 'The good thing about the record is that it's giving people the chance to think about Jackie again, and it's up to those like me to tell people how good he actually was. And a lot of people would say he was a better man than he was a footballer. He was a marvellous man.'

Indeed, as Charlton revealed, Milburn's legend owes as much to his off-the-field persona as his momentous achievements on the field of play. Unlike Shearer, he achieved trophy success with his club; the bedrock of the Milburn legend is the fact that he helped Newcastle win three FA Cups – in 1951, 1952 and 1955. He scored in every round of the 1951 competition, and netted in both the 1952 and 1955 finals, his header in the latter being the second-fastest goal ever in FA Cup final history after being timed at 45 seconds. Just like Shearer, this was a man who consistently performed on the big occasion – he also scored 10 goals in only 13 appearances for England.

Yet Milburn transcended football in a way Shearer may never achieve as he truly was a man of the people; he worked in the pits as a fitter while starting as a footballer, finishing at 8am on Saturdays at Woodburn Colliery, Ashington. After his football career finished, he covered Newcastle for the *News of the World* and the *Sun* for more than 20 years, and remained a hugely popular figure on Tyneside. When he died from cancer in 1988, Newcastle came to a standstill for his funeral as thousands of Geordies mourned the passing of the working-class hero. A statue and a stand bearing his name at St James' Park ensure that he will never, ever be forgotten.

His influence and achievements are immeasurable, yet Shearer has done his best to achieve parity with the original Toon Idol on the football pitch. Milburn's 200 goals came in 397 Newcastle appearances, while Shearer scored 198 times in 380 games. Milburn set the benchmark in inordinate ways and therefore it is no surprise that chasing his most precious achievement, set in 1957, would define Alan Shearer's final season in a Newcastle shirt; it was quite simply, in the eyes of the fans, his *raison d'être*, his *cause célèbre*. And nothing, not even an appalling lapse in form or physiological disaster – the latter of which had befallen Shearer on several occasions – would prevent indomitable Alan from beating it.

It was on 7 January 2006 that he drew level with Milburn's mark of 200 goals, striking just 10 minutes before the end of Newcastle's FA Cup third-round tie with Mansfield Town, who lay 20th in Division Two. The goal itself was unremarkable – a seven-yard shot drilled into the bottom corner, after Albert Luque back-heeled Nolberto Solano's pass into his path. But the quality of the goal mattered little; it was its immense historical significance that counted. What made the strike all the sweeter were the circumstances in which it was achieved.

Fittingly, he registered the record-equalling goal at St James' Park, in front of the Gallowgate End where he used to stand and worship his heroes and, in turn, won the match for his team. His parents and other family members were also in attendance and, touchingly, he dedicated his goal to his mother, Anne, who celebrated her 60th birthday the day after Shearer's moment to cherish. And Shearer celebrated with his team-mates – aptly in the shadow of the Milburn Stand – with his right arm aloft in trademark fashion.

Shearer later enthused of his double century of goals, which came in his 389th Newcastle appearance, 'Thanks to the goal this will be an afternoon I will cherish for the rest of my life. It was fantastic. All my family was here which was important. It's my mum's 60th birthday tomorrow, so she can have that one. They are always here watching the game, and that just made it that much better.'

He went on to pay tribute to the man who inspired him when he was first inculcated with a passion for football. Shearer admitted, 'When I was growing up, all everybody talked about was how great Jackie Milburn was. It wouldn't bother me at all if I didn't score again because just to see my name alongside the great Jackie Milburn is a great honour for me. When I came here and signed, no way in a million years did I think I'd be up there alongside Jackie Milburn.

'I was brought up being told how great Jackie Milburn was. I never had the pleasure of meeting him but I have met some of his family. From what I know, what impresses me most is that he was a man of the people, and that is very, very important. I know that nobody has a bad word to say about him.'

As is his wont, rather than focus exclusively on his own formidable feats, Shearer also went on to allude to the wider significance of his goal for his club. For once, Shearer's detractors could not chide his post-match performance in the media room as he was effusive and engaging, paying tribute to Mansfield for their gutsy display which belied their lowly league status, and never once indulging in personal vanity.

He added, 'You might not believe me but the fact that it was the winner and that put us into the next round is probably more important than me equalling the record, so I am a very happy man right now. It has been a tough time for us recently. No one is trying to hide that fact. We're not playing great, silky football but in the FA Cup it's all about getting through to the next round and we've done that.'

Constantly mindful of others and never comfortable when concentrating solely on himself, Shearer also donated his shirt to the new Newcastle United museum. Like Milburn before him, he has always wanted to give something back to the club who nurtured him and helped shape his legend.

Marginalised somewhat by all the talk of Shearer's career-defining contribution was the fact that Newcastle's narrow win had slightly eased the unremitting pressure on Newcastle's much-maligned manager, Graeme Souness. The Scot preferred not to dwell on his own predicament, though, and instead paid handsome tribute to his talisman.

He said, 'It will take a while for what he has achieved to sink in because he's not the sort of man who thinks about records going into a game. It was always going to happen one day and it's a truly incredible achievement. Getting goals is harder now than when Jackie set the record and I don't see anybody ever matching him.'

Everyone was queuing up to praise Newcastle's legendary number nine, including Shearer's team-mate goalkeeper Shay Given, who opined that Alan had had as colossal an impact on Tyneside as Milburn before him. He commented, 'He's carried this club for a number of years with his goals, his personality and everything else, and he's done the same again. He's made a habit of getting us out of trouble. He's a legend just like Jackie Milburn and one people will still be talking about in 30 years.'

Even Jackie Milburn's widow, Laura, joined in the chorus of approval for Shearer's landmark goal. She listened to the match on the radio and admitted that records were made to be broken and that she was heartened that her late husband's had been overtaken by 'a local lad'.

Mansfield manager, Peter Shirtliff, shrugged off his disappointment at not seeing his plucky side reaping any reward for their battling performance to offer his own eulogy to Shearer: 'He is just awesome. It's a great record and he's a magnificent pro. I'm just sick that their one chance fell to him.'

Meanwhile, Shearer's unbridled joy was tempered by the sad news of the death of Milburn's former team-mate Alf McMichael, who had played alongside Jackie in the 1952 FA Cup final. The full-back was the last surviving member of the 1952 Wembley team, after winger Tommy Walker died in 2005. Yet neither McMichael nor Milburn would have wanted sadness and mourning to overshadow Shearer's joyous day and would surely have been eager that he now went on to become Newcastle's greatest goalscorer.

Suddenly the 'will he, won't he?' murmurings in relation to Shearer and 'the record' were no more. It was inevitable that Shearer was going to be a record breaker; it was just a question of *when* he would become one. The feverish anticipation about his impending feat did not last long and was punctured about a month later on Saturday, 4 February 2006, when Newcastle entertained Portsmouth and the Shearer supposition was ended for good. Once again, the setting and characteristics of the momentous occasion bore all the hallmarks of a fairytale. Triumph overcame disaster as Newcastle appeared a side reborn, reinvigorated rather than demoralised by the departure two days previously of Graeme Souness, who was sacked by Freddy Shepherd and replaced by Glenn Roeder as caretaker boss, with

Shearer as his assistant. There could also be no better place than St James' Park, packed full of 50,000 fervent Newcastle supporters, for Shearer to carve another niche into the annals of Newcastle history.

The tone for yet more joyous history making had been set perfectly before kick-off, according to the *Northern Echo*: 'It started to the refrain of Chumbawumba's "Tubthumping", with its chorus of "I get knocked down, but I get up again". Fitting for Newcastle given everything that happened last week, but also fitting for Shearer given the three serious injuries that threatened to bring his playing career to an untimely end. Assisting Glenn Roeder as his on-field representative, the legendary number nine instigated a 30-second huddle before kick-off. If anyone was going to bring the club together after a week of dissension and strife, it was always going to be him. The fans knew as much, singing "Alan Shearer's black and white army" with an undisguised glee. While the striker has underlined his determination to walk away in the summer, perhaps they know something we don't. Shearer would exude a talismanic presence as Newcastle boss and his on-field prompting on Saturday underlined just how much influence he already wields.

'Cajoling and coaxing his team-mates, the skipper led from the front with a series of clattering challenges and surging runs. Where he was keen to lead, his team-mates were quick to follow and, by the end of the opening 45 minutes, the negativity of the Souness era had all but been dispersed.'

After Newcastle took the lead through Charles N'Zogbia and laid siege to the Portsmouth goal, the odds began to shorten dramatically on Alan Shearer breaking the record, although he was certainly made to endure an agonising wait. He was unable to convert a succession of chances to score the goal he craved and, as Freddy Shepherd would later remark, it almost seemed as if Jackie Milburn's ghost had intervened as a shot-stopping spectre to thwart his record-chasing rival. But Shearer was not to be denied in his dogged pursuit of history and in the 64th minute achieved one of his greatest feats in football. Sensing his moment to pounce and determined that nothing would stop his date with destiny, Shearer took Shola Ameobi's deft backheel in his stride, muscularly evaded the Portsmouth defenders, and calmly prodded the ball under the legs of Dean Kiely in the visitors' goal.

Then, as the *Daily Telegraph*'s Tim Rich observed, 'First there was silence, the spread of tension as Alan Shearer ran on to Shola Ameobi's flick. Then there was the noise. It would have echoed across the Tyne Bridge and into the heart of anyone who has ever loved Newcastle United. The wife of the club chairman, Freddy Shepherd, who was packing to go to Kilimanjaro, heard it three miles away. She had her mountain to climb; Shearer had just conquered his.

'For the 201st time in a black-and-white shirt, Shearer wheeled away, one arm aloft and Jackie Milburn's club record – more burdensome with each game – was gone. In front of the Gallowgate End, where his most fervent supporters sat, he was swallowed up. Then he punched the air and let out a deep lungful of breath.'

An ecstatic Shearer was overjoyed that he had finally put to rest the debate, buzz and the brouhaha about his potential goals tally. He admitted, 'I'm a very happy man tonight. I know what Jackie means and meant to the people. I can now sleep easy that the pressure has gone. I'm a big believer in fate and, if I could have chosen where to do it, it would have been at the Gallowgate End. The reception the fans gave me after scoring will live with me forever. I knew they would do something special, but it was just incredible. Even I was getting emotional after scoring and then, five minutes later, they were still chanting my name.

'They were great to me when I arrived to sign at the Leazes End, but [Saturday's] reception will live with me forever. This ranks up there with anything I have ever done in football and I'm a very happy and proud man.'

After his outpouring of emotion about his glorious goal, Shearer joked that he had deliberately missed scoring what looked an easy chance in Newcastle's previous game against Cheltenham in the FA Cup so that he could score one of his most important goals in front of his home supporters.

And, once again, the ultra-modest striker was keen to allude to the goal's implications for Newcastle's season, rather than to his own legacy, and also touchingly made reference to his former manager. 'The goal is a big bonus, but the important thing was three points because we badly needed them,' added Shearer. 'Anything else would have been a disaster for us – we'd have been in serious trouble. I wish Graeme was here to see it because, whatever anyone thinks of him, he's an honest, decent and genuine man. It just didn't work out for him here because of the injury situation.'

So how did Shearer celebrate his record-breaking feats? Did he indulge in drunken debauchery and madcap antics? No, this is a man who prefers simple and uncomplicated pleasures; after all, a popular myth has it that he creosoted his fence after hearing that his team Blackburn had won the Premier League.

The *Evening Chronicle* revealed that: 'Fresh from his record-breaking performance against Portsmouth on Saturday, we can reveal that the big man splashed out on three pizzas from Papa John's in Chapel House to be delivered to his luxury Darras Hall home. He may be a multi-millionaire, able to afford the finest food and drink in the land, but Shearer's evening of debauchery came to the grand total of just £14.99, plus the generous £5 tip he handed over.

'Details of Shearer's favoured toppings are sketchy but we reckon he might have gone for a "Howay'un" (Howay'un, Hawaiian – geddit? OK, bad joke). Or perhaps he chose a Margherita. It's reliable, a little bland but you know exactly what you're getting. A bit like Shearer!'

Meanwhile, in a repeat of his kind-hearted gesture after his 200th goal, which involved him donating his shirt to the Newcastle museum, he agreed to have his boots – which he had changed before the game to bring him more luck – plated in silver. They then took pride of place in the Gallowgate End museum alongside a host of artefacts from players who had shaped Newcastle's wonderful 125-year history. Promising 'a walk through black and white history', the museum includes prized possessions such as Jackie Milburn's FA Cup winner's medal and Michael Owen's hat-trick ball from England's 5–1 rout of Germany in 2001.

The new exhibit in the showcase of Magpies' memorabilia would be as impressive as anything else on show, according to Newcastle chairman Freddy Shepherd, who added, 'Jackie is held in such esteem but I am sure he would have wanted Alan to have finally done it. I saw Jackie play, but you can't compare the two of them. They are both legends and heroes and they always will be.'

There could surely be no more fitting tribute to number one and two in Newcastle's goal charts than the eight-foot bronze statues of the pair which will be unveiled in the south-west corner of St James' Park during the 2007–08 season. The statues, entitled 'Local Heroes', are being produced by Northumberland sculptor Tom Maley, much to the delight of a proud Alan Shearer, who said, 'I feel very honoured and very proud that these statues are going to be built. It is a great honour that I will be alongside a statue of the great Jackie Milburn. As a kid growing up in Newcastle, I heard so much about his superb career and what he achieved. Never in my wildest dreams did I think that one day I would be mentioned alongside him. I feel very honoured.'

Jackie Milburn's son, Jack Junior, was thrilled that his father's magnificent contribution to Newcastle was to be recognised again. He said, 'This is fantastic news, we are so thrilled. To have the statues of my father and Alan welcoming people to St James' Park will be wonderful.'

Naturally, it is tempting to discuss and compare the respective abilities of Milburn and Shearer, despite the difficulties in doing so with players of different eras, who played in different teams and who were used in different systems. No one can ever categorically state who was better than the other, but such a question will always arouse lively debate on Tyneside from time to time. In many ways, as previously discussed, Milburn and Shearer were very similar, particularly as regards their height and builds. Yet there were also striking differences between the two, as Newcastle club historian Paul Joannou told Reuters, 'Jackie had blistering pace but Alan would be the first to admit he's not the quickest of players. Alan's brilliant in the air while Jackie didn't like the ball there and actually shied away from heading the ball because he had a problem with his neck muscles (fibrositis).

'They were two very different players in so much as "Wor Jackie" was a very mobile roving type of centre-forward and not a targetman like Alan is nowadays. After his first five or six years Alan increasingly played with his back to goal, holding the ball up and bringing others into play.'

What Milburn and Shearer did have in common, however, as Joannou went on to point out, was their 'ferocious' shooting power and their local-boy-made-good images which endeared them to their adoring faithful.

Then, as has been the main thrust of this chapter, these two marvellous men both possessed insatiable appetites for hitting the net time and time again. Milburn still remains Newcastle's highest league and FA Cup goalscorer, with 177 and 23 goals respectively in both competitions, with none other than Alan Shearer in second place in both charts with 148 and 21 goals. Shearer heads the list of the top Newcastle goalscorers in European competitions, with 30 strikes. And he scored the third-most amount of goals in the League Cup in Newcastle's history – netting seven times, behind Andy Cole in first place, who notched 12 goals. However, it is interesting to note that

BREAKING THE RECORD

Milburn and Shearer's respective goal tallies were both inferior to the strike rate of Albert Stubbins, who scored 237 times in only 218 appearances for Newcastle at a time when league competition was suspended during the Second World War.

Ultimately, no definitive decision can be made on who was better than the other. As Milburn's son Jack told the *Evening Chronicle*, 'To compare my dad and Shearer is like trying to predict whether Muhammad Ali would beat Mike Tyson.'

In view of this, it is better to treasure the pair for what they were: Geordie icons and two of the most accomplished centre-forwards that English football has ever produced. The question that should be posed now, and one which will not invite a ready stream of responses, is: Will another local lad come along and threaten Shearer's record? As foreign imports continue to proliferate in English football and in an era where unstinting loyalty to one club is an exception to the norm, it looks an increasingly unlikely prospect. Alan Shearer, like Jackie Milburn before him is, and was, truly one of a kind.

CHAPTER FOURTEEN

Life after Football

A top footballer's career can be richly rewarding. Untold riches, legendary status, glory and adulation can all be achieved within a mere fraction of most people's working lives by the purveyors of soccer brilliance. Yet such delights are not available in inexhaustible supply and can evaporate rapidly as soon as a footballer decides to hang up his boots. And the cruelly unpredictable nature of football, containing potential for sudden injury or unexpected fall from grace, means that a sorry end is always lurking insidiously around the corner for the unsuspecting soccer star.

As discussed in a previous chapter, Alan Shearer stared the stark reality of the horribly abrupt cessation of his career on more than one occasion during his ill-fated, never-ending battle with injuries. His tremendous love of the game he has adored since boyhood sustained him through the desolate days staring dejectedly at the ceiling while lying prostrate on the physiotherapist's couch. Shearer's superlative and sturdy self-belief, coupled with his breathtaking 'bouncebackability', may have a super-human resonance, but, as for any other mortal, nothing lasts forever and Shearer's football career was no different.

In 2006, he could, like so many other footballers, have been faced with much soul-searching and anguished deliberations on how to spend life after such an illustrious and immensely fulfilling career. How could he possibly derive the same success, enjoyment and rewards from his future activities? Kevin Keegan articulated the thoughts of soccer stars everywhere in *The Times* on 12 March 2005: 'The hardest part is, what do you do to replace football? Because there isn't anything.'

Former footballing heroes featured on a BBC television documentary in 2005 could certainly identify with this bleak and unedifying vision. The programme saw Alan Hansen interview a handful of past masters who were struggling to cope with life without the game that had been their livelihood, including Alan Shearer's fellow Geordie Paul Gascoigne. He appeared a faded talent in his late thirties, who was unable to accept that he was no longer captivating thousands with his brilliant skills.

However, Alan Shearer is no Paul Gascoigne. While Gazza's *raison d'être* revolved around kicking a ball, Alan Shearer has sought to broaden his horizons. Indeed, in 2006, as the end of his career loomed, he had a whole gamut of possibilities to pursue, either independently or collectively, including media work, coaching and promotion of charities. Indeed, the guarantee of a handful of vocational options from which to choose had left Shearer in a pleasant quandary.

He said, 'I couldn't tell you what my life is going to be in two years, three years, four years, ten years. I don't know.'

Thankfully, unlike Gazza, he was also not yearning to be back on the football field. 'At the moment, I'm not missing it at all. I haven't really had time to miss it, to be honest,' said Shearer. 'But my body is not taking a pounding. It's fantastic waking up on a Sunday morning and not hobbling to the toilet in the middle of the night with bumps and bruises.'

Meanwhile, he confessed that he was frequently playing his second-favourite sport and many footballers' preferred pastime: golf. A six-handicapper, Shearer's future is sure to include traversing the greens on a regular basis. 'If I'd not become a footballer, I would loved to have been a golfer,' he points out in his autobiography.

He is a regular at pro-am and charity golf events such as The Roxburghe Challenge, which took place in the Scottish Borders in July 2000 and attracted international golf professionals Sergio Garcia, Paul Lawrie and Jesper Parnevik and celebrities such as the Duke of York and actor Hugh Grant. Of Shearer's prowess with a club, the *Scotsman*'s Graham Bean said, 'Shearer played the Roxburghe with typical single-mindedness. You wouldn't find his swing in any golf manual but, typical of the man, it was damned effective.'

Shearer cites Nick Faldo as one of his idols and certain similarities can be drawn between the two men. Both are inveterate grafters and Faldo's obsessive commitment to his game matches Shearer's fixation with football.

Yet Shearer had, by his own admission, never put in much effort in the classroom, so there was profound irony in the announcement that he had been given an Honorary Doctorate of Civil Law in December 2006. This was bestowed on him, and television comedy writers Dick Clement and Ian La Frenais, by Northumbria University, in recognition of their immense contributions to the sporting and cultural landscapes of the North East.

Northumbria University Vice Chancellor, Professor Kel Fidler, said, 'Throughout his career Alan Shearer has been hard-working, committed, disciplined and focused in his endeavours, fighting back from career-threatening injuries with great determination and courage. He is an inspiration to us all.'

ALAN SHEARER

Shearer hailed his degree 'a wonderful accolade', adding, 'Throughout my career I have been keen to learn and develop my own skills and I hope my dedication and approach to my profession is something which can be emulated by the students who are setting out on their chosen career path after collecting their degrees today.'

Playing golf and receiving a degree do not take up much of one's time, however, and cannot compete with the game which Shearer adores and has been involved in since he could walk. Indeed, it was certain that, whatever Shearer decided to pursue in the future once he hung up his boots, it would be football-orientated.

When asked by a caller about his future plans during an interview with BBC Radio Newcastle in 2005, he replied, 'I am going to stay in the game in some capacity whether that's in management or whether that is going into the media. I haven't made my decision yet. Hopefully I will have a choice.'

After he retired, it was also confirmed that he would unsurprisingly maintain links with the club with which he was inextricably linked: Newcastle United. Although management remained a distant prospect on the horizon for Shearer, his employers realised that it would be foolhardy to release a man of his stature and influence and duly made him their sporting ambassador when he retired from playing. One of the demands of the role required Shearer to bring his considerable influence to bear on potential transfer targets for Newcastle. Freddy Shepherd realised that Shearer had been crucial in persuading Michael Owen to join Newcastle, for instance, remarking, 'We will throw him [Shearer] through the door first and, if they [the transfer targets] don't listen to him, they won't listen to anyone. If we have a chance to speak to a certain player we will use Alan. I think we will be using Alan in that capacity this summer, that's a fair assumption.'

In addition to this, his hopes of establishing a career in the media had already been fulfilled, given that in 2004 he had signed a three-year contract with the BBC to become a football pundit. He initially joined Messrs Hansen and Lawrenson to dispense his views on England matches, and then, after retiring from football in 2006, became a regular fixture on *Match of the Day* and a summariser at live matches.

According to the *Daily Telegraph*'s Jim White, this choice of vocation offered a far less pressurised, cosseted, pampered and, therefore, palatable existence than that of management for many former footballers. He explained, 'This would require that, no more than twice a week, you wait at home for a limousine to whisk you to a studio, where you can flirt with the make-up ladies before delivering some off-hand comments about some manager's ineffectual performance. Then, after a convivial drink with the anchorman, producer and your fellow pundit, you will get back in the limo to be home in time to creosote the fence, or whatever it is you like to do in your leisure hours.

'A tough choice. And, given it, is it any wonder that Shearer ruled himself out of the running to take up permanent residence in the manager's office at St James' Park? He is prepared to act as a stand-in. But no more than that.'

If Shearer does decide to remain in punditry, he will be treading a well-worn path followed by an abundance of ex-professionals, White went on to point out. He said, 'The pattern is the same wherever you look... Those who have retired since the wage explosion of the early Nineties have no need to earn huge sums. A couple of hundred pounds for a few platitudes is all they require to punctuate the week's golf. It gives them, they say, the chance to keep in touch with the game, put something back.'

However, was Alan Shearer too dour and unexciting to make a success of a long-term media career? his critics wondered. Could he summon up the requisite emotion and passion with which to embellish his pre- and post-match comments and therefore enhance football aficionados' enjoyment of the beautiful game à la Sky TV's Andy Gray, whose excitable outbursts are as frequent as a Shearer goal used to be? It was a legitimate concern for many observers, given the fact that Shearer had been, at times, an uninspiring interviewee throughout his football career.

Yet if Shearer himself had any doubts about his ability to comment on the game he used to play, then he could draw encouragement in this regard from another erstwhile England legend, Gary Lineker. He, by his own admission, took time to hone his slick media persona when he first attempted to make the transition from the football field to the TV studio in the early 1990s. He undertook voice coaching to eradicate a monotone delivery and eventually succeeded the smooth and assured Des Lynam as the BBC's figurehead of their television football coverage.

Whether Shearer will make such an impression is open to question, but when asked in one interview what quality he could bring to punditry he replied 'commonsense'. In his favour, an in-depth knowledge of the Premiership and its players inform his post- and pre-match discussions on the BBC. He has also developed a growing reputation for forthright, honest comment, reminiscent of fellow pundit Alan Hansen.

For instance, following England's loss to Portugal in the 2006 World Cup, when Cristiano Ronaldo was seen to wink at the Portuguese bench after appearing to provoke the situation which led to Wayne Rooney's sending off, a disapproving Shearer suggested later, 'I think there is every chance that Wayne Rooney could go back to the Manchester United training ground and stick one on Ronaldo.' It was perhaps one of Shearer's most colourful and controversial public statements, a far cry from the colourless and dull reputation he was accused of as a footballer. It also echoed the sentiments of England followers everywhere; and that, as a pundit, can surely be no bad thing.

Yet, according to Alan Hansen, Shearer's pronouncement had been slightly too aggressive and candid. Hansen told the BBC's Jeremy Vine, 'It was actually a great line, 100 per cent spot on, but maybe just the wrong side of the line.'

The reassuring presence of either Hansen or Mark Lawrenson, both of whom are experienced and assured commentators on football, in addition to Gary Lineker, who has transformed himself into adept anchorman from accomplished footballer, will certainly be of great benefit to Shearer as he eases himself into his pundit's role. The BBC does not want flashy and frivolous from its pundits; it requires that they are solid, consistent, professional and knowledgeable, and Alan Shearer fits this template perfectly.

Shearer certainly seems content in remaining in the television arena for the foreseeable future, so much so that he rejected the tantalising chance to forge a coaching career for himself with the England national team. England coach Steve McClaren approached Alan prior to the 2006 World Cup to ascertain whether the Geordie was interested in joining his backroom staff. However, Shearer declined the opportunity, explaining, 'I was flattered when Steve telephoned me just before the World Cup and explained the role he visualised for me, working alongside himself and Terry Venables. I met him upon my return from Germany and was impressed with his plans and his vision for the future. However, I had already told the BBC that I would extend my contract with them and I did not want to break my word.'

Shearer added that he was enjoying being unburdened by the pressures of football, having just experienced his longest-ever family holiday.

And who could blame him for rejecting the opportunity (or should that be poisoned chalice?) to be part of an institution that is forever castigated? Shearer had witnessed for himself how merciless and callous the media can be towards the England manager and his coterie of assistants when he played under Graham Taylor. Although in theory

ALAN SHEARER

Steve McClaren's appointment suggested that a bright new era had been heralded for England following the scandals and misgivings about tactics that had often dogged previous manager Sven-Goran Eriksson, in practice being involved with the English national team is a thankless task. Shearer was probably wise to say 'thanks, but no thanks' to the offer.

Steve McClaren said in response to Shearer's decision, 'I fully understand the reasons behind Alan's decision. I would have loved to have had him on board; he's a top professional and a great guy. As you would expect from Alan, he has chosen to honour a contract to which he had verbally committed – a true mark of the man.'

Shearer may have decided to put a coaching career on the backburner for now, but moving into management has always been mooted as his eventual destiny, with the hot-seat at Newcastle the likely destination. As his football career drew to a close, his name was ubiquitous when a managerial vacancy appeared at St James' Park. Shearer was said to be Newcastle fans' second choice behind then Celtic boss Martin O'Neill to replace Sir Bobby Robson, who was sacked after an indifferent start to the season in 2004. Former Newcastle favourite Chris Waddle was among those championing Shearer's credentials for the job. And, despite the fact that Graeme Souness was chosen ahead of the Toon idol to replace Sir Bobby, the extraordinary events of the spring of 2005 added to the growing belief that Shearer would, sooner rather than later, take control of the club that is entrenched in his heart. In signing a one-year deal to become Newcastle's player-coach, after sensationally opting to continue his playing days, it was widely claimed that Shearer was tacitly declaring that he was envisioning the prospect of steering the St James' Park side's fortunes in years to come. Hailing his decision to remain a Newcastle player, manager Graeme Souness and chairman Freddie Shepherd were united in expressing their shared dream vision for Shearer's eventual destiny.

LIFE AFTER FOOTBALL

Souness said, 'There are no guarantees in management. A lot of top players have tried and found it difficult, but he would have the utmost respect of every single player. I think he's destined to go into management and, if I was a gambling man, I would say he'll be successful at it.' He added, 'I would love to hand over the reins to Alan Shearer as manager of this football club. I want a few years here to be very successful and then hand over a healthy club to him. This is his club.'

Shepherd wholeheartedly agreed, proclaiming, 'Graeme has said he wants Alan to take over when he leaves and, as far as I know, it's what our fans want. I've not said it before – but I am saying it right now. And, remember, I'm no different from the fans because I'm a supporter as well. It's what I want.'

Sir Bobby Robson was also convinced that Shearer was of managerial material, telling the *Evening Standard*, 'First of all, he's a great guy. He's got a tremendous personality and I think he has the leadership qualities that are so important in management. Of course, he's got a status that players will look up to automatically. He's honest, straightforward and direct. He knows what he wants and he doesn't shirk difficult decisions. I think, for instance, that he was right to retire from international football when he did. He's an enthusiast, he works hard and if he gets some experience behind him and has the right people around him he could be successful.'

Another former England centre-forward hero, Sir Geoff Hurst, also provided an endorsement of Shearer's ability to excel in the management arena. He said in the *Evening Standard*, 'Alan has all the right background for management and if he gets the right advice I see no reason why he shouldn't make a success of it.'

With such esteemed football men advancing his management claims, Shearer must have afforded himself some contemplation on the matter.

Shearer had added further credence to the view that he would eventually join the management fraternity by acquiring his UEFA B coaching licence and setting his sights on completing the UEFA A qualification in 2005.

Newcastle's reserve goalkeeper Steve Harper predicted the Lion of Gosforth could, in his new player-coach position, play a pivotal role in helping mastermind a Newcastle revival in 2005–06. He told BBC Sport, 'It's vital to get someone like Alan involved in the club. He's got a wealth of experience. He'll get stuck in next season and that may help our fortunes. The young lads have got a lot to learn from him.'

Taking charge of his beloved club again appeared a tangible possibility at the start of 2006 when Graeme Souness was sacked as Newcastle manager. But, once again, Shearer was adamant that he was not interested in succeeding the Scot in charge of the Magpies. He insisted, 'Let me say here and now that I do not want to be the next manager, the time is not right for me or the club. Things are set up for someone to do well. I hope that someone is the next manager. I just know it will not be me. That is not meant as a slight on the club. I am just thinking of what is best for Newcastle United and, right now, it would not be the best thing to have Alan Shearer as manager.'

Instead, Shearer became caretaker boss Glenn Roeder's assistant. According to Roeder, the move was all part of an eventual progression to a place at the helm of the Tyneside club.

He told the *Sunday Sun*, 'He has all the qualities to be a top, top manager. He is highly intelligent. He has huge motivation. He is someone who takes losing very badly. There are three assets to being a top manager: coaching, man-management and the ability to judge a player. Alan will make a very good coach, using his own voice. Lots of players have the knowledge but they can't get it out of their mouths. Alan is excellent at doing that. As for man-management, he will recognise players are different characters and need different treatment, so that won't be a problem. The third is being able to judge a player. That involves the transfer market, so no one knows that yet. It is a real skill. Some managers have it and some don't.'

So what kind of manager would Alan Shearer turn out to be, as Roeder had contemplated? He has certainly had the good fortune to play under an impressive clutch of managers and has therefore benefited from a diverse selection of coaching methods. The inescapable conclusion one comes to is that his managerial style would be an amalgam of Kevin Keegan and Kenny Dalglish – his twin idols.

His innate love of goals may mean that his tactics would favour Keegan's instinct for attack, although this would be counterbalanced by his appreciation of Dalglish's defensive pragmatism. In terms of his personality, his dour demeanour in post-match interviews would match Dalglish's, yet every now and then his mischievous sense of fun would emerge, in a manner reminiscent of the Scot. Like Keegan, his single-mindedness has infused his major career decisions and would shine through when he was faced with difficult managerial choices.

Otherwise, one could imagine Shearer thriving in adversity as a manager – if his team were in the relegation mire, for example – after being schooled to the hard knocks of football in respect of his serious injuries. Most importantly, he would command the respect of all of his players given his achievements and standing in football.

Irrespective of what Shearer chooses as his future vocation, his football career has bestowed on him huge wealth and his numerous sponsorship deals ensured his coffers would be swollen even after his playing days were over. In December 1997, he signed a 15-year, multi-million-pound contract with Umbro, joining Pelé as a world ambassador for the sports company. His vast fortune consistently put him high on the 'rich list' of Britain's high-earning sports stars during his career. In March 2004, for example, he came fifth in the *Mail on Sunday*'s 'Rich Report' behind the England Rugby team's World Cup-winning hero Jonny Wilkinson.

ALAN SHEARER

His citation read, 'His squeaky-clean image may be from a bygone era but his wages were ahead of their time. One of the best-paid footballers of the Nineties, 33-year-old Shearer has netted £12 million in career earnings so far, and the Newcastle and England striker's support from Umbro, Lucozade, Braun, McDonald's and Jaguar at least doubles his wealth.'

While some footballers are irritated by the demands that sponsorship deals place on their free time, Shearer admits he is more than willing to accede to requests to fulfil his marketing responsibilities. In 2004, he signed a two-year deal to help raise global awareness of Continental Tyres, one of the sponsors of the 2006 World Cup.

The Black Circles tyre website said, 'Shearer will be lending his name to PR, advertising and sales promotion activity and will also be making guest appearances on the manufacturer's behalf.'

Brian Smith, Managing Director, Continental Tyre Group, said, 'We are delighted that Alan – one of the greatest strikers England has ever produced – has joined forces with Continental Tyres to share in the excitement of this incredible sporting event. As a consistently high performer on the pitch, Alan's legendary skills reflect Continental Tyres' core brand values of excellence, precision and reliability.'

Don't be surprised to see more television adverts featuring Shearer promoting the products of his sponsors being beamed into your lounge now that he is a man of leisure. Indeed, perhaps an opportunistic manufacturer of Smoky Bacon crisps could capitalise on Shearer's penchant for the snack – one of his nicknames is Smoky – mirroring Gary Lineker's advertisement of Walker's Crisps.

Bosses of the renowned Geordie brand Newcastle Brown Ale recognised the marketing wisdom in recruiting Shearer to endorse their product as the legend neared the end of his career. To honour his achievement of breaking Newcastle's goalscoring record, the firm created about 2.5 million limited-edition bottles featuring his face on the front. It was the first time in the ale's 79-year history that a celebrity had been shown on the product's packaging. Chris Jowsey, brewery managing director, said, 'Newcastle Brown Ale and Alan Shearer are icons of Geordie culture that inspire a devoted following way beyond their Newcastle homeland. We hope football fans everywhere will join us in a celebration of Big Al's incredible playing career.'

Yet, as touched upon in another chapter, Alan Shearer is not interested in manufacturing himself as a money-making machine, and prefers to use his influence and name to benefit good causes, rather than his own bank balance. His football career may have ended, but his tremendous support for charities will remain for as long as they choose to enlist his help. The National Society for the Prevention of Cruelty to Children recognised that Shearer's wholesome, unsullied character would make him a fantastic figurehead for its endeavours and made him its ambassador in October 2006. Shearer first promoted the charity in 1999 when he took part in their FULL STOP appeal and donated over £400,000 from his testimonial fund to the cause in 2006.

An NSPCC spokesman enthused, 'Additionally, Alan's fundraising includes donation of speaker's fees, auction of his private box at Newcastle United FC, loyal support of NSPCC golf days as well as nominating the NSPCC to benefit from his own Alan Shearer Classic golf event, donating valuable footballing memorabilia. In 2002, the boots he wore to score his 250th goal for Newcastle raised £5,600. Alan's efforts have raised over £70,000 for NSPCC's work with vulnerable children. As with our other ambassadors, Alan appreciates the importance of corporate support in helping to make a difference to children's life and has been instrumental in helping the NSPCC secure key corporate partnerships.

'Reflecting his commitment, he was inducted into the first NSPCC Celebrity Hall of Fame in April 2004. His involvement with young people is extensive; he provides coaching and mentoring to youngsters through Football in the Community links; promotes the Junior Golf to young people through a local golf club, supports their events and attends prize-giving evenings.'

Shearer, who joined Newcastle Falcons and England rugby hero Jonny Wilkinson, as well as Kylie Minogue and Catherine Zeta Jones, as ambassadors for the charity, explained his decision to become involved in the cause: 'As a father, the NSPCC is close to my heart and it horrifies me to think of the many thousands of children still being abused out there. There is nothing more important than stopping this.'

In October 2006, Shearer joined Prime Minister Tony Blair in donating the £1.64 million raised in his testimonial fund to 14 different worthy causes, including the NSPCC. Mr Blair, a self-proclaimed Newcastle fan, gave a glowing assessment of Shearer's charitable donations. He said, 'It's a tremendous honour for me to come along and participate in what is an act of generosity from a man who is remarkable. The pressures and the rewards of being at the top of professional football today are tremendous, but not everyone puts something back. But he has.'

Shearer may even fancy another foray into the film world following his cameo appearance in the 2005 film *Goal!* when he ceases to pull on a black and white shirt. The film was the first in a trilogy of films charting the progress of young Mexican soccer sensation Santiago Munez from the mean streets of Los Angeles to Newcastle United and Real Madrid, culminating in the World Cup finals.

Shearer, who appeared as himself in the film, was praised for his acting skills in the film by one of Hollywood's most promising young actors, Alessandro Nivola, who was one of the central characters, playing Gavin Harris, the jack-the-lad English footballer. He told the *Independent*, 'I was delighted they chose Newcastle for the film. It seems to me that Newcastle are one of the last big English clubs which

LIFE AFTER FOOTBALL

have still got a really romantic air around them. I love the fact that Alan Shearer grew up there, he went back to his home city to play and he captains the side. Alan Shearer in particular seemed very at ease with his lines.'

So, Alan Shearer has no cause to become a bitter and disaffected ex-pro lamenting the passing of time given the ocean of opportunity awaiting him in the future. He has no reason to entertain regrets or rail about the past and has grounds for immense optimism for the future, particularly given that his five-year-old son, Will, has shown signs that he could follow in his father's formidable footsteps.

After his testimonial match against Celtic, he revealed, 'He [Will] loves his football, and if he does I'll be right behind him. It's a wonderful life – in fact, I might have a word with the chairman and see if he wants to sign him.'

The future is bright, the future is Shearer.

Alan Shearer Factfile

NAME: Alan Shearer

DATE OF BIRTH: 13/8/70

PLACE OF BIRTH: Gosforth, Newcastle

HEIGHT: 5'11" (180cm)

WEIGHT: 12st 6lbs (78.99kg)

WIFE: Lainya (married 1991)

CHILDREN: Chloe, Hollie and Will

NICKNAMES: Smoky, Mary Poppins, Captain Fantastic, Super Al.

CLUBS: Southampton (1986-1992), Blackburn, (1992-1996)
        Newcastle (1996-)

POSITION: Centre forward

ALAN SHEARER

INTERNATIONAL CAREER:
- 63 full England caps, 30 goals between 1992 and 2000.
- Debut v France 1992 at Wembley.
- 11 England Under-21 caps, 13 goals.

INTERNATIONAL HONOURS:
- Captained England to victory in 'Le Tournoi', a four-club World Cup rehearsal tournament involving France, Brazil and Italy in 1997.

CLUB HONOURS:
- 1994/95 Premier League champions with Blackburn.

PERSONAL HONOURS (IN FOOTBALL):
- Listed in the FIFA 100 greatest living footballers list.
- Highest ever Premiership goalscorer with 260 goals.
- Most overall goals for Newcastle United: 206.
- Most European goals for Newcastle United: 30.
- Inducted into the English Football Hall of Fame in 2004.
- Named as Overall Player of the Decade, Domestic Player of the Decade, Outstanding Contribution to the FA Premier League and Top Goalscorer in the awards to mark 10 seasons of the FA Premier League in 2003.
- Named Premiership Player of the Decade in April 2002.
- Won Barclaycard Merit Award for scoring 200 goals in Premiership, awarded in April 2002.
- Professional Footballers' Association Player of the Year in 1994/95 and 1996/97.
- Football Writers' Player of the Year in 1994/95.
- Premiership Golden Boot Winner: 1994/95 (34 goals), 1995/96 (31 goals) and 1996/97 (25 goals).

ALAN SHEARER FACTFILE

- Top Scorer for club: 1994-95, 1995-96, 1996-97, 1998-99, 1999-00, 2001-02, 2002-03, 2003-04, 2004-05, 2005-06.

PERSONAL HONOURS (OUTSIDE FOOTBALL):

- Honorary Doctorate in Civil Law from Northumbria University 2006.
- OBE for service to Association Football, awarded by the Queen in June 2001.
- Freedom of the City of Newcastle, awarded in March 2001.

ALAN SHEARER

Playing career (* indicates substitute appearances)

NEWCASTLE

SEASON	COMPETITION	APPEARANCES(*)	GOALS SCORED
2005/06	League	31(1)	10
	FA Cup	3	1
	League Cup	2	1
	Europe	4	2
2004/05	League	26(2)	7
	FA Cup	4	1
	League Cup	1	0
	Europe	9	11
2003/04	League	37	22
	FA Cup	2	0
	League Cup	0(1)	0
	Europe	12	6
2002/03	League	35	17
	FA Cup	1	1
	Europe	12	7
2001/02	League	36(1)	23
	FA Cup	5	2
	League Cup	4	2
2000/01	League	19	5
	League Cup	4	2
1999/00	League	36(1)	23
	FA Cup	6	5
	League Cup	1	0
	Europe	6	2
1998/99	League	29(1)	14
	FA Cup	6	5
	League Cup	2	1
	Europe	2	1
1997/98	League	15(2)	2
	FA Cup	6	5
1996/97	League	31	25
	FA Cup	3	1
	League Cup	1	1
	Europe	4	1
	Charity Shield	1	0
TOTALS		396(9)	206

ALAN SHEARER FACTFILE
BLACKBURN

SEASON	COMPETITION	APPEARANCES(*)	GOALS SCORED
1995/96	League	35	31
	FA Cup	2	0
	League Cup	4	5
	Europe	6	1
	Charity Shield	1	0
1994/95	League	42	34
	FA Cup	2	0
	League Cup	3	2
	Europe	2	1
1993/94	League	34(6)	31
	FA Cup	4	2
	League Cup	4	1
1992/93	League	21	16
	League Cup	5(0)	6
TOTALS		165(6)	130

SOUTHAMPTON

SEASON	COMPETITION	APPEARANCES(*)	GOALS SCORED
1991/92	League	41	13
	FA Cup	7	2
	League Cup	6	3
	ZDS Cup	6	3
1990/91	League	34(2)	4
	FA Cup	3(1)	2
	League Cup	6	6
	ZDS Cup	2	2
1989/90	League	19(7)	3
	FA Cup	1	0
	League Cup	4(2)	2
1988/89	League	8(2)	0
1987/88	League	3(2)	3
TOTALS		140(16)	43